GEORGIAN AND

Portrait of a ......

GEORGIAN AND VICTORIAN BRECON:

Portrait of a Welsh County Town

W.S.K. THOMAS

First Impression—1993

ISBN 0 86383 998 3

© W.S.K. Thomas

Printed by J.D. Lewis and Sons Ltd., Gomer Press, Llandysul, Dyfed.

I'r
Athro Glanmor Williams
Ffrind Ffyddlon a Chynghorwr Doeth

Contents

Preface

The printer's ink was barely dry on my first volume on Brecon before I was reminded by some members of the town community that a companion volume was now needed to bring the history of the borough up to more recent times. Such a follow-up was all the more desirable as the town would be celebrating its 900th anniversary in 1993, and the celebrations would be conducted, in one form or another, throughout the year. And so, once again, it was a case of girding one's loins and getting down to the academic grindstone. Perhaps that is an overstatement since a voyage into waters which have only been partially charted can be a challenge and a most enjoyable experience. The discoveries which are occasionally made can more than compensate for the hours spent in foraging amongst dusty papers and manuscripts, and travelling from one distant repository to another. There are other compensations as well, for the researcher becomes increasingly aware of his indebtedness to those workers who toil in the same vineyard, though seldom does he have the good fortune to meet them in person.

It is also extremely pleasurable to record one's thanks to those who have contributed in one way or another. Foremost amongst these pillars of support is Professor Emeritus Glanmor Williams who gave unstintingly of his time to reading the book in typescript, and his perceptive comments and suggestions have contributed much to enriching and improving the volume. Professor Williams has guided my footsteps since postgraduate days, and I have drawn unstintingly on this well of scholarship, wisdom and experience to my considerable advantage. It is with the greatest affection that I acknowledge my debt to him. Needless to say for any errors that remain I hold myself entirely responsible.

Mr Denzil Hackford, a retired Principal Adviser for schools in Powys, and Mr Stanley Foulkes and Dr W.Ll. Williams, colleagues of mine in High School days, also have a call on my gratitude. While Mr Hackford and Mr Foulkes readily undertook the exacting task of reading the proofs, Dr Williams demonstrated his skill in cartography by preparing the maps on pp. 3, 5 and 126.

Publication in these recessionary times is an expensive business, and I wish to record my grateful thanks to Brecknock Borough Council for its generous financial support which greatly facilitated the publication of this volume. I can only hope that the content will be a means of illuminating the past, as well as helping to satisfy expectations.

My perambulations have taken me to libraries, museums and record offices and I wish to thank the staffs of these institutions for their kindly consideration and help at all times. I particularly wish to thank Mr Ken Jones, A.L.A., the Area Librarian at Brecon, and his assistant, Mr Chris Price, for their active and enthusiastic co-operation. My demands upon their time and patience must, I feel, have been considerable. Another who deserves special mention is Mr Gordon Reid, the County Archivist, who, despite having only recently been appointed to the post, proved a valuable ally.

I wish, also, to express my gratitude to those senior citizens of Brecon whom I engaged in endless discussions about the town's past. They must all be extremely thankful that the work is completed since, for them, it was becoming a hazard even to appear in the streets.

And finally I wish to express my heartfelt thanks to my wife for sharing with me life in Brecon in a bygone age and never once complaining.

W.S.K. Thomas
Brecon, 1993

Illustrations

Maps

Introduction

During the Middle Ages, ever since its foundation by Bernard de Newmarch in 1093, Brecon had been an important frontier town and a considerable market and manufacturing centre. As a frontier town it was the nerve centre of an extensive lordship, since within its castle was housed the administrative machinery of the seignory. Here were located the chancery and the exchequer, the armoury, the prison, and the law courts, and here also were to be found the apartments for the use of the lord when he chose to be in residence. But the town was, in addition, the hub of the economic life of the lordship and, indeed, all trading activities within Brecknock were controlled by the borough's burgesses who had been granted by charter a monopoly of trade, and the right to hold weekly markets and annual fairs. Even Llywel, a distant 'vill' on the road to Llandovery, was kept in a condition of servitude to the parent body at Brecon. This duality of function ensured that, despite the snares and challenges of the later Middle Ages represented by such events as the occasional onslaughts by Welsh princes, the visitation of the Black Death, and the rebellion of Owain Glyndŵr, the town survived. It was even put to the torch, but from the ashes it rose again.

The Acts of Union 1536/43 resulted in the borough losing one of its main pillars, since its role as a frontier town was relegated to limbo by this legislation. Furthermore, the ambiguities in these acts led to a considerable loss of revenue. However, in addition to retaining one of its original functions as a market, the town donned another mantle as it now became the county town of a newly constituted shire, and the venue for the holding of the Assize Courts. It was further granted the right to return a representative to Parliament and, unlike the other shire towns of Wales, no out-boroughs were to share in the election.

But Brecon's growth and development were greatly inhibited by its isolation geographically, since the town was surrounded by an inhospitable terrain. The few roads that did exist were mere dirt tracks, impassable in winter and, as the local rivers were not navigable, goods had to be transported on horseback or by wagon. In Georgian and Victorian times this isolation became a thing of the past with the improvement in the roads and bridges, the building of the canal, and the construction of railways. These developments were inextricably linked with the quickening pulse of both agriculture and industry in Wales. Improving landlords had to get their perishable produce quickly to market, and the booming populations of the new industrial conurbations of south Wales provided hungry mouths in plenty to feed. Breconshire, as a result, became a veritable granary for an industrial proletariat, and the role of the West Country and Ireland in that respect suffered in consequence. Pack horses and wagons became a common sight on the roads leading to the south, whilst on the canal heavily laden barges plied their busy trade. The onset of steam diminished somewhat the trade along the roads, and gradually relegated the drovers to the realm of folk history. For the canal, on the other hand, the appearance of the steam engine, spelt the death knell, for this artificial waterway was destroyed as a commercial enterprise and became, after a period of considerable neglect, a tourist attraction.

The 'revolution' in agriculture and industry which characterised Georgian and Victorian Britain, and the improvements and expansion in the means of communication, had far-reaching effects on Brecon. From being a small market town it seemingly overnight acquired a quasi-metropolitan status. The opportunities for employment provided by the improvements in the roads, and the advent of the canal and railway, the greatly expanded activity on the farms in response to developments at Merthyr, Dowlais and elsewhere in south Wales, led to a population explosion in the borough, and to accommodate this demographic expansion housing development on a considerable scale had to be embarked upon, particularly in the extra-mural areas. And the borough's new-found prosperity was reflected not only in its physical expansion; it was demonstrated as well in the upgrading of the houses and business premises in the centre of the town. Brecon financiers like the Wilkinses oiled the wheels of industry in south Wales, as they were the paymasters of the hordes of workers employed in the iron foundries and pits. The currency of the 'Old Bank' at Brecon had a wide circulation in Glamorgan, and the activities of the bank were not confined to financing iron. Money was also lent to farmers and drovers, and ploughed into the construction of canals, railways and ships.

This frenetic activity within the town attracted lawyers like bees to the honeypot and a few of these, like the Bolds, amassed considerable wealth and became leading members of the town community. Tourists, whose comments are a quarry of useful information, visited the town in increasing numbers to enjoy such attractions as the castle, the priory church and the 'gaer', the opportunities for boating on the rivers and lakes, the town's numerous walks, and sightseeing and rambling in the hills and mountains which encompassed the borough. Even the local beer proved a source of delight. Attempts were made by the corporation to improve the town's aspect, and particularly did this apply to the approach road from the east through the Watton, since it was made wider where it entered the town and attention was devoted to Captain's Walk to enhance its beauty.

But some visitors, while they rejoiced in the town's many fine buildings, did not hesitate to comment also on the drabness of the dwellings of the poor, particularly those situated in the vicinity of the castle, the Struet and Llanfaes. These damp miserable hovels were a breeding ground for all kinds of diseases, and tuberculosis, especially, found a congenial home there. The town was visited twice by cholera, the most dreaded of diseases, and the number of dead in *Beili Glas* testified to the virulence of the attacks. The mortality rate was such that the corporation had to acquire a new burial ground at Cradoc Road. Infant mortality in the town was high, with children dying at birth or very soon afterwards, and the substandard nature of the dwellings in so many instances was only one of the factors at work. An insufficiency of drains, the practice of disposing of sewage in the streets, an impure water supply, and the still rather primitive state of midwifery were all to play their part.

This poverty and deprivation were underlying causes of much of the lawlessness in the borough, which was exemplified in the fact that the most common crime of all was theft, either of animals or from the person. Punishment for breaches of the law was severe, and felons could be whipped, pilloried, placed in the stocks, sentenced to periods in the town's gaol, transported for life to the colonies or to Botany Bay, and even hanged. Hanging was a public spectacle watched by hundreds, even thousands of people, and the practice was continued outside the prison in Llanfaes until 1861. However, after 1835, law and order, which had been the responsibility of twenty-four constables, two to each of the twelve wards in the town, became the province of a properly constituted police force, when three police officers, wearing distinctive uniforms, made their appearance in the streets of the town.

But the calm that generally prevailed amongst the noise and bustle of a thriving market town and busy service and administrative centre was occasionally broken by rioting. This was certainly the case in 1831, when reverberations from the Merthyr riots led to such agitation among the prisoners in the town's county gaol that visits by relatives and friends had to be stopped. In the same year, the narrow streets of the ancient borough were to echo to the noise of violence as mobs ran amok in the main streets, breaking windows, and screaming for reform. Change was in the air as the industrial proletariat in south Wales, profoundly dissatisfied with their working conditions, agitated for improvements in their daily lot which they felt could only be achieved through the reform of Parliament. The Parliamentary Reform Act 1832 having failed to satisfy their expectations, the Chartists embarked upon a concerted campaign of action, often accompanied by disorder, to secure further changes in the franchise, and in Brecon they held their noisy meetings in various inns scattered over the borough. Nor was the unrest of the 1830s and 1840s confined to the town. In 1844, two miles north of the borough, on the road leading to Builth over the Epynt mountain, Rebecca and her daughters put in a fleeting appearance and destroyed a tollgate.

The enhanced importance of Brecon as a business centre during Georgian and Victorian times, as the town responded to expansion in agriculture and industry, contributed to a subtle change in its character. While in earlier centuries the gentry had stood at the apex of the social pyramid, as was demonstrated by the manner in which their dwellings dominated the townscape, in the eighteenth and nineteenth centuries this primacy came to be undermined by the commercial interests. And there was another equally subtle factor contributing to a change in the town's ethos. This was the gradual replacement of Welsh by English as the language spoken by the majority of the inhabitants. This transformation in the linguistic scene was mainly attributable to the general use of English as the medium of instruction in the schools, at both primary and secondary level. The effects of this anglicisation can still be discerned today as English is the predominant language heard in the streets.

However, despite the busy lives led by so many of Brecon's citizens, there were abundant opportunities to indulge in pleasurable pursuits. The upper echelons of society entertained on a lavish scale, attended society balls in their best finery, placed wagers on their favourite horses in the local races, and graced the town's theatres. They went boating on the canal, rivers and lakes, fished for salmon and trout in the streams, shot grouse on the heather-strewn hills, and hunted the fox and the hare with the hounds. Bowls, tennis and fives occupied the attention of the more energetic among them, as did cycling and rambling. There were also pastimes which could be enjoyed by both rich and poor alike, and these embraced cock-fighting and supping in the numerous inns located in profusion in the town. Cricket, football and rugby football attracted hordes of enthusiastic followers, and some of these games were played by children in the streets much to the annoyance of the city fathers.

This complex society was presided over until 1835 by a closed corporation, a body which had been created by the charter granted by Philip and Mary to the borough in 1556. Power was vested in the hands of a bailiff, two aldermen and twelve capital burgesses, and this oligarchy of families was closely knit by ties of kin and friendship. Prior to the passing of the Municipal Corporations Act, their main interest was in the more profitable aspects of town life, like the markets and fairs, and their general conduct of affairs was tainted by more than a hint of corruption. Borough property was regarded as an asset to be exploited exclusively for their benefit, since they were the ones who leased it, and on terms which can only be described as extremely favourable.

1835 was a real watershed in the history of town government at Brecon and elsewhere. Following the passing of the Municipal Corporations Act in that year, when an unrepresentative, and possibly quite corrupt, body was replaced by a new corporation comprising a mayor, four aldermen, and twelve councillors elected by the ratepayers, far-reaching, and much needed reforms, were introduced. A police force was immediately established for the better enforcement of law and order; a new workhouse was erected in Llanfaes, and a new market hall in the Struet; the town's aspect was improved, and greater attention was paid to the paving of the streets; a Board of Health was set up, and cleaner water was provided through the opening of new filter beds in St David's. The town, also, came to be covered by a network of sewers. Street lighting, first by gas and later by electricity, was introduced, and state schools, both elementary and secondary, built. These developments amounted to a virtual revolution in town administration; changes which went a long way towards remedying the deficiencies that had prevailed under the former system.

This closed shop at Brecon, by virtue of the union legislation 1536/43, had the right to return a burgess member to Westminster. As a result, parliamentary elections had developed into public trials of strength and influence between rival gentry families. The Brecon seat, during Georgian and Victorian times, was contended for by the great houses of Gwernyfed, Buckland, the Priory, and Tredegar; and during the eighteenth century, for the most part, the Tredegar interest was to prevail in both county and borough. These were contests that led to a perceptible pounding in the heartbeat of Brecon.

Considerable ingenuity was displayed in manipulating the

borough electorate; so influence with, or control over, the bailiff could be crucial. As the returning officer he was in a position to admit unqualified voters who would support a candidate of his choice, whilst refusing to accept the votes of those who would have espoused a rival. Open resort was made to the bribery of voters, and since corruption was endemic in Georgian and Victorian society, no stigma or shame was attached to the practice. In these situations the power of the purse was paramount. While in the period preceding 1832 elections had been representative of contests between powerful local rivals, after the passing of the First Parliamentary Reform Act issues such as policy and principle began to determine the outcome of elections. The great days of the manor houses were over; the political clout exercised locally for so long by the great landowners was on the wane.

The Parliamentary Reform Act 1832 had greatly augmented the electorate since the vote was extended to the £10 householder. The manipulation of the town's voters now became increasingly difficult, and the stranglehold which the Morgan family of Tredegar had succeeded in placing on their necks was finally loosened though not entirely broken. Until 1884 when Brecon—and Llywel—finally lost its right to return its own member to Westminster, the borough representation was shared between gentlemen as disparate as Charles Pratt, Howel Gwyn, Edward Hyde, Gwynne-Holford and Cyril Flower. Further reform of Parliament in 1867, 1884, 1918 and 1928 resulted in the enfranchisement of all male and female adults in the town, and the cumulative effect of all these acts was to make Parliament a completely democratic institution.

But an even more powerful force in the lives of the citizens than politics was religion, and a characteristic feature of the religious scene from the Anglican Settlement of 1559 down to the eighteenth century was the dominance of the Anglican Church. The vast majority of the inhabitants of Wales worshipped at its altars, and it was a church also which the people had taken to their bosoms. This situation applied particularly to Brecon, whose insular situation fostered a conservative temper which made the town a bastion of Anglicanism.

However, the health of this state church left much to be desired. It can, at best, be described as somnolent. Its leaders were hardly equipped to be great spiritual heads since for the most part, they were Englishmen who regarded their Welsh bishoprics as stepping stones to more lucrative preferment in England. Inevitably, their stay in Wales was only too brief, and as for the most part they were non-resident, this situation inevitably led to a general neglect of episcopal duties. Between these English bishops and the lower clergy, who were recruited from native society, and were Welsh in speech and sentiment, there existed an unbridgeable divide. The evils of pluralism and absenteeism were not exclusive to the higher clergy; they were to be found amongst the lower orders as well and this, coupled with their ignorance, meant that the faithful were not provided with spiritual nourishment. These were the ills within the church which were to be exploited to the full by the Methodists.

The 'older Dissenters', the Baptists and Independents, had made inroads into Brecon and Breconshire long before the Methodists arrived on the scene. Indeed, they may well have prepared the ground for the seed which the Methodists scattered so liberally, for it would appear that Methodism prospered where Dissent was strongest. The Baptists became entrenched in Kensington, once the heart of Catholicism in the town, and here they were to build two chapels; the Independents, on the other hand, established their cause in Lion Street and Glamorgan Street. By the Victorian period these chapels had become far too small to accommodate their rapidly expanding congregations, and so they were either rebuilt or enlarged, and in a far more ornamental style to satisfy the new tastes in architecture.

The need for a regeneration in church life, allied with the vice and profanity in society, led in the Georgian period to a great 'Methodist Revival' in both England and Wales. The leading ark bearers in Breconshire were Howel Harris, Daniel Rowland and William Williams, though John and Charles Wesley were also to make their presence and influence felt there. The impassioned sermons from the pulpit of these fervent preachers secured scores of conversions, and the Methodists erected their chapels, both English and Welsh, in Llanfaes, the Struet and Lion Street.

This enormous expansion of Nonconformity effected a cataclysmic change in the religious and social map of Wales. People left the established church in droves and found a more congenial spiritual home in the chapels. The church at Brecon, with its three ancient foundations, which had occupied a seemingly unassailable position in their affections, lost much of its attraction, and almost sixty per cent of worshippers changed their allegiance and began to attend one or another of the numerous chapels which had sprung up with mushroom rapidity. During the first fifty years of the nineteenth century no fewer than five new chapels were constructed, while another two were entirely rebuilt. Socially, religion, which had once been a unifying factor in the fabric of Welsh society, now became a divisive force with this split between church and chapel, *pobol y llan a phobol y capel.*

By mid Victorian times the church had been overwhelmed by a great Nonconformist tide and it was not until about 1840 that it began the long delayed task of putting its own house in order. Non-residence amongst the archdeacons at Brecon became a thing of the past, and in the latter half of Victoria's reign church funds were used for the restoration of the decayed fabrics of St John's, St Mary's and St David's.

Inextricably linked with the church from very early times was education, and even during the Middle Ages there were church schools in the town. In Henry VIII's reign, Christ College was erected on the site of the dissolved Dominican Priory in Llanfaes by Bishop William Barlow. Despite the vicissitudes in its fortunes, it survived the test of time to develop into one of the primary public schools of Wales catering for day pupils as well as boarders.

In the late seventeenth and eighteenth centuries, in an attempt to save souls through the provision of a religious education, national philanthropic societies like the Welsh Trust and the S.P.C.K. established schools. A teacher in one of the S.P.C.K. schools, Griffith Jones of Llanddowror, continued the good work of dispelling the mists of ignorance by establishing Circulating Schools. In the Georgian period an elementary education was also provided in private schools like Boughrood House and the Blue Coat Schools for boys and girls which were sponsored by charitable citizens. The charity school tradition was continued into Victoria's reign through the establishment of the Benevolent Schools, which based their practices very largely on those employed in the British and National Schools. The National School Society, which was closely identified with the established church, built two schools in Brecon, while the British Society, which had close ties with Nonconformity, established one. However, these more formal agencies for the provision of elementary education were still inadequate, and this situation opened the door for the appearance of Dame and Private Adventure Schools which provided a low standard of education in buildings that were completely inadequate.

The Victorian era also witnessed the proliferation of Sunday Schools which were attached to the churches and chapels, though the church Sunday Schools never achieved the degree of success attained by their Nonconformist counterparts. In these schools large numbers of children—and in the case of the Nonconformist Sunday Schools, adults as well—were taught to read the Scriptures. But the Nonconformist Sunday Schools were institutions which did more than simply teach the art of reading; through the diversification of their activities they were to become the *foci* of life in the local community.

These were the schools in Brecon which, in 1846, were placed under the microscope by the commissioners appointed to examine the state of education in Wales. However inadequate their backgrounds for the task, and however prejudiced their outlook, their report, dubbed 'The Treason of the Blue Books', highlighted grave deficiencies in the schools and provided a much needed impulse for reform.

Another landmark in Welsh education was the enactment of Forster's Education Act 1870 which attempted to remedy the deficiencies in the Voluntary system. Board Schools were established, and in Brecon two of these made their appearance, one in

Llanfaes and the other at Mount Street. In the wake of the passing of the Welsh Intermediate Act 1889 the town was further provided with two secondary schools, one for the girls at Cerrig Cochion and the other for the boys at Cradoc Road. And for those boys wishing to enter the ministry there was a Congregational College available locally.

From the viewpoint of educational provision, Brecon at the close of Victoria's reign was one of the more fortunate towns in Wales, as there was a rich variety of schools both elementary and secondary, state and private. A sound educational system had been put in place, and it was not until the passing of Butler's Education Act 1944 that it was subject to any drastic revision.

Chapter 1

THE ARTERIES OF COMMERCE

Brecon, which by the eighteenth century had developed into one of the principal inland towns of Wales, had done so despite the fact that it was, geographically, rather isolated, since it was surrounded by hostile hills and mountains, great stretches of open moorland and, in the west, a considerable forest (*Fforest Fawr*). The borough had grown and prospered because of the operation of a multiplicity of factors. During the Middle Ages it had become the hub of the economic life of the seignory of Brecknock. Indeed, the town's charters had conferred on it a complete monopoly of all trading transactions within the lordship, and Llywel, a distant 'vill' in the west on the road to Llandovery, which might have disputed that supremacy, had been made subservient to the jealous parent body and remained so until 1884. But together with being a market centre for an entirely rural hinterland, with the emphasis very much on the rearing of cattle and sheep, the town was also a manufacturing centre, and in their half-timbered dwellings, with their gable ends facing the street, craftsmen such as corvisers, glovers, saddlers, curriers, tanners, tilers, masons, glaziers, joiners, carpenters, tuckers, weavers, tailors, and smiths plied their busy trades. Moreover, its role as a trading and manufacturing centre had been reinforced in the sixteenth century by the Acts of Union 1536/43. By this legislation Brecon became not only the county town of the newly constituted shire of Brecon, endowed with the right to return a burgess member to Parliament; it also had conferred on it the status of an assize town, a venue for the holding of the Court of Great Sessions. Twice annually, there-fore, much to the unfeigned delight and satisfaction of the local innkeepers, hordes of noisy, fractious litigants thronged the narrow streets of the ancient borough.

In the eighteenth century, the faint stirrings in the industrial bosom of Wales, which had been discernible in Elizabeth I's

1

reign, now increased in tempo and the Principality bore witness to an Industrial and Agrarian Revolution. Obviously far-reaching changes of this magnitude were partly caused by, or led to, improvements in the means of communication. Hence the revolution in transportation during Georgian and Victorian times with improvements in old roads and the building of new ones, the widening and extension of bridges, the cutting of canals, and the laying down of tramroads and railways. Brecon was to figure prominently in all these developments—it had to or stagnate—and these were changes which were to promote still further the borough's growth and prosperity and effect changes in its character.

Roads and Bridges

Despite its isolation geographically, Brecon was the focal point of a network of roads radiating out in all directions, and the routes of today's roads differ but little from those that existed in Georgian and Victorian times. The road due west via Llanfaes led not only to Merthyr Tydfil by way of Glyn Tarell (it was realigned about 1830), it also, about ten miles further on at Sennybridge, bifurcated, one branch leading to Crai and Ystradgynlais, and another proceeding to Trecastle (Llywel) and Llandovery. Another highway proceeded in a south-easterly direction, through the suburb of Watton, and then to Tal-y-llyn, Crickhowell, and Abergavenny. It joined the present A40 at Tal-y-bryn, just beyond Llansanffraid church;[1] a third went due north, over the Epynt mountain, to Builth, while a fourth led to the north-east, and linked Brecon to Talgarth, Hay, and Hereford.

These roads, as with roads generally in Wales, were in an appalling condition. Since the departure of the Roman legions in the fifth century A.D., few new roads had been constructed in Wales and so the roads around Brecon would have been dirt tracks and bridleways riddled with ruts, boulders, and puddles. Indeed, in winter they became quagmires and virtually impassable. By an act of 1555 the responsibility for the maintenance of

2

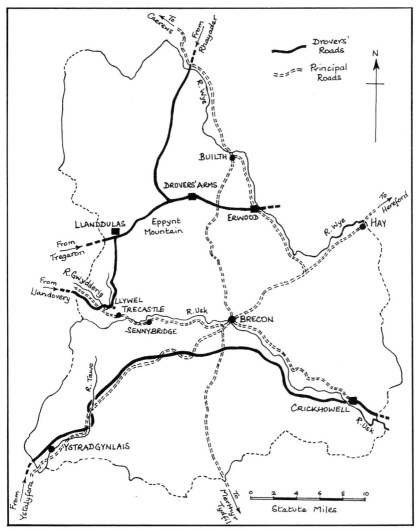

The Highways

the roads had been placed squarely on the shoulders of the parishes, and overseers of the highways were empowered to recruit male parishioners, the *corvée*, for six days in the year, to perform running repairs, a duty which they were reluctant to

3

perform since they received no payment for their labours. And so little more was done by them than to fill in holes, which could be feet deep, and to remove obstructions like fallen trees and boulders. They tended to view these six days as holidays, and such was the neglect of the roads that various parishes around Brecon were prosecuted. Thus, in 1798, the parishioners of Glyn Tarell and Dyffryn Honddu were charged with neglecting the roads between Brecon and Merthyr, and between Llandyfaelog and Upper Chapel.

People embarked upon their journeys by road weighed down by a sense of trepidation, and even dread, and such were the hazards to be faced that some deemed it advisable to make their wills, or to receive a blessing from their parish priest. One traveller remarked that 'nothing but love of glory should tempt a man to pass along them'. It is hardly surprising, therefore, that at journey's end the weary traveller would heave an immense sigh of relief and mutter a heartfelt 'God be praised'. Daniel Defoe, an intrepid traveller together with being a prolific writer, averred that to the English Breconshire was known as 'Breakneckshire', a dire comment on the state of the highways.

Prior to the improvements in the condition of the roads introduced by the Turnpike Trusts, a familiar spectacle on Brecon's roads had been strings of horses and mules, with panniers strapped to their backs full of agricultural produce like grain, making their way slowly to the iron and coal districts of south Wales which, after all, were not too far distant. On the return journey they would be laden with coal which was being extensively used to burn lime, and as a fuel to warm the family hearth, particularly in urban centres such as Brecon. The route invariably used was through the Taff valley and past the Storey Arms. Though much of this coal was destined for Brecon, a great deal was sold much further afield, in places as distant as Hay and Knighton and even Hereford.

The initiative for introducing improvements in the roads was taken by local landowners of substance who petitioned Parliament for powers to form companies known as Turnpike Trusts for the express purpose of raising money to effect repairs. They achieved this by issuing road bonds on which a fixed rate of interest, usually five per cent, was paid. The first Breconshire Turnpike Act was passed in 1767 though, regrettably, no copy of it is now available. However, a second act, passed twenty years later in 1787, sheds a great deal of light on the previous one. It

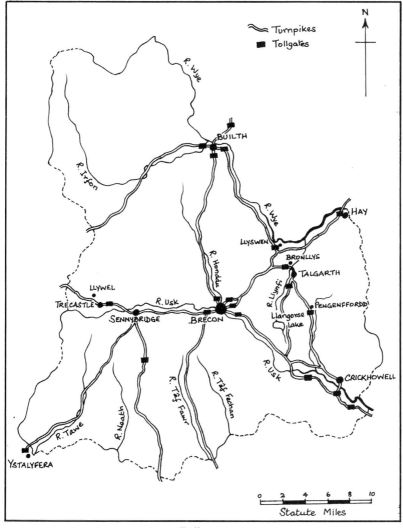

Tollgates

appears that in the Act of 1767 a Board of Trustees was established and £10,000 was to be borrowed for making and maintaining roads in the county. The act of 1787 lists a number of exceptions from the payment of tolls. These included horses conveying stones, lime or any material needed for road repairs; carts carrying dung and lime to be used as fertilizers locally; hay and corn in the straw stored locally and the products of local farms; going to or returning from church or chapel; attendance at funerals; horses being taken to the farrier's to be shod; carriages carrying mail; horses of soldiers on the march; vagrants with passes; and finally voters travelling to register their votes for the knight of the shire. However, while previous to the Act vehicles carrying materials for use in the town of Brecon were exempt from toll, under the new act tolls had to be paid, and on Sundays they were even doubled.

Considering the burden that tolls placed on the shoulders of farmers, it was understandable that they should attempt to evade payment, and they displayed considerable ingenuity in their attempts to achieve this. A favourite ruse was to cover a load on which toll was due with something which was free from such payment, such as covering a load of bricks with corn in the straw or manure; another common practice was to avoid the tollgate entirely by encircling it, a practice made possible when the land around consisted of unfenced common or was owned by a sympathetic landowner.

At the commencement of the nineteenth century, in 1809, a single trust was established for the county known as the Breconshire Turnpike Trust. The trustees, all prominent men in the life of the county, included Hugh Bold, an attorney, Richard Crawshay, the Merthyr iron 'king', Thomas Coke, a Wesleyan missionary, Benjamin Hall, later Lord Llanover, Theophilus Jones, the eminent antiquary, Thomas Wood, the county member at Westminster, and Penry Williams, the squire of Penpont. The trustees had to be possessed of estates of the annual value of £80 or own estates to the value of £2,000 over and above their debts.

The toll charges were specified in the act and these included for

6

Rebecca destroys a gate

each horse or beast not drawing a vehicle, $1\frac{1}{2}d.$; for animals drawing a vehicle, $4d.$; carts carrying lime with wheels less than six inches wide, $3d.$; those with wider wheels, $1\frac{1}{2}d.$;[2] for every score of oxen, $1s.$ $3d.$; for every score of calves, swine, goats, sheep or lambs, $7\frac{1}{2}d.$

Lime was of paramount importance to farmers as it was extensively used as a fertiliser. This meant a journey to the lime kilns, and since these could be a considerable distance away, tolls would have been collected at several gates, a situation greatly resented by the farmers. This smouldering discontent was one factor underlying the Rebecca riots when, between 1838-43 (though there were minor convulsions after this date), tollgates were destroyed by Rebecca and her daughters throughout south-west Wales. However, it was in the summer of 1844 that Rebecca made one of her rare appearances in Breconshire when, on a Saturday night, she destroyed the gate at Tair-derwen, two miles outside Brecon on the road to Builth over the Epynt mountain. This was not the only gate that was to be found near the town. There were four others, so that taken together they formed a tight ring around the borough. A similar situation existed at Hay,

Swansea, and Carmarthen, so that these four towns gave the impression of being under siege.

The trusts, doubtless aware of the resentment felt by small farmers, attempted to address the grievance by reducing the number of gates (the side-gates at Llanfaes and Tair-derwen were removed), and by lessening the burden of toll on lime. They instituted a system by which farmers fetching lime from the kilns paid toll at one gate only on the outward journey. If the return journey was completed on the same day then no additional toll was charged. To take full advantage of this concession the farmers would assemble with their carts at the first gate at midnight so that they could be home within twenty-four hours. Brecon farmers were helped still further for it was stipulated that no toll was to be charged at any gate between the town and the kilns at Dorlan Goch, which were not far removed.

The trustees were also allowed by the legislation of 1809 to erect 'stones and posts on the sides of the road with inscriptions on them denoting the number of miles and distances of places as they shall think proper'. Anyone convicted of defacing these signs would be fined £5, a very substantial sum indeed. Many of these stones placed along the roads to the town have survived, and they can still be seen by the observant traveller.

A Toll-gate House

The gates of a trust were generally let by auction to the highest bidder, usually for a period of three years, though the gates in Breconshire were let on an annual lease. The Shire Hall, Brecon, was the venue for such an auction in 1802, when all the gates in the county were up for lease. In 1839 the gates in the Watton,[3] Pencelli, Cefn Brynich, and Groesffordd were put up for auction. For this purpose they were grouped together and leased for one year for £656, the lessees, all local men, being William Lewis, John Griffiths, a draper, and Rees Evans, a tailor. They were permitted to pay the purchase price in monthly instalments of £54 15s. 4d.. A condition of the agreement was that the lessees were responsible for repairing the toll-house windows together with the boxes belonging to the side-gates,[4] a situation which possibly had arisen because these were targets for attack. From the money collected in tolls at the gates around Brecon, it becomes very clear that increasing use was being made of the town's highways. In 1801 the Brecon gates realised £504; thirty years later the amount collected was £1,864, an expansion of the order of 270 per cent.

The roads around Brecon thus maintained by the trust would have consisted of broken stones since John McAdam's principles of road construction were now being generally adopted. Maintenance and repairs were carried out by men in the regular employ of the trust since they were found to be more efficient than casual labour. Local farmers tendered for the hauling of stone and were paid about 8d. a cubic yard. For breaking the stone into suitable sizes the workmen, who had to provide their own hammers, received between 8d. and 1s. a cubic yard. Other items of equipment like wheelbarrows, scrapers and rakes were provided by the trust. On average it cost the trust about £29 a year to maintain every mile of principal road. Other responsibilities of the trust included the building of the toll-houses—they cost in the region of £40 to erect—and the payment of the toll-keepers, who received between 2s. 6d. and 6s. a week.

One of the effects of the improvement in Brecon's roads introduced by the Trust was that commodities, hitherto carried on the backs of mules and horses, were increasingly carried in horse-

The Warehouses in Church Lane

drawn wagons. The produce was stored in Brecon itself—and the large warehouses of Messrs George North, one of the firms participating in the trade with the industrial towns of south Wales, can still be seen behind St Mary's church—before being conveyed in wagons to Merthyr. Involved in this traffic also were the farmers of west Wales and *cardi* carts laden with produce, particularly butter and pork, could be seen in the autumn and early winter making their way through Brecon to the industrial areas of Glamorgan and Monmouthshire. Some of the carts would turn off the main road at Sennybridge, and proceed to Merthyr and Dowlais through Defynnog and past the farm now known as Forest Lodge; others would turn off at the Tarell bridge on the outskirts of Brecon, but most would carry on through the town, the drivers stopping overnight at the 'Bridge-End Inn' near the Usk bridge leaving their carts unattended on the roadside by Christ College.

The normal practice followed by the drivers was to leave home on Monday and return home by Friday or Saturday, Sunday being a day of rest. The carts would leave Brecon through the Watton, and turn off the main road at the lock bridge near Cefn-brynich farm before proceeding to Llangynidr. They were then faced with the uphill climb over Tre-fil mountain to the works. There, waiting for them, were the merchants, people like Brychan of Rhymney and Jayne of Nant-y-Glo. Together with carrying foodstuffs, the drivers also acted as unofficial postmen. The demand for labour in the industrial valleys had largely been supplied from rural west Wales, and so contact with home could be maintained by mail delivered by these carriers.

The delivery of the official mail could also be expedited by good roads. Brecon was an important staging post on the mail road between London and Ireland, and many are the buildings in the town provided with arched entrances leading to cobbled rear yards—the Wellington Hotel is an excellent example—which bear testimony to this significant phase in the development of road communication.

Other coaching inns included the 'Castle', the 'Bell', and the 'Golden Lion', possibly the most prominent of them all. The premises of the 'Golden Lion', situated in Lion Street, and until comparatively recent times the site of the offices of the Breconshire Coal and Lime Co., were very substantial since there were stalls for about fifty horses, and attached to the hostelry were 52 acres of land near the town. A well-known host in the latter half of the eighteenth century was Thomas Longfellow, and until 1792 he was proprietor of the 'Bell Inn' also. His profits enabled him to purchase Peytin Du and Peytin Gwyn, both substantial residences situated just north of the town, and the present day market place was the site of what was known as 'Longfellow's Garden'. He died on 30 June 1814, and was buried in the chancel of the Priory church. Together with being universally known, he was also greatly respected, despite his

11

garrulity, though there were some who were very critical both of his fare and his hospitality. One traveller voiced his opinion of the host of the 'Golden Lion' in the following manner: 'My dinner consisted of a large piece of salmon, to begin with, and a roasted sirloin of beef, of which I eat 2 lbs, washed down by a bottle of port, in which I received some assistance from the master of the inn, Mr Longfellow, a talkative, conceited blockhead, who was full of conversation.'

From Brecon there was a daily coach service to Merthyr run by a Francis Moore, and this reflects the paramount position occupied by that town in the blossoming industrial activity in south Wales. On Tuesdays, Thursdays, and Fridays there were services to Hereford, and from there to the west of England and to the Midlands; to Llandrindod Wells, by way of Upper Chapel and the Epynt mountain; and to Bristol via Crickhowell, Abergavenny, Raglan, and Chepstow. Travel by coach was not cheap, since there was a charge of 1s. 3d. per mile, and labourers, paid around 8s. a week, would hardly have been found riding on one.

Despite the improvements introduced by the Turnpike Trusts, coaches were still subjected to heavy wear and tear, and at Brecon there were facilities both for repairing coaches and for building new ones, and amongst the early coach builders were craftsmen such as Benjamin Thomas and James Sims. This trade was carried on in the town until the advent of the motor car, and one

Travel by coach

12

of the last coach builders was Herbert C. Rich, whose business premises were located in the Watton, and it was after this family that Rich Way was named. In October 1876 H.C. Rich placed the following advertisement in the local paper:

> Herbert C. Rich, Coach Builder, Brecon
> New and Second-hand Carriages
> of every description always on Sale
> Repairs executed promptly and with the
> Best material and workmanship

Together with normal damage consistent with heavy and regular use, coaches were also damaged through accidents. These could result from reckless driving, or from driving under the influence of drink. Reckless driving often resulted from coachmen laying wagers as to who would get to a certain destination first and, occasionally, an innocent carter would get involved in a collision with a coach swaying from side to side as it was being driven at breakneck speeds; accidents were also caused by drink and drive coachmen, and this is precisely what happened on 18 December 1835 to the Gloucester and Carmarthen mail. The driver, Ned Jenkins, possibly to fortify himself against the rigours of the weather, had partaken too liberally of the cup at the Castle Hotel, Brecon. Some seven miles outside Trecastle he had overtaken a carrier's cart returning from the Breconshire hills, probably with a load of lime, and the coach had gone over the side and ended up in the Gwydderig river. Miraculously, no one was killed, though one passenger suffered a deep cut on his chin for which he was handsomely compensated. Another passenger, Colonel Sackville Gwynne of Glan-bran Park, Llandovery, was so enraged that, after he had recovered his breath, he proceeded to put the boot into the coachman's posterior while chasing him down the road. Accidents such as this were infrequent occurrences and Brecon inns, furthermore, do not appear to have harboured any 'gentlemen of the road' who would invite terrified travellers to 'stand and deliver'. There were no Welsh Dick Turpins lying in wait for the unwary on the roads outside Brecon.

The arrival of the railway at Brecon meant that considerably less use was made of the roads, since movement by rail was quicker and infinitely more comfortable. The income from tolls dropped substantially as more and more gates were removed. In 1843 the annual revenue from the 33 Breconshire gates and bars on 183 miles of road had amounted to £6,476; by 1875 the income from 23 gates on 118 miles of road had fallen to £2,125 and it was in this year that all the gates around Brecon were removed.

Opinion generally was moving sharply in favour of the total abolition of the trusts and John Lloyd of Dinas, a prominent landowner in the county, agitated vigorously towards this end, and acted as honorary secretary to the movement's committee. With the establishment of the Breconshire County Council in 1888, the Turnpike system came to an end, and responsibility for the roads now became part and parcel of the jurisdiction of the new council.

Bridges

In the will of Roger Gody, a burgess of Brecon, dated 10 June 1407, four bridges are mentioned at his hometown. They were called 'Redebrewysbrugge', 'Stonebrugge', 'Laddynbrugge', and 'Hoddenbrugge'. Three of these crossed the Honddu and led to the castle and priory; the fourth carried the main road west across the Usk. These bridges were stone-built and can be seen quite clearly on Speed's map of 1610, and in the ichnograph of the town by Meredith Jones in 1744. They were a constant source of expense to the town and county as they were subjected to constant pounding from the flood waters of the Honddu and Usk. John Leland in his Itinerary observed that in 1535 the bridge over the Usk had been destroyed by flood water caused not by torrential rain but by snow melting on the mountains. It took nearly thirty years to replace this bridge—the river could, after all, be forded at this point—and it was only in 1563 that the new bridge was completed and Thomas Churchyard, a poet of Elizabeth's reign, was greatly impressed by it. In 1794 the bridge was widened to accommodate the ever-increasing amount of traffic on the roads, the work being entrusted to Thomas Edwards, a member of the famous bridge-building family of Eglwysilan in Glamorgan. The expense involved amounted to £1,000 and included the addition of two extra arches at the Llanfaes end to make the gradient to the centre of the bridge easier. This expansion meant that a smithy at the west end of the bridge had to be removed since it prevented the water from flowing beneath the two new arches. The smith, Richard Balcot, was, however, awarded four guineas in compensation. Theophilus Jones in 1809 described the renovated bridge as being wide enough to enable 'two waggons, with ease, to repass each other'. However, even the handiwork of such a redoubtable builder as Thomas Edwards could not withstand the continuous hammering it received from the flood waters of the Usk, and in 1801 the bridge had to be repaired yet again. Edwards had undertaken to keep the bridge in good repair for seven years, and to his widow it appeared that the stipulated period had elapsed. She protested, but finally agreed to pay £150, a very shrewd move, since at the next meeting of the Quarter Sessions the justices awarded the contract to John Maund—he lived at Tŷ Mawr in the parish of Llanelli—who undertook to repair the bridge for £423. He further agreed to maintain it for twenty-one years for an annual payment of five guineas.

The three bridges across the Honddu had come to be known by now as the Priory bridge, the Castle bridge, and the Aberhonddu bridge, and all three suffered constant damage from floods. There were disastrous floods in 1853, 1873, and 1876; and in the flood of 1853, the Castle bridge lost one of its piers, while the Honddu bridge, which had been widened in 1840 by Thomas Prosser of Llanfihangel-Cwm-Du at a cost of £236 10s.—it was a great favourite with artists—was swept away completely. A plaque on the wall at the bottom of Ship Street still indicates the great height of the water at that point.

The Honddu bridge was rebuilt immediately and a contract was drawn up between Walter Jones, a Brecon builder, John Jones of Llanspyddid, and Evan Jones, a local gentleman and clerk of the peace of the county, for the erection of a three-arch stone bridge with a span of 65 feet at a cost of £230. This bridge

15

again was destroyed by flood water in 1873 and in the following year an iron bridge was erected in its place.

So important were these bridges to the inhabitants of Brecon that, even from very early times, leading citizens had felt obligated to leave legacies in their wills for their repair and maintenance. Roger Gody (d. 1407) left 6s. 8s. for the maintenance of the bridge called 'Redebrewysbrugge' and a similar amount for the bridge named 'Stonebrugge'. To the bridges called 'Laddynbrugge' and 'Hoddenbrugge', and the latter was situated near to the fulling mills (*pandai*), he donated 3s. 4d.. Sir John Price of the Priory (d. 1555), a leading citizen of the town, was another worthy gentleman who made provision in his will, and he left £10 to be spent at the discretion of the bailiff and his 'two eldest brethren towards the mending of the bridge upon Usk'.

The Brecon and Abergavenny Canal

The act which gave birth to the Brecon and Abergavenny canal was passed in March 1793 and was entitled 'An Act for making and maintaining a navigable canal from the town of Brecknock to the Monmouthshire Canal, near the town of Pontypool, in the county of Monmouth, and for making and maintaining railways and stone roads from such canal to several ironworks and mines in the counties of Brecknock and Monmouth'. The Brecon and Abergavenny Canal Company held its first meeting—and doubtless enjoyed the hospitality of the proprietor, Thomas Longfellow—at the 'Golden Lion' in Brecon on 16 May 1793, and present were a few shareholders who were prominent in the Monmouthshire Canal Company. These included the Duke of Beaufort, Sir Charles Morgan of Tredegar Park, the member of Parliament for the borough of Brecon, Sir Robert Salusbury of Llanwern, Monmouthshire, and a few of the leading ironmasters of Merthyr Tydfil, industrialists like Richard Hill of the Plymouth works, and Samuel and Jeremiah Homfray of Penydarren. But most of the proprietors were local people, and in their midst were to be found the Wilkinses of the Old Bank at Brecon, an institution founded in 1778 by Walter and Jeffreys

Wilkins who had made a considerable fortune in India. A two-county organisation for the company was established initially, since the necessary capital had been equally subscribed, but this joint arrangement was abandoned in 1804.

The Brecon canal was launched for the most laudable purpose of lowering the price of coal and lime at Brecon. By the act a body consisting of landowners possessed of estates of the value of £100 a year was established to arbitrate in disputes which might arise between the company and the owners of land through which the canal passed; they could also determine the amount of compensation to be paid for disturbance and damage. The company was to provide watering places for cattle which had been deprived of those which they had been accustomed to use, and mills and dwelling houses were likewise to be provided with alternative supplies of water if the normal means of supply had been interfered with.

The company was empowered to raise £100,000 through the sale of shares, the value of which was not to exceed £100, and no person was to hold more than 50. The proprietors could raise a further £50,000 among themselves if it was deemed necessary. Persons guilty of obstructing navigation on the canal, or who deliberately or carelessly left open any locks, valves etc, would be fined, though the maximum penalty was not to exceed £5.

The act empowered the company to build tramroads up to eight miles from the canal, thus greatly extending its catchment area. However, if the company did not wish to do so, then colliery owners were given this authority. Owners of land through which the canal passed could erect wharves and charge rates for their use. These landowners, also, together with the lord of the manor if the canal passed through a common, had exclusive rights of fishery. They further had the right to use pleasure boats on the canal, free from the payment of toll, as long as the boats did not exceed five feet in breadth and twelve feet in length, did not make use of any of the locks, and were not berthed in the canal basin itself.

Strangely enough, the Brecon and Abergavenny Company commenced operations by building a tramroad from the Gelli-

Felen colliery in the Clydach valley to Gilwern. It then continued by bridge over the Usk to Glangrwyney where a forge worked pig-iron brought from Ebbw Vale. The engineer employed was John Dadford and the work was completed in August 1794. The rails and sleepers were provided by the Penydarren iron works, though the sleepers were later changed to wood. This tramroad cost £6,167 and another £900 had to be paid for the bridge.

The cutting of the canal by hard-living, hard-swearing, and hard-drinking navvies who were predominantly Irish, from Gilwern to Brecon, was started early in 1797, and by November of that year Llangynidr bridge, 8½ miles away, had been reached. The remaining ten miles from there through Tal-y-bont to Brecon were completed on 1 December 1800, and on the 24 December the first boatload of coal was brought to Brecon from the Gelli-Felen colliery situated on land belonging to the Duke of Beaufort and operated by one Edward Kendall. It was claimed that the canal had reduced the price of coal at Brecon from about 14*d*. per cwt. to 9*d*., thus effectively realising at least one of the objectives which its proponents had in mind.

A Canal Scene

The canal was 4½ feet deep and three yards wide, and the barges were capable of carrying twenty-five tons. Undoubtedly, the main engineering features of this section of the canal are the high embankment and single-arched aqueduct at Gilwern, the tunnel at Tal-y-bont, and the four-arched aqueduct over the Usk below Brecon. These were engineered by Thomas Dadford using local contractors.

In March 1802 the decision was made to extend the canal southwards from Gilwern to Llanfoist, the site of the Abergavenny wharf, and Thomas Cartwright, who had replaced Dadford as engineer, made the survey. By 14 January 1805 this stretch had been completed, by which time almost £130,000 had been spent. Canals, indeed, were very expensive to build. Direct trading by the Brecon and Abergavenny Canal Company was now handed over to the newly formed Brecon Boat Company, first mentioned in 1796, and though largely owned by canal shareholders, it was independent. The leading lights were Jeffreys Wilkins, John Lloyd, John Peirce, and John Powell the solicitor, all from Brecon. In 1801 the Boat Company leased a colliery at Clydach, and after this date Brecon and its hinterland were very largely supplied with coal from this source. The Clydach colliery also provided Hay with its coal. The carriage of coal from the Forest of Dean pits up the Wye had proved unsatisfactory, particularly when the river was in flood, and so a tramroad, beginning at the public wharf at Brecon, was opened to Hay on 7 May 1816. Together with the wharf at Brecon, there were further wharves at Tal-y-llyn, Talgarth, Glasbury, Winforton and Eardisley. The gauge was three feet six inches and the trams carried between 1½ and 2 tons. On the return journey they carried corn and other farm products.

Another colliery was leased by the Brecon Boat Company in 1820, and in the hey-day of the trade sixteen boats, each carrying 21 tons, were to be seen conveying the coal along the canal to Brecon. 'All the country-side came for their supply of coal, and in the late Autumn every farmer came and fetched his stock of Coal from the Brecon Boat Company's wharf . . . the yard at Brecon was always well stocked for winter'. The Boat Company also

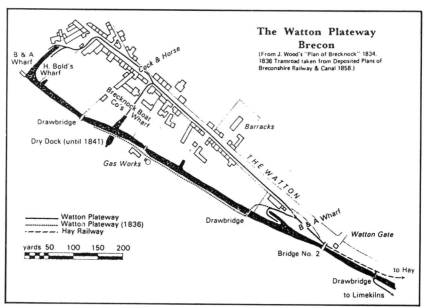

The Watton Plateway
Brecon
(From J. Wood's "Plan of Brecknock" 1834.
1836 Tramroad taken from Deposited Plans of
Breconshire Railway & Canal 1858.)

B & A Wharf
H. Bold's Wharf
Cock & Horse
Brecknock Boat Co's Wharf
Drawbridge
Dry Dock (until 1841)
Gas Works
Barracks
THE WATTON

— Watton Plateway
········ Watton Plateway (1836)
·—·—·— Hay Railway

yards 50   100   150   200

Drawbridge
B & A Wharf
Watton Gate
Bridge No. 2
to Hay
Drawbridge
to Limekilns

The Watton Plateway

owned limestone quarries, maintained lime kilns, and supplied lime.

In 1812, despite the fact that the original proposals envisaged no link, the junction with the Monmouthshire canal was effected 'amidst the acclamation of a very numerous body of the inhabitants'. The offer of £3,000 from the Monmouthshire Company had proved too tempting, though the union was to be long delayed owing to funds running out, and it was only the threat of litigation by the Monmouthshire Company that finally persuaded the Brecon Company to raise the necessary additional capital. Work had commenced upwards from the junction, and there were few snags, though the aqueduct at Pantymoile had to be rebuilt, and the wharves at Brecon and Gilwern extended. 'The 'Plan of Brecknock' by J. Wood shows four wharves at Brecon in 1834. The total cost of the canal and its tramroads now amounted to well over £200,000, though the opening of the extension led to an appreciable increase in the company's revenue, raising it from £5,365 in 1810-11 to £8,849 in 1813-14.

Coal and coke were certainly very important products carried on the tramroads. But these tramways were also used to link the canal with ironworks and limestone quarries, and lime, like coal, was of particular importance since it was extensively used by farmers as a fertilizer and by builders to make mortar. Other merchandise carried on these tramroads to the canal included, naturally enough, agricultural products and building materials like foreign timber, stones and bricks. In the year ending 29 March 1823 the total canal revenue was £10,221 of which £9,602 was received from tolls. The tonnage carried on the canal amounted to 86,944 and by the tramroads to 27,024. A further breakdown of the figures provides the following statistical information (to the nearest round figure):

	Canal tonnage	Canal tolls	Tramroad tonnage	Tramroad revenue
Coal and coke	32,613	£3,618	16,558	£513
Iron	32,742	£3,528	5,927	£232
Lime and limestone	14,748	£319	1,161	£6
Merchandise	3,243	£1,052	151	£6
Other traffic	3,598	£297	3,227	£32
	86,944	£8,814	27,024	£789

It was clear that the company was not making the profits that had been expected. This was possibly due to the competition from the Monmouthshire Company which led to a price war. So damaging was the conflict that by 1833 the Brecon and Abergavenny Company had had enough, and it now put out feelers for union with its rival, though nothing was to come from these approaches. However, the main reason for the decline in revenue was the competition from the railways. The iron trade was lost as a result of the construction of the Merthyr, Tredegar, Abergavenny, and Brynmawr railway in 1862 so that the Brecon Boat

Company was forced to stop trading in 1865, while much of the coal trade was lost to the Brecon and Merthyr railway in 1863. It was this competition that led to the Brecon and Abergavenny Company offering itself for sale to the Monmouthshire Company, and on 29 September 1865 the deal was concluded. The purchase price of £24,750 meant a share value of £25, whereas previously shares had been almost unsaleable though a few had been sold for £8 each. The Monmouthshire Company was eager to buy for two reasons: first, to prevent the remaining trade of the Brecon and Abergavenny Company from falling into the hands of a rival; and secondly, since the Newport Dock Company had been permitted to divert water from the Monmouthshire canal in 1854, the additional water needed to maintain an adequate level along the whole length of the canal to Newport could only be provided from the river Usk. This situation greatly disturbed John Lloyd of Dinas who led a spirited public campaign to have the practice stopped, since 17-18 million gallons were removed every twenty-four hours without compensation of any kind being paid.

By the turn of the century only one boat, the market boat from Newport, travelled the entire length of the canal though two or three worked the upper reaches. The last toll on the canal was collected at Llanfrynach in February 1933.

Today the canal is used mainly by pleasure boats and barges, a role which had been anticipated in Victorian times. A favourite pastime with our ancestors in those days was boating and punting, and the canal at Brecon was extensively used for that purpose on long hot summer days. Herbert Rich, the coach builder with premises in the Watton, had been the proud possessor of both a boat and a boathouse.

Railways

An Act of Parliament passed in 1859 gave the green light for the construction of a railway from Pant to Tal-y-bont and thence to Brecon. It embraced sections of two of the oldest tramroads in Wales. A railway from Brecon to Merthyr had been projected as

22

early as 1838, but nothing had come of it despite the efforts of the great Dowlais iron master, Sir John Guest.

Clearly, a railway to the south linking Brecon to the industrial Leviathans of south Wales was needed, and several Brecon men of means, including J.P. de Winton, the banker, and the solicitor, Henry Cobb, set about planning it. The expanding populations of industrial towns like Merthyr and Dowlais had to be fed, and there was an ever-increasing demand for rural produce such as flour, oats, beans, cattle, sheep, and pigs. Some of these necessities were certainly being provided by the farmers of Breconshire and west Wales, and pack-horses and wagons, laden with goods, were familiar sights on the roads. But a far greater quantity came from the West Country (Somerset and Devon in particular) and Ireland, since it was cheaper to buy there. A ton of goods could be brought from Ireland to Merthyr for 6s. to 7s.; a haulier, to transport that same ton from Brecon to Merthyr, would charge as much as 20s. to 25s. In 1859 to send a sack of flour from Brecon to Merthyr cost 2s. 6d. But Merthyr could obtain flour from Bridgwater in Somerset for 9d. to 10d. a sack, and for 1s. 3d. a sack when delivered from the furthermost districts of Ireland.

Industrial expansion in the Merthyr area also greatly increased the demand for pitwood, and some 9,000 tons per annum were needed at Dowlais alone and possibly 20,000 tons a year in the area as a whole. Breconshire had an abundance of timber 'unsaleable except as firewood 20 miles west and north of Tal-y-bont'. Its potential in this particular commodity was estimated at 20,000 tons of pitwood and 15,000 tons of ash and oak each year. Dowlais obtained much of its timber from southern Ireland paying freight charges of 3s. a ton for the transit across the Irish Channel to Cardiff, and a further 3s. to 4s. a ton for the carriage of the timber on the Taff Vale line northwards from Cardiff. In 1859, at Dowlais, the price of pitwood was 28s., and of timber 110s., a ton. At Tal-y-bont pitwood sold for 14s. and timber for 70s., a ton, and the maximum haulage rate by rail from Tal-y-bont to Merthyr was assessed at not more than 3s. 6d. a ton.

The foundries and mines at Merthyr made use of numerous horses. Some they owned; others they hired. In 1859 at the Dowlais works there were 250 horses and their annual consumption of hay amounted to 700 tons—much of it brought from Bridgwater—and 650 tons of oats and beans, the oats imported wholly from Ireland, with some beans from Carmarthenshire. Little of this food came from the fields and meadows along the banks of the Usk. The advent of the railway changed all this, particularly after the opening of a through service from Brecon to Merthyr via Pontsticill junction and Cefn Coed-y-Cymer in August 1868. In a report published in November 1868, it is noted that large consignments of potatoes, vegetables, and fruit now reached Merthyr from Breconshire.

There was a general air of euphoria in Brecon in the years immediately preceding the opening of the Brecon to Merthyr Railway fostered by an intensive propaganda campaign to dispel prejudices and to win the hearts and minds of a conservative populace. The advantages were painted in roseate colours, though time was to demonstrate that some of the claims made were exaggerated. Much was made of the claim, borne out by later events, that the prices of essential commodities would be greatly reduced at Brecon by the coming of the railway. Coal, as a domestic fuel, was burnt in considerable quantities, and was being sold at Brecon for 17*s*. a ton. A cold winter could cause the price to escalate, since in a severe frost the canal would freeze over. This was exemplified in the winter of 1860-61, and such was the demand for coal that the Brecon wharves were cleared of their last reserves. The coal now had to be carried in carts and wagons from Tal-y-bont, some seven miles away, and the price soared to 23*s*. 6*d*. a ton. The railway certainly had the effect of lowering the price of coal at the town, and on 30 January 1863 the *Brecon Journal* advertised that John Prothero was offering Dowlais coal for sale at the following prices:

	In Trucks	Per Ton	By scales per cwt
Tal-y-bont	9*s*.8*d*.	10*s*.3*d*.	6½*d*.
Brynderwen	10*s*.4*d*.	11*s*.3*d*.	7*d*.
Brecon	11*s*.0*d*.	11*s*.6*d*.	7½*d*.

In June 1863 the Breconshire Coal and Lime Company Ltd. announced its intention to sell coal at certain stations on the Brecon and Merthyr line. The prices quoted were: 10*s*. a ton at Tal-y-bont, 10*s* 9*d*. at Talyllyn, and 11*s*. at Brecon. It further declared that coal could be delivered to all parts of Brecon town for 12*s*. or 12*s*. 6*d*. a ton, depending on the distances involved.

A commodity that was of considerable importance to builders and farmers alike was lime. Since the railway ran close to limestone quarries situated between Pontsticill and Dowlais, it was claimed that the price would be greatly reduced. At Merthyr lime sold at 4*s*. 8*d*, a ton; at Tal-y-bont it was selling at 12*s*. a ton or 1*s*. 8*d*. a barrel. With rail transport it was felt that lime could be sold at Brecon for 10*d*.-12*d*. a barrel.

There were also arguments advanced of a wildly speculative nature regarding the merits of the railway. Quiet, respectable Brecon would become a recreation centre for the toiling masses in the foundries and mines, and the town's prosperity would obviously be enhanced by this influx. Furthermore, the visitors would be greatly delighted by Brecon's own ale, 'a prime ale, made of water, malt and hops, without the infusion of tobacco or any article of a deleterious nature'.

People were also reminded of the large number of horses employed in the mines and foundries whose manure was deposited on the slag heaps 'vitiating the air'. This useful by-product could be carried by rail at not more than 1*s*. 9*d*. a ton, and could be sold to the farmers in the Usk valley for 3*s*. a ton thus enriching still further the soil.

Together with the industrial proletariat, ladies of fashion 'from beyond the mountain' would be attracted to 'fashionable' Brecon, situated as it was in a 'gentlemanly' county. And not only to Brecon. The spa towns of Llandrindod Wells and Llanwrtyd would also be opened up. The prospects seemed endless.

Brecon became the hub of a network of railways radiating in all directions. The first line projected, naturally enough, was the Brecon to Merthyr. This was in 1859 and when, on 1 May 1863, this line was opened to traffic, Brecon had entered upon the age of steam. Others followed in quick succession as the railway

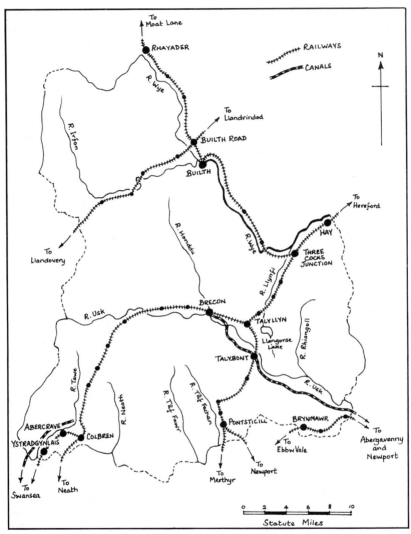

Links by Canal and Rail

mania hit the town. The sod was cut in Penlan Park in August 1863 by Lady Tredegar for the Hereford, Hay, and Brecon, though the scheme was then abandoned in favour of the present route. In September 1864 the Mid-Wales railway, extending from Brecon to Llanidloes was opened, forming at Talyllyn a junction

26

with the Brecon and Merthyr, and at Three Cocks with the Hereford, Hay and Brecon. Three years later, in 1867, the Neath and Brecon was opened. These links, controlled by separate companies, which did not make for much economic sense, were served by the Watton, Mount Street, and Free Street stations. The Watton was erected by the Brecon and Merthyr company (B & M) just above the canal basin, and near the new race course, identified now as Island Field. It included an engine shed, turntable, and goods sidings, and at the west end a single rough platform with a low building. Mount Street was erected by the Neath and Brecon Company as a temporary halt, but conditions at Watton becoming rather congested, the Mid-Wales Company in 1868 elected to use Mount Street as its passenger terminus.

But there was general agreement that a single station for general use was required, the two sites under consideration being Mount Street and Free Street. After considerable lobbying the latter site was chosen, and the B & M started the building of a handsome station at the point where the lower Watton line joined the high level line. The contract was for £2,000 though, in the event, a larger sum than this was expended. The station buildings

The Watton station viewed from the west

27

The Watton station viewed from the east

Mount Street Station: As it is today

Free Street Station: a close view of the large decorative building

28

included a ticket office, waiting room, offices for all the companies using it, a main and an island platform, a signal box, and turntable. The station was opened for traffic on 1 March 1871.

The railways, by offering a faster and more effective means of marketing, were certainly of benefit to the farmers. The citizens of the borough benefited in two ways: many found employment on the railways, and secondly, the prices of certain essential commodities, especially foodstuffs and coal, were reduced. Socially, travel further afield, and particularly to the coast, could now be undertaken with ease and a considerable degree of comfort. On the other hand the railways sounded the death-knell for the drovers (*porthmyn*), familiar figures on the Welsh rural landscape for centuries. They now gradually faded away, though their roads in the vicinity of the town, all heading east, are still faintly visible, and drovers' inns, their watering places at night, in and around the town, are still a continual reminder of their importance in the Welsh economy in bygone years. Furthermore, the arrival of the steam locomotive at Brecon, and the ensuing competition, put paid to an already languishing canal, and this artificial waterway continued to survive simply as a source of water and a playground for those with an interest in aquatic pursuits.

NOTES

[1] This route was later changed to run past Llansanffraid church as it does today.
[2] Narrow wheels did far more damage to road surfaces than broad wheels with the result that maintenance costs could be significantly increased.
[3] The gate in the Watton had been provided with a lamp.
[4] Side gates were usually chains placed across a lesser road where it met a major one. The smaller amount of traffic on these side roads would not have justified the employment of a toll-collector. Wooden boxes, therefore, were provided and road users were expected to place their toll in these.

Chapter 2

THE SOCIAL AND ECONOMIC PULSE

Topographically, Brecon still retained many of the features which had distinguished it at the end of the Middle Ages and, in this respect, we are fortunate to have the descriptions and impressions of English travellers. While they had previously been accustomed to proceed on the 'Grand Tour' of Europe, the outbreaks of the French Revolutionary and Napoleonic Wars (1793-1815) had effectively put an end to this practice. And so their gaze had moved westwards to what was, to them, darkest Wales. Their observations on the country's landscape and antiquities are a veritable mine of invaluable information, since they provide graphic descriptions of ancient monuments, castles, imposing county seats and parish churches, together with genealogies of the leading local families.

The Norman castle, built on its eminence overlooking the rivers Honddu and Usk, was still an object that attracted interest. However, it no longer presided over the town in all its majesty and grandeur since by Georgian times it was in an advanced state of decay. When John Leland undertook his celebrated itinerary of King Henry VIII's kingdom in the 1530s he had described the castle at Brecon as 'very large, strong and well mainteynid; and the keep of the castle is very large and faire'. John Speed, in 1610, presented a quite different image. To him the 'stately' castle was already in a ruinous condition. In 1787, the Hon. John Byng visited the site and declared that 'nothing now remains but a small bastion, at the hill top, where stood Ely tower, the area is converted into a bowling green; and the old hall which fronts the bridge, forms one side of a five's court'. Twenty years later, according to W.F. Mavor, 'various ugly cottages', had made their appearance in the immediate vicinity of the fortress, and a tennis court had also materialised. In the early decades of the nineteenth century, the area was subject to further building development and, in 1811, Nicholas Carlisle noted that 'Sir Charles Morgan has lately

30

built an Inn on the site of the ancient castle, of which a few ruined walls are now the only remains'.

The medieval town, separated from its castle by the deeply incised Honddu valley, had been surrounded by a defensive wall, about 1066 yards in length and elliptical in shape. The wall had been crowned by ten towers, some semi-circular and others square in shape, and served by four major gates. In 1830 two of the original gates were still in existence, although extremely ruinous, and here and there the remains of a few crumbling towers and short stretches of wall were still discernible. The moat, which had also encompassed the town on the landward side of the wall, had disappeared, largely filled in by débris and refuse deposited there by the townspeople. Thus, by Georgian times, with the advent of more stable and settled times, the medieval defensive features had already decayed and, in some instances, completely disappeared.

The four stone bridges of Brecon, three crossing the Honddu, and one crossing the Usk, also came in for comment. In 1833 Samuel Lewis describes these bridges, in sequence downstream, in the following terms: 'the first, which is of stone . . . is kept in repair by the inhabitants of the Borough; the second . . . has two arches, and between them a very massive pier, that anciently sustained a drawbridge, and is now thrown open to the public, and the expense of keeping it in repair is defrayed by the lords of the manor of Brecknock; the third . . . is an old bridge of stone, consisting of three heavy arches, and is kept in repair by the inhabitants of the Borough'. Llanfaes bridge, according to Lewis, was 'a substantial stone structure of seven arches leading to the parish of St David and lying on the Turnpike from Brecon to Carmarthen'.

It was understandable that visiting clergymen should have shown most interest in the town's ecclesiastical buildings. The Rev. J. Evans in 1804 averred, erroneously, that 'there are three churches, the most considerable of which is St David's, where prayers are read in Welsh twice a week'. He added that 'what is considered as the superior is the Collegiate Church endowed by Henry VIII out of spoils of the religious houses incorporating at the same time the foundation of Abergwily'. In 1811 Carlisle elaborated on this description by recalling that 'within the precincts of the Collegiate Church of Christ . . . are the church, a dwelling house (the residence of two or three Bishops of St David's), a barn, and out houses, a schoolroom with rooms above, a small cottage adjoining, two cottages formerly constituting part of the Porter's Lodge, three or four more on the western side of the road leading from the church, and five or six acres of excellent pasture or meadow-ground—the whole being Extra Parochial'.

The priory church, by virtue of its historical associations with the Benedictine monks, and as the home of the town's craft gilds, was frequently visited. The Hon. John Byng was the only traveller to report in detail on his inspection of the building, and his observations were rather unflattering to say the least. Doubtless his judgement had been clouded a little by frustration arising from his inability to secure satisfactory accommodation, which had been totally taken over by the retinue of the bishop of St David's. His possibly jaundiced view of the church was reflected in these words: 'I began my survey of the town, and first to the priory church, a well built venerable pile near which are two good houses, built from the ruins of the priory-house. The inside of this church is a filthy display of Welsh dirt—pews falling down—and every part like an hogs stye'.

The town also housed the county gaol. Following the decay of the castle the common gaol, which had for so long nestled within its sturdy walls, was transferred to a site near the Struet gate. It remained in the possession of the Corporation until 1842 though, after 1800, it was rarely used as a place of confinement, the borough magistrates preferring to commit offenders to the county gaol. John Howard, the famous philanthropist, visited the gaol in 1779 and reported that 'it now consists of only two rooms, 7½ feet square; no fireplace, no allowance, no court; no water; the house quite out of repair'. Matters had not improved by 1778 when Howard declared that 'no alteration had been wrought in the prison, and there were still no prisoners'. The county gaol which had been erected in the Watton in 1690 was also visited by Howard. It then stood on the site currently occupied by the Trustees Savings Bank. The renowned prison reformer paid his first visit in 1774, when he declared that the annual salary paid the gaoler was £31 10s. and from this sum he was expected to feed the prisoners. The prison, according to Howard, was sadly in need of repair, with debtors and felons huddled indiscriminately together in two courts. These were nothing more than dark dungeons where prisoners were not even allowed straw on which to lie.

The Corporation, certainly since the sixteenth century, was in possession of another cell near the bridge which spanned the river Usk. It was referred to as *Porth Bach*,[1] and 'in this hole, not fit for a dog, drunkards were sometimes confined for the night'. In 1776 it was removed to enable the entrance to the town from the west to be widened.

In 1781 a new gaol, designed to hold twenty-four persons in so many separate cells, was erected on a site on the east bank of the Tarell in the parish of St David's. The builder was a local man,

(Dewi Davies, *Law and Disorder*, p. 35)
Governor's House

33

County Gaol within the walls

Andrew Maund. The accommodation comprised 'five day rooms, one work room, and five airing yards, in one of which is a tread wheel applicable either to the introduction of soft water for the supply of the prison, or to the working of a trucking mill'. In 1858, at a cost of £5,000, a new male wing was added containing forty cells, each of which was to hold three prisoners. What remained of the old gaol was razed to the ground in 1870, and a replacement block was built at a cost of £8,000. At the same time, adjacent to the gaol, a house was provided for the prison governor, the money for this purpose being borrowed from the Crown Insurance Company at 4½ per cent interest. It was agreed that the loan should be repaid in thirty equal instalments. While the prison was being rebuilt, the prisoners were transferred to the gaol in Hereford at a cost of 10*s*. per person.

Topographers, generally, were impressed by the general aspect and housing of the borough. H.P. Wyndham described the town as large, populous and handsome, while, in 1802, G. Manby, who expressed similar sentiments, added that it 'had three principal streets, and among them several houses more elegant than is usual in such distant towns'. Two years later, the Rev. John Evans,

34

lavished encomiums on the beauty of the town: 'Though old, it is for the most part handsomely built, the houses good, and the streets spacious, well paved, and generally clean'.

However, these were tributes from travellers who viewed the town through rose-coloured spectacles. The low quality of some of the housing in the borough impelled a few topographers to attempt to redress the balance by commenting on the less desirable features of the dwellings. In 1806 W.F. Mavor declared 'that the town consists of three principal streets, but they are in places too narrow and except at one entrance, we saw few houses that might be called handsome'. Nevertheless, he did concede that 'its two old churches and its different bridges, give it some degree of distinction. The cottages built around the castle came in for considerable criticism, and they were described as 'miserable habitations'. Warming to the same theme, B.H. Malkin, in 1803, wrote of the housing plight of the poor: 'With respect to the town itself, it is one of the best built in Wales, in point of accommodation for persons of fortune and condition; but very mean, and often ruinous, in the streets occupied by the poorer inhabitants, and miserably deficient in its general arrangements. Neither is it neat and cleanly, except in the principal situations, which is inexcusable in a town, situated on a gentle slope, rising from the confluence of copious and rapid rivers'.

Though the commercial character of the main streets of the borough must have been evident to even the least percipient of observers, the premises of the professional, retail and craft services still did not evoke any comment. From this singular lack of attention it can, with confidence, be deduced that this aspect of the townscape was very low on their list of priorities. The one significant exception is the Gild Hall, situated in the High Street, which combined the functions of a borough and market hall. The first town hall had been built in 1624 by John Abel, a Herefordshire man. In 1770 it was restructured at the joint expense of the corporation and county, though the town's parliamentary representative made contributions as well. Samuel Lewis describes the building in this manner: 'On the first floor a spacious room in which the public business of the corporation is transacted, and

35

the sessions and courts for the borough, and the assizes and quarter sessions of the county . . . at the east end is a room for the accommodation of the grand jury, and for the preservation of the public records of the borough; The basement story (*sic*) is appropriated as a market place,[2] and beneath it are spacious vaults, in which leather and other articles of merchandise are stored: the attic story was used as a receptacle for arms and military stores prior to the erection of the armoury, in 1805'.

In 1888 this town hall, which had long been in need of enlargement and renovation, was rebuilt at a cost of £3,000. The basement, which had served as a corn market and where the stocks, used for the punishment of those guilty of minor offences had been kept, was converted into a Council Chamber and Borough Police Court, a Mayor's Parlour, and Town Clerk's office, an arrangement which enabled the whole of the first floor to be used as an assembly room. To add to the attractions and usefulness of the building, a 'drum-face' clock was placed over the main

The Gildhall with the ground floor an open market *c.* 1870

entrance. The cost of these alterations was wholly defrayed by Colonel John Morgan of Bank House, Brecon, who had inherited considerable wealth from his uncle, a private banker.

When the canal finally made its appearance in the town in 1800, the event did not go unnoticed, and the Rev. J. Evans and J. Britton commented on its commercial possibilities.

But it was an ever-changing townscape, and the town's aspect was particularly modified during the first fifty years of the nineteenth century. Samuel Lewis, in 1833, was favourably impressed by recent changes, and he commented that 'considerable alterations have been made of late years, with the view of improving the entrances to it, on the line of the principal thoroughfare: at the eastern extremity, the barracks and a row of genteel houses called Jeffreys Place have been erected; and the Usk bridge gate, and several houses adjoining it have been taken down'.

In 1805 the government had erected a red-brick building in the Watton alongside the road leading into Brecon from Abergavenny. It was a two-storey structure designed for the storage of powder, arms and ammunition. The lower storey, in 1813, was fitted up as an armoury equipped with racks for the reception of 15,000 muskets and bayonets, and 1,500 swords. This development allayed the fears of those inhabitants who had slept uneasily in their beds when the gunpowder had been stored in the town hall. Later, the armoury was converted into a barracks with accommodation for 270 men. It was from these barracks that, in 1831, soldiers had been sent to suppress the Merthyr rioters of that year and they had left from the Castle Hotel under the command of Guildford Onslow. Eight years later, in 1839, more troops were dispatched from there to quell the Chartist Riots in Llanidloes and Newport. But there were disturbances in the countryside as well, and in 1839 Rebecca and her daughters had embarked upon the destruction of toll gates in south-east Wales. Following the destruction of the gates at Efailwen and Maes-Gwyn, the Home Office ordered a detachment of twenty-five soldiers to proceed from their barracks in Brecon to Narberth. Their arrival at that little town on a Sunday morning, with bayonets fixed, occasioned considerable outrage and they were roundly condemned by a leading dissenter. A battery of artillery was also stationed in the barracks until the artillery wing was converted into quarters for the staff of the Third Battalion South Wales Borderers. Prior to the construction of the barracks, troops had been accommodated at the 'Old Lion Inn', which had been adapted for the purpose. This arrangement brought to an end the inconvenience and expense of having soldiers billeted in private houses and inns.

In 1873 the barracks acquired an enhanced importance following Lord Cardwell's army reforms, since Brecon was established as the military centre for the counties of Brecknock, Radnor, Montgomery and Monmouth. The barracks now became the home of the South Wales Borderers, and it was a company from this regiment which covered itself in glory in the Zulu War of 1879. In its desperate, but successful, defence of the mission at Rorke's Drift, following the disaster at Isandhlwana, when a combined British and native force of 1,300 men was annihilated, seven Victoria Crosses were awarded for conspicuous gallantry. In the long annals of British military history, since the first presentation of the medal, this achievement has never been surpassed.

The relationship between the military and the civilian population of Brecon was invariably good, and this was reflected in the fact that on 1 October 1827 Major Ross and the officers of the 23rd Regiment of Foot were formally thanked by the corporation for the excellent behaviour of the soldiers under their command during the period they were stationed in the town. This is not to deny that individual soldiers could fall from grace, and this is exemplified in an incident which occurred on a Saturday evening in 1833. A young carpenter by the name of William Lewis was making his way towards Brecon from Merthyr when, about a mile and a half from his destination, he was overtaken by two soldiers from the 11th Regiment. One of the soldiers drew his bayonet and, with the butt-end, he struck Lewis a violent blow on the head laying him senseless on the road. In this condition he was wounded several times and his watch was stolen. The culprits were never identified.

The Barracks in the Watton *c.* 1910

Near the east gate of the town, in 1842, a new county hall was built of pure Bath stone. It was designed in the Grecian Doric style by T.H. Wyatt of London and built at a cost of about £12,000 by Samuel Hancorn of Brecon. Thomas Roscoe describes the building as 'forming a beautiful object to great (*sic*) the traveller's sight as he enters the town by way of Crickhowell. It stands upon a area, along the side of which extends a public promenade called Captain's Walk, pleasantly shaded by poplars and sycamores, with the Usk flowing merrily at its base'. It was at this time, also, that Captain's Walk was greatly improved, and the Bulwark and Glamorgan Street considerably widened.

Other desirable features which attracted visitors and evoked approving comment were the Roman remains at the *Gaer*, and sight-seeing and climbing excursions in the Beacons. The town further boasted two mignificent public walks which did not escape the attention of even short-term visitors: one lay beneath the old town wall alongside the Usk, and the second was the Priory walk commencing at St John's church. J.T. Barber, in the early years of the nineteenth century, waxed lyrical about 'a luxuriant grove impendent over the brawling Hondy, once assigned to the meditations of monkish fraud, but now more happily applied to the use of townspeople, and enlivened on fine evenings

39

by a brilliant promenade of Cambrian beauties'. It appears that, even in those days, they had what, in popular parlance, is now referred to as 'monkey parades'.

When describing society in Brecon in Georgian and Victorian times, it is both desirable and necessary to establish the size of the unit with which we are dealing. From 1801 onwards a fairly reliable source is the official census taken decennially; but, prior to that date, estimates only of population are possible, based on such evidence as chantry returns, hearth tax returns, episcopal returns, parish records and subsidy rolls. The difficulty is further compounded by the unreliability and incompleteness of these records. However, despite the deficiencies, it is possible to demonstrate how the number of townspeople grew steadily, part-icularly between 1800-50, and how this expansion was reflected physically in the extension in housing which took place, mainly in areas lying outside the limits of the old town walls. Within the walled area, on the other hand, change was very largely confined to the general refronting of the houses which occurred in the nineteenth century, giving the town very much the appearance which it assumes today.

Towards the close of the Middle Ages, the population of Brecon could not possibly have fallen far short of 800 and may

The New Shire Hall, 1842. The buildings to the left stand on the site of the County Gaol, 1690

have been considerably greater. By 1563, basing our estimate on the bishops' returns to certain interrogatories which the Privy Council had directed them to complete, the population of the town would appear to have been in the region of 1,998, making Brecon one of the largest towns in Wales. In the first half of the sixteenth century, therefore, the borough may have experienced a demographic explosion since the town's population may have increased by as much as 150 per cent. The increase is attributable to the operation of two factors: natural growth, and the influx of people from the town's hinterland attracted by the promise of greater opportunities and higher wages. This process had been greatly facilitated by the passing of the Union legislation 1536/43, by which the Welsh were given the same legal rights as Englishmen. During the following one hundred years the rate of population growth slowed down dramatically, for the Hearth Tax returns of 1670 demonstrate that there were 442 households in the town, providing an estimated population of 2,069 souls, an increase of four per cent only. This relative decline was evident in other parts of Wales, and was possibly caused by such factors as disease, famines, casualties and outbreaks of the plague. According to the census of 1801, the population of Brecon stood then at 2,898; by 1851 it had grown to 6,098 and by the turn of the nineteenth century it had fallen back slightly by 5,901. A breakdown of the figures provides the following interesting statistical information:

Census Returns

District	1801	Year 1851	1901
St John Upper	849	1,903	1,668
with Venny Fach	129	164	-
St Mary's	1,109	2,218	2,616
Military in Barracks	-	271	-
Christ College	-	101	-
Castle Inn	-	22	-
St David's, Lower	618	1,281	1,457
St David's, Upper	193	138	160
Totals	2,898	6,098	5,901

Between 1670 and 1801 Brecon's population would appear to have increased by some forty per cent, while during the next fifty years, 1801-51, there was a further graphic expansion of 110 per cent. This was followed, on the other hand, during the last fifty years of Victoria's reign by a fall of some three per cent.

An increase of this nature can obviously not be explained entirely on the grounds of natural growth, since the average household size between 1801-51 was 4.75. In other words, households in Brecon consisted of the parents and two or three children. There would obviously have been considerable movement into the town from outside, and people would have been motivated to do so by the borough's increasing prosperity, and the diversification of employment opportunities. A barometer of this growing affluence was the expansion in the number of houses, and while in 1801 there were 540 houses in Brecon, 499 inhabited and 41 uninhabited, by 1861 this total had increased to 1,266, of which 1,155 were inhabited and 111 uninhabited, an increase of 134 per cent. The expansion in the provision of houses was particularly noticeable between 1801-31. The intercensal increases in houses were taking place mainly in the extra-mural areas, in suburbs like Llanfaes (St David's Lower), and around the Priory and Castle (St John's Upper). The increases within the walls, in St John's Lower (St Mary's) were of a much lower order. This development in the townscape is exemplified in the following table:

Districts

Parish	St David's Lower (Llanfaes)		St John's Upper		St John's Lower (St Mary's)	
	No.	No.	No.	No.	No.	No.
1801						
1811	+ 51	+ 43.6	+ 121	+ 66.5	+ 45	+ 18.7
1821	+ 88	+ 52.4	+ 65	+ 21.5	+ 29	+ 10.1
1831	+ 38	+ 14.8	+ 69	+ 18.8	+ 81	+ 25.7
1841	+ 29	+ 9.8	+ 32	+ 7.3	+ 17	+ 4.2
1851	-17	- 5.2	- 5	- 1.0	+ 26	+ 6.3
1861	+ 12	+ 3.9	+ 5	+ 1.0	+ 15	+ 3.4

The development of the town, particularly in the extra-mural areas, is further vividly illustrated when a comparison is made of John Speed's map of 1610, Meredith Jones's plan of 1744, and John Wood's plan of 1834. Speed's map had depicted three major roads converging in the High Street, with well defined

ICHNOGRAPHY
of the Town of
BRECKNOCK,
From a Plan by Meredith Jones,
Surveyor.
in 1744.

REFERENCE.

1 St John the Evangelist's	16 Glamorganshire Street
2 The Priory House Cloisters &c	17 Captain's Walk
3 The Castle	18 Watton Gate
4 Castle Bridge	19 Watton
5 Upper Bridge on Dᵒ	20 Old Bowling Green
6 Lower Dᵒ	21 Water Gate
7 Struet Gate	22 Bridge Gate
8 High Street superior	23 Usk Bridge
9 Town-Wall	24 Usk Mill
10 St Mary's Chapel	25 Struet
11 The Bulwark	26 Lion Lane
12 High Street inferior	27 Church Street
13 Ship Street	28 Heol rhydd
14 Wheat Street	29 The Postern
15 St Mary's Street	30 Pen y drif

43

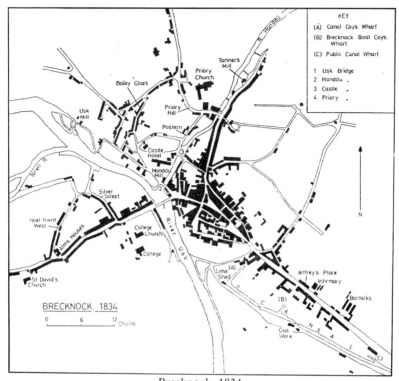

KEY

(A) Canal Coys. Wharf
(B) Brecknock Boat Coys. Wharf
(C) Public Canal Wharf

1 Usk Bridge
2 Honddu
3 Castle
4 Priory

Brecknock, 1834
Based on the Plan of John Wood

ribbon development outside the North Gate, East Gate and West Gate. Within the walls the arrangement of buildings—and building density was high—corresponded very closely to the twentieth century pattern. Meredith Jones's plan embraced a wider area, and demonstrated how the west bank of the Honddu, the district in the vicinity of the castle and priory, had been colonised during the intervening period. In Llanfaes there was a continuous rib of building from the Usk bridge to Ffrwdgrech road junction to the west of St David's church, and along *Heol Hwnt* and Silver Street there was an arc of residential development. On the east bank of the Honddu, to the north of the Struet Gate, there was little density change in building. Wood's plan, almost a century later,

44

confirms the trends revealed in Meredith Jones's map, and captures the continuance of residential development to the west of the Honddu at *Beili Glas*, Priory Hill, Postern and Pendre. It further reaffirms the gradual infilling that was taking place in Llanfaes, and provides annotated detail relating to building development in the Watton. Alexandra Road and Camden Road, on the other hand, prominent features on today's townscape, were relatively free of development at this time.

The diversification of employment opportunities after 1811 exercised a pronounced effect on population by encouraging a labour drift from unskilled agricultural occupations, and a numerical increase in what is described as 'other occupations' can be attributed, in part, to the concealed sectoral employment increase in transportation. It would appear that nearly fifty-five per cent of the total active male labour force aged at least twenty years was employed in retail trades and handicrafts, whilst unspecified non-agricultural labour accounted for a further twenty per cent. A numerical indication of the town's employment structure can be provided by extracting blanket employment statistics from Census Enumeration Abstracts. This is exemplified in the following tables:

Brecon's Employment Structure

Occupation of Families

Year	Agriculture		Trade and Handicrafts		Other		Total
	No	%	No	%	No	%	
1801	272	11	654	25	1,650	64	2,576
1811	205	26	375	48	196	26	776
1821	174	18	574	58	240	24	998
1831	92	8	609	53	448	39	1,149

Occupations of Males over 20 in 1831

Occupation	St David's (Llanfaes)	St John's Upper	St John's Lower	Total
Total Males	303	477	463	1,243
Agriculture	88	6	12	106
Non-Agricultural Manufacturing	4	-	1	5
Retail trades and handicrafts	171	245	264	680
Banking and Professions	6	20	69	95
Labourers	4	184	62	250
Other Males	29	8	29	66
Servants	1	14	26	41

Furthermore, there were in St David's, three male and thirty-two female servants under the age of twenty; in St John's, five of the male servants and fifty-one of the female servants were under that age, and in St Mary's, whilst the number of male servants under twenty was fifteen, the number of females was 175.

The arrival of the canal in Brecon in 1800 was certainly an important consideration underlying the town's growing prosperity and increasing numbers, since it opened new markets and provided extended facilities for the tranportation of merchandise. Brecon, as a consequence, became an important distribution centre for a considerable hinterland. The tramroad between Brecon and Hay, which opened in 1816 and remained fully operational until 1864, enabled the town to penetrate into areas to the east which had hitherto been supplied up the Wye valley. Again, the improvement in the roads effected by the Turnpike Trusts also accelerated the town's prosperity as goods which had earlier been carried in baskets, on the backs of horses and mules, to great iron centres such as Merthyr, Dowlais and Ebbw Vale, to feed their ever-expanding populations, were now conveyed increasingly in wagons. The existence in Church Lane of large warehouses, and the proximity to these of a basket maker's shop, are eloquent witnesses to the scale of the operation. And the influence of the arrival of the railway must never be underestimated since the opening of the Brecon to Merthyr line (1868) enabled the county to become a granary and market garden for the valleys of south Wales.

Brecon also profited from the fact that its marketing and service facilities, both for the benefit of its own citizens, and for that of its hinterland, remained buoyant throughout the nineteenth century. But particularly significant was its role as the principal market town of a rich shire, which had taken considerable advantage of the 'New Agriculture', to pay rich dividends. Samuel Lewis in the third decade of the century remarked that 'the markets are on Wednesday for butchers meat and vegetables, and on Saturday, which is the principal market, for corn and provisions: the charter of the borough also grants another market on Friday. The fairs are on the first Wednesday in March, May 4th, July 5th, September 9th, November 16th principally for horses, cattle, sheep, agriculture produce, hops, wool, leather, and pedlery: those in May and November, of which the latter is the larger, are also statute fairs for the hiring of servants'. The town also provided a comprehensive range of professional, financial, legal, retail and craft services. The extent of this provision can be gauged from the following table:

	High Street	The Watton	Llanfaes	Ship Street	The Struet	Castle Street	Lion Street	The Bulwark	Watergate	Beili Glas	Pendre	Priory Hill	Mount Street	Wheat Street	Other localities	Totals
Total Functions Recorded in each Street	82	68	67	50	50	24	19	14	6	5	6	5	6	8	27	437
I Professional & Financial																
Academics	1	2	2		1		2	1			1				2	12
Architects		1														1
Attorneys	1	1			2	1		1						2		8
Auctioneers	1							1	1							3
Bankers	2	1			1		1									5
Chemists & Druggists	4			1		1										6
Dentists		1														1
Fire and Office Agents	5			4	4	1	1	1								16
Surgeons		1						2	2						1	6
Surveyors		2	1					1						1	2	7
	14	9	3	5	8	3	4	7	3	-	1	-	-	3	5	65
II Crafts																
Builders		2														2
Carpenters and joiners		4	5				1									10
Painters, Plumbers	1		2		2		2				1					8
Plasterers												1	1			2
Stonemasons			6								1	1			1	9
Agricultural implement makers		1	1		2											4
Blacksmiths	1	2	2	2	1										3	11
Boot/Shoemakers	5	2	5	2	3	2					1		2		2	24
Brazier & tinplate workers				1	1										1	3
Brewers		1			1											2
Cabinet makers					1	1	2	1					1			6
Coopers		1													2	3
Curriers and leather cutters			1	1				1								3
Hairdressers	1			1	1			1								4
Iron & brass founders				1											1	2
Maltsters		2			1									1	1	5
Millers		1			2										1	4
Printers	1						1	1								3
Saddlers	2		1			1	1								1	6
Skinners			1		2											3
Straw-bonnet makers	1	2		1		1										5

48

	High Street	The Watton	Llanfaes	Ship Street	The Struet	Castle Street	Lion Street	The Bulwark	Watergate	Beili Glas	Pendre	Priory Hill	Mount Street	Wheat Street	Other localities	Totals
Tailors	2	1	3	2	2		1		2					1	1	15
Tanners/ Fellmongers		1														1
Watch/clock makers	2		1		1											4
Wheelwrights		1	2											1		4
Woollen manufacturers			2									1			1	4
Others etc.		2			2		1						1			6
	16	18	37	11	19	8	8	5	-	2	3	3	5	2	16	153

III Distribution	High Street	The Watton	Llanfaes	Ship Street	The Struet	Castle Street	Lion Street	The Bulwark	Watergate	Beili Glas	Pendre	Priory Hill	Mount Street	Wheat Street	Other localities	Totals
Agricultural	1	1														2
Coal and Lime		4					1									5
Hops	4			3												7
Slate		2														2
Timber		2														2
Manure and guano	1	2														3
Wool	2															2
Booksellers	3					1										4
Butchers	2	2	1	1		1	1									8
China and glass	3	1	1													5
Confectioners	2	1		2												5
Grocers and tea dealers	5		1	1		1										8
Hatters	1			4		1										6
Ironmongers	3	2	1	3												9
Linen and Woollen Drapers	7			3			1									11
Milliners	2	3		1	3	2	2		1							14
Seedsmen	1	1		3	1							1			1	8
Shopkeepers	5	8	7	6	1	15	1		2	3		1			1	50
Tallow Chandlers			1		1											2
Retailers of beer		1	4						1			1			1	8
Wine and Spirits	4			1												5
	46	30	16	28	7	21	5	1	3	3	1	2	-	-	3	116

IV Hostelries	High Street	The Watton	Llanfaes	Ship Street	The Struet	Castle Street	Lion Street	The Bulwark	Watergate	Beili Glas	Pendre	Priory Hill	Mount Street	Wheat Street	Other localities	Totals
Eating house keepers	1						1									2
Inns and Hotels			2		1											3
Taverns/Public Houses	4	11	11	3	5	1			2		1		1	3	2	44
Post horse keepers	1			1	1										1	4
	6	11	11	6	5	3	-	1	2	-	1	-	1	3	3	53

49

Compared with previous centuries there was a considerably extended scale of service provision in Victorian times. However, E.I. Spence and, later in 1810, the Rev. J. Evans and J. Britton, were all agreed that 'there are here at present no manufactures of consequence', and this sentiment was to be echoed by Samuel Lewis in 1833. The production of woollen cloth had experienced a relative decline—only four were connected with this activity—but the leather trades still occupied a position of some importance, with 37 craftsmen involved. These were made up of 24 shoemakers, 3 curriers, 6 saddlers, 3 skinners, and one tanner. In 1860 John Murray was to confirm that both wool and leather featured prominently in the town's export trade, and John Gorton in 1833 asserted that textile manufacturing embraced 'cloth and cotton stockings'. What impressed B.H. Malkin in 1803, and with some justification, was the making of hats, and it would appear that by mid-century there were five straw-bonnet makers and six hatters practising their skills in the borough.

The nerve centre of the business world in Brecon—and this, possibly, was as to be expected—was in the High Street (82 service functions) with the Watton (68 service functions) and Llanfaes (67 service functions) in hot contention. It is significant that both the Watton and Llanfaes lay on the principal road running east to west. This 'midland' route commenced at Gloucester and then took in Ross, Monmouth, Abergavenny, Brecon, Llandovery and Carmarthen where it intercepted the southern route from Bristol via Newport and Cardiff. Least well provided were Watergate, *Beili Glas*, Pendre, Priory Hill, Mount Street, Wheat Street, Belle Vue, Church Street, Chapel Street, St Michael Street, Mill Street, Mount Pleasant and Glamorgan Street. For the upper echelons of urban society residing in Glamorgan Street, Lion Street and the Bulwark, the absence of services would have been of no great consequence since the diverse services offered in the High Street were only a stone's throw away.

In the High Street was also located Wilkins' Bank. Today the building is a branch of Lloyd's. It was from this bank that money was conveyed weekly to Merthyr Tydfil to pay the wages of those thousands of workmen employed in the iron foundries at Cyf-

50

arthfa, Penydarren, and Dowlais together with the employees of the Abernant Coal and Iron Works in the Aberdare valley. Indeed, Wilkins' notes became the paper currency for the whole of north Glamorgan. Brecon, as the financial centre of the south Wales iron industry—its financiers were up to their elbows in iron —was a veritable power house, and its economic status was such that it attracted solicitors like bees to the honey pot. The town was renowned for its lawyers, and included in their ranks were people of the eminence of Sir John Meredith, who was Howel Harris's attorney. He had also been high sheriff of Brecknock and Radnorshire. Another luminary was Hugh Bold, described in 1775 by the Moravian missioner, La Trobe, as the most eminent lawyer in the town. He acted for the Cyfarthfa iron works. Further, Brecon was the home town of Theophilus Jones, author of easily the best of all the old 'county histories' of Wales. And here also resided John Wilkins who was a banker as well as a lawyer. By 1858 there would appear to have been eight attorneys with offices in the borough.

As a banker John Wilkins, from 1760 onwards, was John May-bery's partner in the ironworks located in the Priory Groves, on the banks of the Honddu, about a mile from the centre of the town. The furnace and forge at Brecon, and the forge at Pipton on the Llynfi stream near Glasbury, had been established by Benjamin Tanner, an ironmonger of Brecon, and Richard Wellington, a gentleman of Hay, as co-partners in 1720-3. The original lease of the land at Brecon had been granted by Edward Jeffreys of the Priory (the Camden family). The site offered considerable advantages since an old corn-mill had previously stood there, and a mill-pond and leat were ready to hand for conversion by the new lessees. Furthermore, the water power of the Honddu, a swift flowing river, was sufficient to drive the huge bellows necessary to produce a strong blast of air without which a sufficiently intense heat could not be produced to smelt the iron ore.

To this furnace at Brecon the iron ore and the limestone required for fluxing were conveyed in sacks on the backs of horses and mules from Hirwaun, some eighteen miles distant; and the abundant oak and other woods of the district, after being

Old Forge, Brecon

burnt to make the charcoal, supplied the fuel. The coppice woods in Cwmdwr valley, beyond Llywel, and those far away up the Wye valley, and across the Epynt mountain at Llangamarch and Llanwrtyd, had also to be requisitioned. A forge was added at a later period to the Brecon furnace. Pipton, on the other hand, was a forge and nothing more, and it may be assumed that it had been fed by a supply of pig-iron from the Honddu furnace. It is quite possible that the iron so manufactured was taken to Hay, six miles from Pipton, and carried by barge down the Wye to Chepstow, and thence to Bristol. The transportation costs were high, and the price of iron was dear also, probably exceeding £20 a ton.

It was in 1753 that the Brecon works were bought by Thomas Maybery for £400, and he immediately conveyed them to his son, John. The Mayberys were iron masters from Powick Forge on the Teme in Worcestershire. The working of iron on a large scale at Hirwaun, particularly after the introduction of coke—burnt steam coal—as a smelting agent, effectively sealed the fate of the Brecon works, and production there had ceased long before 1800.

Wilkins' Bank or the 'Old Bank' had been established at Brecon in 1778 by four partners, including Walter and Jeffreys Wilkins, sons of the lawyer industrialist John Wilkins (1713-84). Each of the partners had contributed £1,000. John Wilkins, as Deputy Clerk for the Brecknock Circuit of the Court of Great Sessions, was the holder of a profitable legal office in Brecon, and he may well have contributed towards the establishment of the bank. The Jeffreys family of Llywel, the maternal relatives of Walter and Jeffreys, may also have invested in it some of the wealth gained by them in the City of London and elsewhere. However, it has been suggested that the main promoter was Walter Wilkins (1741-1828), who had amassed a considerable fortune in India before becoming a banker and, later, Whig Member of Parliament for Radnorshire.

During the first half of the nineteenth century, the affairs of the bank were dominated by John Parry Wilkins (from 1839 he came to be known as John Parry de Winton), who was the son of Jeffreys Wilkins. He became a partner in 1796 or immediately afterwards. A shrewd and highly respectable banker, he spent the years 1826-32 as the first agent of the Bank of England branch at Swansea. He relinquished this post, and its salary of £1,000 a year, to take a half share in the Brecon branch, and to resume his position as its manager at an annual salary of £250.

Apart from paying the wages of iron workers, and in July 1839 the agent of Wilkins and Co. at Merthyr required about £5,000 in gold to provide the monthly wages for the iron workers, it also lent money on long term to the iron masters. In 1813 Wilkins and Co. had a loan of £54,000 outstanding on mortgage to Anthony Hill and Co. of the Plymouth Iron Works. However, the larger part of its dealings was with the agricultural population, since it made loans to farmers and particularly to the drovers. In 1832 the Bank of England branch opened a loan account for John Parry Wilkins and the Brecon branch to enable them to assist farmers in Carmarthenshire and Breconshire. But advances were made especially on the promissory notes of drovers to enable them 'to go to the fairs'. The drovers required large sums of money to buy cattle in Wales, and to pay for taking them to the markets in the

53

Midlands and the south-east of England. The bank would advance for two or three months on the promissory note of a drover, and the amount lent would usually not exceed £2,000.

Wilkins and Co. had considerable interests also in transport enterprises. The bank promoted the construction of both the Glamorgan and Brecon canals, and John Parry de Winton was one of the principal promoters of the Brecon to Merthyr railway project and one of the directors of the railway from its incorporation in 1859. The bank further participated in the ownership of small ships, of Llanelli registration, between 1840-90. During the years 1851-69 the banker, Henry Jones Evans of Llanelli subscribed sums of between £99 and £1,000 on mortgage for twelve sailing ships and, in the record of his investment of 1859 in the sloop *Lady Louise*, he is described as a 'banker of Wilkins and Co. Llanelly'.

In 1890 the Wilkins' Bank merged with Lloyd's Bank, and while the 'Old Bank' had been launched with an operating capital of £9,000, the amount paid in consideration to its partners in 1890 was £290,000.

The craftsmen and shopkeepers, who constituted the preponderant middle-class element in the town, lived in narrow fronted dwellings with the workshop or shop on the ground floor facing the street, and with the living quarters above on the first floor. These were the habitations which, during the course of the nineteenth century, were generally refronted. The upper middle class, on the other hand, the academics, merchants, architects, attorneys, surgeons and bankers dwelt in large comfortable well-furnished houses removed from their business premises. In fact they vied with the gentry in their degree of comfort, and there would have been little to differentiate between their life styles. What distinguished them from the gentry was that while they were still directly involved with the town's commerce and trade, the gentry were not. The latter's imposing stone-constructed houses were built and supported from the profits of landowning. For the efficient running of their large households and for purposes of entertainment, these wealthy families required the services of maids and manservants, and in this respect it is worthy of note that in St John's Lower (St Mary) there were 175 female servants and 41 male servants.

However, despite this economic parity, socially the apex of local society was occupied by representatives of the landowning class, who used Brecon either as a permanent residence, or as a winter one, at a time when it was neither easy nor fashionable to spend the winter in London. They resided for the most part in Glamorgan Street, Lion Street and the Bulwark. Many of their habitations, though now largely used for other purposes, still retain their gardens and are, even today, a noticeable feature of the townscape. But these unquestioned leaders of Brecon society were not only considerable employers of labour, they were the conduits by which considerable amounts of money were poured into the local economy, and their continued interest in the countryside from which they were sprung was reflected in the fact that they were committed supporters of the County Agricultural Society. Discerning visitors were acutely conscious of the social standing of this group, and were agreed with the Rev. E. Spence that 'the society here is more select than in any other town in South Wales, from its chief inhabitants consisting of very old and respectable families who have retired on their fortunes'. To Benjamin Malkin, Brecon 'appears in most respects to be a very desirable residence, and is much inhabited by clergy and gentry of independent fortunes. It is quiet and orderly, to which the blank calendar of the judges bears no unfrequent testimony'.

Malkin was justified in mentioning the clergy, since there was a strong ecclesiastical element in the town. Brecon, as a pleasant enough place to live in, attracted the clergy in droves, and it is small wonder that Theophilus Evans should have preferred to reside in Llanfaes, leaving his other cures, Llangamarch, Llan-wrtyd, and Abergwesyn in the charge of a difficult young curate, William Williams of Pantycelyn. Not that Williams himself, either, had any great desire to live within the bounds of these parishes. There was a whole row of parishes fringing the Epynt (Trallong, Merthyr Cynog, Llanfihangel Nant Bran, Llandeilo'r Fan) which can hardly have ever seen their incumbents except on

Sundays. And in Brecon, also, was the College of Christ, which was a school and a corporation of non-resident prebendaries, who delighted to visit Brecon as a change from their remote vicarages in north Brecknock and Radnorshire.

But while the wealthy paraded their wealth by living in spacious edifices, the poor inhabitants, on the other hand, occupied low-quality housing, and their hovels were equally as arresting a feature of the townscape. J.T. Barber commented that 'Its once magnificent castle . . . is so choaked (sic) up with miserable habitations, as to exhibit no token of antique grandeur'. Malkin, while observing that Brecon was one of the best built towns in Wales from the standpoint of the habitations of the affluent, declared that 'it was very mean, and often ruinous, in the streets occupied by the poorer inhabitants'. The areas that he referred to embraced Llanfaes, Heol Hwnt, Kensington, Mill Street and the Struet.

The cottages of the poor were small and very crudely constructed. They usually consisted of only two rooms, one on the ground floor and one directly above. The room on the first floor was a bedroom and was used by the whole family. It would appear to have been badly ventilated, since the windows were rarely opened and, in many cases, they were incapable of being opened. Where there were no windows, light and ventilation were provided by means of small skylights set in the roof. Roofs were usually tiled or thatched, and the supporting walls comprised rough stubble-stone masonry. The mortar used was inferior in quality, with the result that during the wet seasons the cottages were extremely damp. There was no provision for drainage. Families, usually one to each cottage, paid rents which varied from £2 to £5 per annum. The household furnishings were extremely basic and crudely made of wood. Unlike the larger and wealthier households, where kitchen ranges, with ovens, had been introduced, heating in the living room was provided by a small grate, though the high price of coal precluded its regular use. The bedroom, on the other hand, had no form of heating.

The poor in Brecon would have represented a considerable element in the town population. They lay on the unprivileged side of the social divide, and from birth they were afforded few opportunities for improving their status. Until the passing of the Poor Law Amendment Act in 1834, the main feature of poor relief at Brecon, and elsewhere in Wales, had been determined by the Poor Law Act 1601. By this legislation the care of the poor had been made the responsibility of the parishes, and a very important distinction was drawn between the able-bodied vagabonds who could work, and the old and impotent who were incapable of labour. The former were to be set to work in a house of correction or the gaol, while the latter were to be provided with relief, either by alms or by supplying them with stocks of hemp, wool and similar material to work on. For this category of poor, parishes could build 'convenient houses of dwelling'. Poor children were to be apprenticed, and begging was made illegal. The scheme was to be financed by the imposition of a compulsory rate on householders, to be administered by officers known as overseers appointed by the justices. In the wake of this legislation, a house of correction was erected in the Watton, but in Brecon, as in other towns in the Principality, the indigent were to benefit also from the charitable instincts of some of the wealthier citizens, and this benevolence could take the form of money, food and clothes.

This tradition of charitable giving to alleviate the distress of the poor was maintained throughout Georgian and Victorian times. Archdeacon Richard Davies did his utmost to relieve their necessities, and he initiated many a scheme towards this end. In 1820 he was in receipt of £195 19s. 9d. to be distributed among the poor, and he used the money to purchase coal, bread, and blankets for them. He provided succour for the poor in other ways as well. Once, during a particularly severe winter, when heavy snow had caused deep distress among the destitute, he employed them, at his own expense, to clear the snow from the streets of Brecon. On another occasion, when their suffering was acute, he found work for them in whitewashing dwellings in certain districts of the town and in making drains.

On occasions the whole community rallied to the relief of the poor, and meetings were held in the town hall to organise collections. And wealthy individuals, before departing this earthly abode to meet their maker, would appease their consciences by leaving money in their wills to be devoted for charitable purposes. George Price Watkins of Penoyre, the founder in 1832 of the infirmary in the Watton, left the proceeds from £1,000 invested in three per cent stock to be divided 'among such decayed, discrepit (*sic*) inhabitants not receiving parish relief', while Sir Joseph Baily of Glanusk Park left £20 to be distributed annually among them.

This kind of relief did not touch directly a main cause of the suffering of the poor, namely the low wages of many of those in employment. In 1785, the Berkshire magistrates meeting at Speenhamland, had decided to supplement wages where necessary in order to raise them to subsistence level. The general adoption of this system throughout England and Wales had disastrous consequences, since workers lapsed into a condition of moral and economic degradation. An outward index of the disaster was the poor rate which became a crushing burden, particularly on agriculture, since the rate was levied upon land. The evil had to be tackled, and so in 1834 Lord Melbourne's Whig government passed the Poor Law Amendment Act. The Speenhamland System was swept away, and outdoor relief was forbidden except to the aged and infirm. Parishes were grouped into Unions, and any able-bodied person applying for relief had to enter a workhouse where the workhouse test was applied. Within each Union the administration of these regulations became the responsibility of a Board of Guardians elected by the ratepayers.

Following this legislation Brecknock, in the autumn of 1836, was divided into Unions, and within the Brecon Union, which consisted of forty-two parishes, tenders for a new workhouse were immediately sought. The new Union workhouse was erected in 1839 on an eminence overlooking St David's church, on land granted by Sir Charles Morgan, and far enough from the town centre to satisfy the delicate susceptibilities of the borough's middle class. Added pressure for a new workhouse to replace the inadequate building in Mount Street had been created by the increasing number of vagrant poor passing through the town en route to the industrial valleys of south Wales, and by destitute Irish fleeing from famine in Ireland following the potato blight of the mid 1840s. Conditions within the workhouse were probably Dickensian and, like little Oliver Twist, inmates might well have asked for more. The system of poor relief established in 1834 endured until 1894. It was then partially superseded as the functions of the Guardians were taken over by the recently formed District Councils. Today, the workhouse at Brecon has been adapted for another purpose, namely, as a geriatric hospital. The pitiful state of the poor in Brecon will help, somewhat, to dispel the cosy image of Victorian family life captured on canvas by painters such as Charles Lucy in his 'Sunny Hours of Childhood'.

The physical expansion of the town, its increasing prosperity (despite the large number of poor people) and growing import- ance in Georgian and Victorian times made the building of a new market both necessary and desirable. It was necessary because the farmers preferred not to do business on the lower floor of the Gild Hall; rather were they disposed to sell their produce in the inns and the open streets without payment of tolls, with the result that

St David's Hospital, Llanfaes.
On this site stood the Brecon Union Workhouse

59

these streets were obstructed and 'rendered dangerous and inconvenient to the inhabitants and public at large passing through the same'. This practice also contributed to the streets becoming filthy, and a breeding ground of disease, and visitors to the borough were not slow in complaining about the lack of cleanliness. To the Corporation the building of a new market hall was desirable because it would enhance the dignity of the borough. It was generally felt that no market town was worth its salt unless provided with a proper and well regulated market place.

These considerations led to an application by the Corporation to Parliament for an act enabling it to erect a new market hall, and on 8 May 1838 the 'Act for providing market places and for regulating the Markets within the Borough of Brecon, in the County of Brecon', received royal assent. Together with the erection of a new market hall, the act also made provision for the establishment of a cattle market and the building of an abattoir.

The new market was erected on the site of the 'Queen's Head Inn' and gardens. A number of dwelling houses were appropriated as well as a shop, a tan-yard and a malt house. The hall, designed by T.H. Wyatt, was built by a local builder, Thomas Griffith. Though the original estimate was £2,280, the final bill amounted to £4,500. A stretch of Castle Street was widened, and Sir Charles Morgan of Tredegar donated £200 towards this end. On 4 April 1840 the market was officially opened by the mayor, Mr Henry Lucas.

In the act of 1838 it was decreed that once the new market had been opened, no agricultural produce could be exposed for sale within the borough. However, fish, vegetables, poultry, eggs, butter and fruit could still be sold from door to door when carried in hand baskets. Furthermore, once the abattoir had been constructed, animals could not be slaughtered in any other place. The Coporation was to furnish weighing machines in or near the market place and charge people for their use. The market tolls were also laid down in the act, and there were two categories of toll payers: those who rented permanent stalls and traded in 'enclosed, covered shops' throughout the week, and those who made use of the market on market days only, that is, on Wednesdays and Saturdays. Some of the tolls charged were as follows:

Butcher's stall for a whole week—4s.
Butcher's stall on market days only—2s. 6d.
For those not occupying a stall—the selling of a carcase of a bull or steer—2s.
of a calf, pig or sheep—6d.
Fruit and vegetable stall for whole week—3s.
on market days only—1s. 6d.

From the commencement the new market hall proved a financial liability. This may well have been because farmers, notoriously conservative in their outlook, and having traded for centuries in the streets or inns, were reluctant to change their habits. In 1842 the Corporation decided to let the tolls and, having advertised for tenders, accepted one for £500 to run for the twelve months from June 1842 to June 1843.

The mismanagement of the market was such that in 1862 the decision was taken to privatise it and the responsibility for running it was transferred to a company. The tolls had amounted annually to no more than £320. Since the Corporation claimed £210 a year towards its general finances, this left only £110 to pay the interest on borrowed capital and other expenses. The Corporation had also failed to fulfil some of its obligations under the terms of the act of 1838. A slaughterhouse had not been provided, and the cattle market and fairs were still being held in the streets of the town.

The fixed capital of the new company was to be £3,000, the money to be raised by selling 300 shares at £10 a share. Four directors were appointed: John Parry de Winton, John Evans (a banker), Joseph Bass and William de Winton. The Corporation was still to receive its slice of the cake, £210 a year, and the company was empowered to provide a cattle market with an abattoir adjacent to it. Those wishing to sell produce in the streets had to obtain a licence to do so, for which £1 a year was paid. Failure to obtain one could result in a fine of up to £2. The company was permitted to let the market tolls together with those of the fairs, cattle market and slaughterhouse. The markets and fairs were to be advertised by the town crier who was to be paid for his services from market levies. Animals (cattle, sheep and pigs) driven through the streets of the town were still subject to a drift toll.

By 1878 a cattle market had been established in *Clawdd y Gaer* and it is still located there. Furthermore, a slaughterhouse had been provided in Free Street though it was never used as the Local Government Board felt that the site chosen was unsuitable, and that it did not conform to local health requirements. But in order to remove all cattle trading from the streets, a larger cattle market was required, and the company also wished to let the tolls by auction rather than by tender. And so in 1878 the Brecon Market Amendment Act was passed. The cattle market was enlarged, and all cattle sales in the streets of Brecon came to an end. However, the ban did not apply to horses, and horse trading continued in the streets of the town, though mainly in Llanfaes, until fairly recent times.

While the bill was passing through its various stages, a petition was received from the residents of Llanfaes, headed by the Rev. Rees Price, vicar of St David's, Conway Lloyd of Dinas and the

Brecon Market at the turn of the century

Rev. J.D. Williams, headmaster of Christ College. In 1876 Llanfaes had been subject to heavy flooding, houses and shops being under four feet of water, and so they wanted a clause inserted in the bill to prevent a recurrence arising from the depositing of rubbish in the river Usk. Since the slaughterhouse in Free Street could not be used, the company had erected another behind the market hall in Market Street or Horn Lane as it was then called. The temptation to dispose of the offal in the nearby river might well have proved irresistible. It is possible that it was because of the justifiable fears of the citizens of Llanfaes that a new and spacious abattoir was built near the canal bank on its present location. The petition having evoked no official response, Mr John Lloyd of Dinas undertook a study of the problem, and in the light of his findings decided to raise an embankment at the *Gwttws*. This barrier greatly alleviated the situation.

In 1897 it was decided to hold an *eisteddfod* at Brecon, 'the proceeds to be devoted in aid of the outlay made by the conversion of the dairy, produce and provision areas in the General Market into a spacious hall—a much needed want in our town—suitable for holding large assemblies as well as for its original purpose'. The *eisteddfod* proved a success, and the significant amount of money raised was used to adapt the market hall. Apart from some minor alterations, the market hall of 1897 is the one which still serves the town of Brecon today.

The town's increasing size and rapidly growing population considerably exacerbated the problems of health and hygiene, with the result that the spectre of death found a congenial home there. One grave problem was undoubtedly poor housing, for while the affluent dwelt in homes which were 'large and good', and provided with proper water closets, the habitats of the poor were far from hygienic. The materials used in their construction, the size of rooms and lack of ventilation, the poor water supply and lack of drainage meant that all kinds of diseases could thrive within. Observers commented upon the inadequacies of their water closets since 'one is made to serve for several houses and these are in many instances placed in exposed situations, in others close to dwelling houses in confined courts. The necessaries empty generally into open cesspools which are cleared by manual labour, and the contents carried away for manure'. Refuse water was invariably disposed of in the streets, a most unhealthy practice when it is considered that the town's drains were very inadequate. Sewers were virtually non-existent and in 1845 Sir Henry de la Beche complained that 'there are no sewers in the town with the exception of a small one, two feet in diameter, in Castle Street'. The drainage from 48 horses stabled at the barracks ran into the canal, hardly contributing to its attractions as an amenity.

But undoubtedly the principal factor exercising a deleterious influence on health was the problem of a pure water supply. In previous centuries the town had been provided with its water from a pond in Glamorgan Street, situated to the south of St Mary's church, and from numerous public and private wells such as the Maendu Well, the Priory Well, one situated near the street called 'Well Street', another in the Postern, close to the bed of the Honddu, and St David's Well near the workhouse. In 1776 the Brecon Town Improvement Act empowered a body of commissioners to pave, light and clean the streets as well as to arrange for a proper supply of drinking water. They built a reservoir below the Priory churchyard, a singularly unsuitable situation as it was surrounded by trees. To this reservoir water was pumped from the Honddu through the old engine house, and then gravity fed into the town along wooden pipes laid by one Benjamin Grazebrook of Stroud. The water was unfiltered 'so that when the river is discoloured . . . by . . . floods, the leet waters are coloured also and pumped into the reservoir'. G.T. Clark, who arrived in Brecon in 1849 as an inspector appointed under the terms of the 1848 Health Act, added that the water was contaminated by 'decayed leaves from the trees in the Grove falling into the open Reservoir'. Between 1811-13 these wooden pipes were replaced by cast iron ones, the contractor being Thomas Proberts of Abergavenny. Under the terms of the contract he was also to pave and pitch the streets.

With this background of dirty streets, sub-standard housing, completely inadequate sewers, and polluted water, it is hardly

64

surprising that Brecon should have been affected occasionally by outbreaks of cholera, a disfiguring disease which struck with great speed, and whose victims were predominantly the elderly, the young and the underprivileged. The new killer struck first in Sunderland in October 1831. The next thirty-five years witnessed three more attacks of this scourge: 1848-9, 1853-4 and 1866. Brecon suffered from two of these visitations, in 1849 when two people died, and 1854 when 57 succumbed to the disease. It is worthy of note that of the eight Welsh towns affected in 1854 only two, Brecon and Caernarfon, were not important industrial centres.

A central figure in the battle against the epidemic in 1854 was Dr Thomas Prestwood Lucas.[3] He had succeeded his father in his Brecon practice and as physician to the infirmary in the Watton. Dr Lucas was in no doubt as to the cause of the outbreak; it was the ill-timed cleansing of an open sewer in *Beili Glas*. He reports that it was 'in consequence of the long continuance of dry weather in a very filthy state. Its contents were carried to a part of a field near the row of houses . . . & there left'. In his view it was the accumulation of this filth that was responsible. His appraisal of the situation was incorrect. Though he was plainly puzzled by the fact that some of the filthiest areas in the town like Llanfaes, and the upper end of the Struet, did not produce cholera, he failed to make the crucial connection with the water supply to the afflicted premises.

The real villains were the Madrell brook and the well in close proximity to it. The Madrell rose on the southern slope of Pen-y-Crug and emptied into the Usk by the Promenade. It acted as a sewer and a source of water for washing for houses near its path. The well at *Beili Glas* was occasionally polluted through the overflowing of the Madrell, which ran into a culvert within two yards of it. There was a concentration of infected houses along the course of the stream between the Priory church and the Usk, in Nicholas Row, Priory Row, London Row, Black Boy and Mill Street.

Forty-one victims were buried in the church yard of St John's and of these 33 came from *Beili Glas* or adjacent areas. Most were labourers or craftsmen, and the area where they lived constituted a 'working class' district. Among this number, also, were nine widows, a clear indication of the desperate plight of these unfortunates in days when pensions and national insurance payments were not available.

The burial of so many bodies in St John's placed considerable pressure on space there, and this meant that either the burial ground was extended, or a new cemetery had to be provided. The former course of action was successfully resisted by powerful local landed interests, and prominent in this lobby was the Marquis of Camden. And so on 19 October 1857 it was decided to purchase, for £620, five acres of Court farm from the trustees of Sir Charles Morgan. It was in this manner that the Municipal Cemetery in Cradoc Road came into existence.

However, lessons were learnt from the cholera outbreak. The Madrell was covered over for most of its length, and by 1880 Brecon had been provided with a network of sewers leading to a sewerage farm and tank at Brynich, a mile and a half to the east of the town. The scheme was one of downward filtration, and the engineer responsible was Samuel Harper of Merthyr. J.R. Cobb also proposed, in a private bill, to supply the town with better water and a drainage system, but the opposition of the Corporation led to his dropping the bill. The Corporation itself now took some of his proposals on board, and on 9 January 1866 the first sod of the new filter beds was cut by the Mayor, Alderman Prothero, on land above the workhouse and about a mile from the town. These developments represented considerable advances in protecting the health of the populace by the turn of the century. Particularly was this so when taken in conjunction with regulations concerning the abatement of filth in houses, lodging houses and the market—these premises had to be connected with sewers—and the prohibition on the keeping of pigs in close proximity to living premises.

But cholera was not the only disease to cause an alarming mortality rate in the town, especially among babes and the very young. From a report on the causes of death in the town over a five year period leading up to 1848, the following are listed as the commonest:

Small Pox—4	Apoplexy—9
Measles—8	Paralysis—6
Scarlatina—45	Convulsions—107
(Scarlet Fever)	
Whooping Cough—24	Bronchitis—24
Dysentery—4	Pneumonia—29
Diarrhoea—21	Phthisis—145
	(Tuberculosis)
Cholera—2	Dropsy—26
Hydrocephalus—12	Child Birth—10

Since measles and whooping cough were not at this time officially certifiable diseases, doubtless many cases would have gone unrecorded. However, despite the frightening nature of some of these statistics, the report ends on a very complacent note 'Thus one can see that Brecon, as a whole, was an exceptionally healthy town during the '40s'.

It was the devastating rate of infant mortality which detracted somewhat from the cosy Victorian image of Brecon as a comfortable county and market town noted for its elegance and 'style', and set it on a par with an industrial metropolis like Merthyr Tydfil to the south. In both towns death in the age group up to five years accounted for almost a third of the total number of deaths. This contrasted unfavourably with a figure of one in four for the gentry class in Brecon for the same age group. When one considers the damp, badly-ventilated dwellings of the poor, and the ill-drained swamps of Llanfaes, where the settlements of Heol Hwnt and Silver Street were expanding rapidly, it is hardly surprising to discover that Tuberculosis was the deadliest killer of all.

Poverty and deprivation were causes of much of the lawlessness in Brecon during Georgian and Victorian times. The most common crime of all was theft, either of animals, particularly sheep, or from the person. Pigs, geese and horses were also taken, the latter because they were in great demand in the mines and iron works of south Wales. From a list of fifteen prisoners incarcerated in the county gaol in 1800, no fewer than nine had been guilty of stealing clothes and, of these, three were sentenced to seven years transportation. Margaret Jenkins, aged thirty, had stolen wearing apparel, while John and Anne Owen, aged forty-nine and fifty respectively, had illegally appropriated for themselves a piece of blue cloth. David Phillips, accused of sheep stealing, had been sentenced to death, and the youngest of the prisoners, John Jenkins, a boy of twelve, had been sentenced to two years solitary confinement for putting poison in a tea kettle 'to injure his master and family'.

Theft was punishable in several ways. The usual penalty was imprisonment and the prisoner could be put in irons, kept in solitary, or made to walk the treadmill. Thieves could also be sentenced to transportation to the colonies or to Botany Bay. The pillory, 'branding on the cheeke', and the whip could also be their lot. Occasionally they might even be hanged, though this extreme form of punishment was invariably reserved for murderers or those guilty of attempted murder. Since hangings at this time were public spectactles hundreds, even thousands, of people would be attracted to the gaol to witness the macabre proceedings. During the period that John Lazenby was governor of the county gaol in Llanfaes—he was appointed governor in 1837 and remained in the office for some forty years—three men were hanged for homicide. On 10 April 1845 Thomas Thomas was hanged for shooting a Cardiganshire butter farmer, David Lewis, at Trecastle; James Griffiths suffered a similar fate in 1849 for murdering a fellow servant with an axe at Cwmgwdi; and on 23 April 1861 William Williams was executed for shooting his aunt at Crickhowell. This was the last occasion on which a public hanging was to take place at Brecon. The motive behind all three killings was financial gain.

Prison could also be the fate of those who had incurred debts of £2 and over, though in most gaols either a separate building, or separate rooms, were provided for them. Creditors responsible for having debtors placed behind bars have been castigated as heartless, grasping individuals, but this was not usually the case, since it has been estimated that only one in ten debtors found themselves in a debtors' prison. There was a great deal of public sympathy for those imprisoned for petty debts, as it meant that a man could be separated from his wife, children and family for a considerable period of time. Public concern expressed itself in the formation of a society for the discharge and relief of persons imprisoned for debts throughout England and Wales, and one of its founder members was the Rev. John Neild who had reported on conditions in the gaol at Brecon in 1806.

Within the county gaol in Brecon the daily regimen for prisoners was generally hard even though discipline, at times, was lax and prisoners, with the help of relatives and friends on the outside, could make good their escape. The fare was meagre consisting in the main of gruel, potatoes and bread, a monotonous and ill-balanced diet, relieved occasionally through the generosity of public benefactors who would provide money, food, clothes, wood and coal. In 1830 the prisoners in the county gaol publicly expressed their thanks 'to the Rev. Canon Williams of Abercamlais for a most excellent dinner of roast beef and plum pudding supplied to them on Christmas day'. But the prisoners suffered most from the cold, and when a number of justices inspected the county gaol in 1841 it appeared to them that the method of warming certain areas of the prison was 'cruelly insufficient, and particularly during inclement weather'. Problems could also be exacerbated through overcrowding and in the 1840s, in order to relieve pressure on space, an application was made to the Home Secretary for permission to transfer some prisoners to a gaol in one of the neighbouring counties.

The relative calm which generally prevailed in the streets of Brecon was occasionally disturbed by the incidence of rioting, and this was particularly true of the year 1831. The 1830s and 1840s were decades which witnessed considerable unrest and discontent in the industrial towns of south Wales where the workers were agitating for reform. Apart from a small forge on the banks of the Honddu, Brecon had remained impervious to industrialisation with its most unpleasant social consequences. However, the

69

Merthyr riots of 1831—and travel by coach had doubtless helped to speed up the dissemination of news—were still to cause reverberations in the town. Notice of the rioting caused considerable unrest among prisoners in the county gaol. They became turbulent and unruly, with the result that privileges, such as the weekly visit from relatives and friends, were withdrawn.

On a Friday night in 1831 Brecon's streets erupted into violence. It had been rumoured in the town that the effigy of a gentleman, opposed to reform, was to be burnt in Llanfaes, and considerable numbers of workmen assembled determined to prevent this from happening. This disturbance was doubtless related to the Merthyr riots, but the trouble may also have been caused by the country-wide agitation for parliamentary reform. Nothing transpired in Llanfaes. Instead, the effigy was paraded through the main streets of the town, accompanied by shouts of 'Watkins and Reform'.[4] Thirty-five panes of glass in the front windows of the house of the Rev. Thomas Vaughan in Priory Hill were broken. The mob then pursued its way through the town, systematically breaking the windows of gentlemen's residences. In the Watton they attacked the house of Major Price, a worthy, charitable and popular man. The rioters further declared their intention of freeing the prisoners in the town and county gaols. They averred that in the county gaol the prisoners were 'obliged to live on bread and water'. The rioters only dispersed after the magistrates had threatened to read the Riot Act. Seven or eight of those involved were arrested and released on bail and, to prevent a recurrence, 250 male citizens were sworn in as special constables.

However, Brecon was not finished with protest yet. Dissatisfaction with the terms of the 1832 Reform Act had led to the growth of Chartism among the industrial proletariat and these Chartists, in an attempt to win support in rural areas, organised a meeting in the town. The first venue was the 'Black Cock Inn' but the landlord, on discovering the true purpose of the gathering, had everyone evicted. The Chartists then moved to the 'Bull's Head', where a journeyman plasterer was elected as chairman. Many of the worthy citizens of the borough attended from sheer curiosity, though huntsmen in their midst attempted to disrupt proceedings by blowing their horns. The meeting became so unruly that it was decided to adjourn proceedings until the following night. In the meantime mine host in the 'Bull's Head' was given to understand that he was not to receive such characters in his house, and the next meeting, of necessity, was held in yet another inn, the 'King's Head' in Kensington, where the chair was occupied by David Jones, a carpenter. The Chartist missionary from Brynmawr promised that John Frost himself would come to address them. And so would Feargus O'Connor, 'a nice man . . . who had plenty of tongue and plenty of money'. A paper containing several resolutions was then read. One related to the forming of a society, each member to pay a penny a week; the tenor of another was that the society should act as a moral force—as opposed to physical force—to obtain a Charter. The chair would appear to have received little support from the floor and nothing was achieved.

Prior to the passing of the Municipal Corporations Act in 1835, policing in the borough of Brecon was largely the responsibility of constables, two being appointed to each of the twelve wards in the town. Nominally under the control of the bailiff and magistrates and unpaid, it can be assumed that they did not display great zeal in the performance of their duties. Frequently the office was filled by a deputy who received a half guinea or a guinea for his services. However, this system of policing was so inefficient that some of the leading citizens of the town had formed an association to which each member paid an annual subscription. The money so raised was to be expended on the rewarding, and payment of expenses, of those providing information which led to the apprehension and conviction of felons. The Brecon Association or Society was known as 'The Brecon Uskside Association for the prosecution of Felons'.

In the 1820s a development of the utmost importance took place where policing was concerned. This was the establishment of the Metropolitan police by Sir Robert Peel in 1829. They were to be efficiently trained, and adequately paid, and they were to be a civilian and not a military force. All over the country local

71

authorities imitated Peel's organisation and established police forces of their own though Brecon, doubtless because of the expense involved and the additional burden on the rates, was slow to follow. It was the Municipal Corporations Act 1835 that was instrumental in galvanising the borough into some kind of action. By the terms of the act, the new town councils were to nominate from their own body a sufficient number of councillors to form a Watch Committee. This body, in turn, was to appoint 'a sufficient number of fit men to act as constables for preserving the peace of night and day'. Brecon was provided with three police officers, and they were to wear a distinctive uniform. Each was issued with a blue coat and a police hat 'marked in white on the right side, and the collar with B.P. No 1, B.P. No 2 and B.P No 3 and that all the clothing of the Town Crier and Police Officrs be considered Corporation property'. In 1835 the three officers in Brecon were Jonas Williams, the town gaoler and chief police officer, David Davies and John Waters. Jonas, at a salary of £7 10s. for a period of three months, was to patrol the beat in the upper division of St John; David Davies's sphere of responsibility was Ship Street and the parish of St David's (Llanfaes), and John Waters's beat was the Chapelry of St Mary (the town centre).

The need to extend this organisation into the rural areas resulted in the passing of an act in 1856 which made compulsory the establishment of a county police force on a full-time, regular and paid basis. Counties had been empowered to do this in 1839, but the legislation was permissive in character, and consequently few did so. It was a different story in 1856. Breconshire jumped to it, and a Chief Constable was immediately appointed in the person of Lieutenant E.R. Gwynne from a list of thirty applicants, most of whom had military backgrounds or were possessed of previous police experience with other authorities. Gwynne was to remain in this office for forty-eight years—until his retirement in 1905. The total strength of the county force under his command was twenty-nine, scattered over fourteen districts and, apart from Gwynne, it consisted of two Superintendents, six sergeants, and seventeen constables. Brecon, as the county town and administrative headquarters, was allocated six and Brynmawr and Ystradgynlais, on the industrial fringe of the county where a greater degree of disorder and unrest could be expected, were allotted four and three respectively. The other districts had to be content with two or even one.

While the upper echelons of the force were chosen from candidates with a certain social cachet, the lower ranks were recruited from the labouring classes, for whom appointment to the force meant escape from the drudgery of work in a factory or on a farm. It further meant job security, respect, an opportunity for promotion and, to cap it all, a pension on retirement. In 1890 the police were awarded a pension after twenty-five years service or after fifteen if warranted on medical grounds.

The establishment of a county police force inevitably resulted in the provision of station houses which could be used as lock-ups as well as homes. After 1857 these were established in such places as Builth, Hay, Gilwern, Tal-y-bont, Cefn Coed, Crickhowell and, in 1874, Brecon. The Brecon station was a substantial building adjoining the shire hall and overlooking Captain's Walk. In 1842 a smaller lock-up had been built in the Postern in close proximity to the Honddu.

(Dewi Davies, *Law and Disorder*, p. 107)
Postern Gaol

The Police Station, Captain's Walk

Just as Brecon had acquired a quasi-metropolitan status in Georgian and Victorian times, so also, during these centuries, was there a subtle, but very gradual, change in the character of the town. Until the end of the seventeenth century, Brecon had been a borough with a distinctly Welsh flavour. Many of the streets had Welsh names such as Heol-y-Llygoden (Mouse Street), Lôn-y-Poptŷ Boeth (Lane of the Hot Bakehouse). Groes Heol (Cross Street) and Heol Rydd (Free Street). And the language generally spoken in the streets had been Welsh. Indeed, according to Hugh Thomas, the Breconshire Herald, writing in 1698, it was 'as good as any in Wales'. Furthermore, when Hugh Thomas wrote, though there were some 400 families living in the borough 'scarce thirty were of English name and descent'.

However, the primacy of the Welsh tongue was to be challenged and then overthrown in the eighteenth and nineteenth centuries. It was not a phenomenon which occurred overnight. It would appear that the Welsh language was first corrupted through the increasing adoption of English words, a 'Wenglish' mentality, before it was finally overwhelmed by the English tide. Eminent people living within the borough were very conscious of what was happening. There is the testimony of the Rev. D. Charles, Principal of Trefeca. In 1847 he declared before the Education Commissioners that 'The English Language is fast gaining ground in the neighbourhood, so much so that the Welsh will not continue to be the prevailing language in a few years. The admixture of both English and Welsh in the dialect at present spoken render it highly desirable that the people be correctly taught in the language they will have to use in the future'. John Williams, editor of the *Silurian*, also appeared before the commissioners, and confirmed that the English language was gaining ground, and that it was 'desirable that it should be better taught . . . in his neighbourhood it is true, the employments of the population are entirely connected with agriculture, but great numbers every year obtain work in the iron and coal districts and for these employments an imperfect knowledge of English was an obstacle to promotion'.

But the transformation of the linguistic scene partook of the nature of an autumnal rather than a cataclysmic change, and this is borne out by the evidence of the Rev. Henry Griffiths, Principal of the Independent College, Brecon. While agreeing that English was gaining ground, he argued that the speed of change 'was not as fast as Englishmen are apt to suppose. Very few pulpits or Sunday schools have changed language within the memory of man'.

There were a multiplicity of factors at work accounting for the virtual demise of the Welsh language in the town. Undoubtedly the most important was the use of English as the medium of instruction in the schools. It was the language generally employed in the elementary, Sunday, private and secondary schools. It was only in the Circulating Schools of Griffith Jones (one only in Brecon) and the Congregational College that Welsh found favour. Again, sermons from the pulpit, from those of dissenting chapels as well as from those of the church, were increasingly in English, and in the Victorian era it was the 'done thing' to attend a place of worship on Sunday since it conferred a veneer of respectability. The gentry, still in early Victorian times the natural leaders of Welsh society, though their authority was increasingly being undermined by growing commercial interests, had become anglicised by the end of the seventeeth century, and it was inevitable that the society over which they presided should ape their ways. The local newspaper, the *Brecon County Times*, established in 1866 with Edwin Poole as editor from 1873, was written entirely in English, and the influence of the printed word could be paramount. English, furthermore, was the language of local administration, together with being the language employed in the law courts, though interpreters were available. The language of the drill square in the barracks was English, and many English regiments were stationed there. And English was also the tongue of the increasing number of visitors who arrived at the ancient borough and the appearance of the stage coach, and the advent of the railway, had contributed immeasurably to the ease and comfort of travel.

For rich and poor alike, within this closely knit community at Brecon, there were opportunities for relaxation, and time to indulge in pleasurable pursuits. Indeed, the pursuit of pleasure would have occupied the waking hours of most of the urban gentry and many pastimes such as entertaining on a lavish scale, society balls, horse racing, hunting, theatre visits, bowls and fives would have been virtually exclusive to them. Their impressive mansions, serviced by liveried servants, were convenient adjuncts of a luxurious life style. In these elegant homes they wined and dined each other, and played card games and dice, particularly during the long winter evenings. Society balls were also held in the Castle Hotel and the Gild Hall, and on these gala occasions it is easy to imagine young ladies of fashion flirting outrageously with the young blades from the regiment. Flat racing was mooted in 1825 and the first meeting was held in 1828 on a field alongside the river Usk at Abercynrig. Though a stand had not been provided, the races had come to rank as second to none in the Principality. Eminent peers like the Duke of Beaufort and Lord Tredegar were enthusiastic patrons, and the county and borough members of Parliament were also closely associated with the course. Some of the best bred horses, including St Leger favourites, were entered for the races and 'The Steward's Cup', worth £100, was one of the valuable trophies competed for. Furthermore, a pack of hounds was kept in the town, and afforded excellent sport on two or three days a week. The 'sport' included hare coursing, and it is sobering to discover that the mountain hares were 'little and good' and that they 'thoroughly understood their business'. The art of fly fishing indulged the fancies of many, and the followers of Isaac Walton could walk the banks of the Usk and the Honddu, together with their tributary streams, and demonstrate their skills in catching the trout and salmon to be found there in such abundance.

Another great attraction was the theatre and English strolling players entertained the 'genteel' element within the town population. By the Licensing Act 1737 these players were liable to punishment as rogues and vagabonds, and a way had to be found to circumvent the law otherwise actors could not play at marts, fairs, horse-races and cock-matches, or entertain audiences with 'good plays and waggon loads of scenes and adopted habits'. A single actor could escape the clutches of the beadle by becoming a 'lecturer'. Having put together a few observations on human nature, he would journey from town to town playing at the inns or gentlemen's houses. The most interesting of these was Le Sieur Rea. An Irishman with a thick brogue, he had adopted the French title for business purposes. In 1773 he pursued his way from Carmarthen to Brecon giving performances en route at Llandeilo, Llangadock and Llandovery. In Brecon he gave his 'Grand Medley' at Mr Longfellow's 'Golden Lion Inn'.

Some of the companies which visited Wales in the second half of the eighteenth century were very respectable. One such company was established by John Ward, who took the London theatre as his yardstick as he wished to win the support of polite society. His company came to Brecon in 1755 and played there for eight weeks in May and June. The length of the visit would seem to suggest that this was not the company's first introduction to the town. During the stay Sarah Siddons, Brecon's most famous daughter, was born at the 'Shoulder of Mutton' on 5 July. She was not christened until the 14 July when the event was

Sarah Siddons

recorded in St Mary's Parish Register. The entry reads: 'Sarah, d. of George (sic) Kemble, a commedian, and Sarah, his wife'.

Sarah's father, Roger Kemble, had joined the company at Birmingham in 1752. The following year he married Ward's eighteen year old daughter at Cirencester. He was a suave, genial man and she, a dignified and determined girl. Both were regular actors in the company that presented Rowe's *Tamerlane* and Foote's *The Englishman at Paris* to the 'polite and crowded audiences at Brecon.

The company visited Brecon again in 1758 and two years later it fitted up a theatre in the great room of 'The Bell' in High Street Superior. The fare provided was varied and included *The Suspicious Husband* together with Carey's ballad-opera, *The Contrivances*. Ward himself delivered a new prologue entitled 'On the King of Prussia—and the Present Time'. On Easter Monday, at the same venue, the company performed *Macbeth* with a 'Prologue on Shakespeare' by 'the Rev. Mr Greene, master of the Stratford Free School'.

Ward knew how to please. He used the best of the old and the new plays, and the topical items which he introduced were also of interest. He made the temporary theatre, whether in barn, hall or inn, the centre of polite provincial life, and brought London tastes and diversions to the country towns. These little theatres became *foci* of English culture in Wales.

Early in 1784 another resourceful Irishman, John Boles Watson, who had played with Roger Kemble and inherited his circuit, brought his 'Cheltenham Company of Comedians' to Brecon, where it was to present attractions which included paintings and scenery 'newly done by Mr West of the Royal Academy, London'. In 1787 he opened a new theatre in Brecon and acted there from February to April. This theatre was established in the Watton, behind the 'New Inn' and for many years entry was effected through the inn itself. Andrew Maund's last will and testament confirms that he was the owner of both the 'New Inn' and the theatre, and that he and John Boles Watson had entered into some form of partnership concerning the playhouse.[5] The theatre was fitted up and decorated by Abbott, and among the plays presented were *Alexander the Great, The School For Scandal*, and General Burgoyne's comedy, *The Heiress*.

The Theatre Royal at Brecon was situated to the east of the T.S.B. It is now a carpet warehouse

In 1789 one of Watson's actresses, a Mrs Hudson, appeared at Brecon alone and gave an entertainment called 'As You Like It'. Her performance concluded with 'A Commemoration of the King's happy recovery—The Royal Procession to St. Paul's'. She delivered her lecture in the great room of 'The Bell' which had also been used by Ward and Kemble. The room was described 'as fitted up with proper scenery, a stage and every decoration necessary to form a complete theatre'.

December 1789 witnessed the arrival of Watson himself in the town, and he acted in the 'Theatre, Brecon', probably the Theatre Royal in the Watton. The most important of his presentations was *Don Juan* or *The Libertine Destroyed*. This was not Mozart's opera, but a ballet with 'Music by Monsieur Gluck as lately performed at the Royalty and both patent theatres'.

Watson died in 1813 and his son took over. In the Theatre Royal at Brecon there was a display by the tight-rope walker, Richer; and Watson junior, in his introductory remarks, was careful to give thanks to the magistrates and the ladies and gentlemen for the 'liberal encouragement conferred upon his father for the last thirty years'.

The Royal at Brecon was also to welcome Andrew Cherry, the first manager of the new theatre at Swansea (1807) who had been a leading actor at Drury Lane. The need to find fashionable audiences during the winter months led him to Brecon where his company played before packed houses. His audiences had the good taste to appreciate the 'classical elegance' of his theatrical decorations, and in January 1808 they generously patronised Miss Cherry's benefit performance of *Ella Rosenburg* and *All in the Wrong*.

The Victorian era bore witness in the provinces to a growing indifference to the theatre. Though border companies still visited Wales, the hazards of the strolling life were increasing for them. The new standards of propriety certainly affected attendances. The increasing emphasis on respectability and outward piety meant that serious men and women ceased to frequent theatres, which were regarded as the haunts of the feckless and the frivolous. Gentry patronage in many instances was withdrawn, and the provincial theatre was doomed. By mid-century it had come to be held that any gentleman who supported players was either gay or eccentric. Methodism also played a part in the decline, since the prophets of the new awakening warned their followers against players whom they considered to be the children of the Devil or, worse still, the offspring of the English Devil. To thoughtful men it was clear that a certain degree of immorality accompanied performances and in Wales, as in England, the playhouse attracted prostitutes. It would appear that the Methodists had some grounds for complaint. Expensive stars, transported around the country in fast coaches, added to their woes; so did the insatiable demand for novelties. Even the new fashion of dining late compounded their problems. Those hostile to the stage gained the ascendancy, and the traditions of the English theatre in Wales were gradually forgotten.

The Crisps, a border company whose circuit included Worcester, Hereford, Shrewsbury and Chester, strained every sinew to sustain the theatre. In 1822 the company opened in Brecon and during the next eight years Charles Crisp was to play at his 'elegant little theatre' in the town. His seasons lasted four months, and among his patrons were Mrs Wilkins of Penoyre, Mrs Powell of Cantref, and the officers of the Royal Welsh Fusiliers. In 1824 his theatre was lit by gas and, five years later, he introduced a pair of famous actresses, the Misses Tree, to the town. He varied his plays, and he could claim with every justification that his seasons provided 'a continued round of novelty'.

However, the changed climate in Victorian times meant that the days of the Theatre Royal were numbered, and the last recorded performance took place in 1870/71. There had been a degree of intimacy about the Georgian theatre, and the halls had been small, enabling a close rapport to be established between actor and audience. The Victorian taste for lavish performances meant that larger theatres were required and, after 1871, when drama was performed at Brecon-or concerts given—they were presented at the recently-built market hall. For the great stars the coming of the railway offered an even faster means of transportation and when Adelina Patti, arguably the greatest of the

Victorian divas, sang at the market hall, she arrived there from her home at Craig-y-Nos by courtesy of the Brecon to Neath railway.

The game of bowls also had its army of dedicated followers, and its popularity was demonstrated by the fact that there were bowling greens at the Castle Hotel, in Llanfaes and in the Watton. Fives was another attraction. This was a ball game played by two or four players in a court enclosed on three or four sides, the hard ball being struck with the hand which was usually protected by a glove. On 23 February 1786 the following challenge was published in the *Hereford Journal*:

'Brecon Fives Court
There are two men in the town of Brecon who will play a Rubber at fives, with battleboards, in the court of Brecon Castle against any two men in the Kingdom of One Hundred Guineas . . . If any chuse (*sic*) to accept of the challenge they may apply to Mr Jones at the Castle aforesaid'.

A spectator sport which attracted people from all walks of life was cock-fighting. Contests of this kind, held either in a church-yard or in specially designed cockpits, were bloody affairs but nonetheless extremely popular. On 16 May 1775 a cock-fight at the 'Greyhound Inn', Bridge Street, Llanfaes was advertised in the following terms:

'A cock Match to be fought at the Greyhound Inn between the gentlemen of Brecon and the gentlemen of Carmarthen on the 29th May instant. Twenty-one Cocks on each side for Four Guineas a Battle and Fifty the odd, and ten byes for Two Guineas a battle'.

Leisure hours were also spent in the convivial atmosphere of an inn, and Brecon was liberally supplied in this respect since a 'drink map' of 1834 reveals the existence of forty-seven in the town and its suburbs. Llanfaes could boast twelve, the Watton ten, the Struet four while the remainder were scattered over the town itself. Beer was quaffed in large quantities, and for many it represented a temporary escape from the miseries of a humdrum existence. It is hardly surprising, therefore, that reports of proceedings in Police Courts reveal that drunkenness was one of the commonest offences. In a typical quarterly report to the Standing Joint Committee of the Police Authority in 1898, twenty-six persons were proceeded against on grounds of drunkenness, and twenty-three were convicted, while fifty-four were accused of being drunk and disorderly and of these fifty-three were found guilty. However, these proceedings did have their lighter moments particularly when it was reported in the *Brecon and Radnor Express* that one good soul was prosecuted for being drunk in charge of a donkey. Such was her state of inebriation that she had no control over the animal, and found it difficult to clamber back into the cart. Her defence had been that she was rheumatic. She was ordered to pay seven shillings costs.

Drink resulted in all sorts of antisocial behaviour, such as breaking gas lamps, shop windows, robbing gardens, assaults in the streets and wife beating, particularly on Saturday nights. It was the opinion of at least one policeman that Llanfaes, an area with a great deal of poor housing, was the worst district in the town, and police did not dare venture there singly on Saturday nights. Gas lighting had first been introduced into Brecon in 1822, and it was employed as a form of lighting in the schools—though masters were encouraged to be frugal in its use—in the theatre, in the larger houses, and to illuminate the streets. It was the gas standards in the streets that were the objects of attack by drunkards, though mischievous boys also delighted in breaking the glass with their slings and catapults and had to be dealt with by irate town magistrates. The introduction of gas lighting, and of petroleum lamps, effected the demise of the tallow chandlers represented by several reputable families in Brecon, notably the Winstones and the Prices of Bridge Street.

But the inns were also closely associated with gambling and an inhabitant of the town, who wished to remain anonymous from fear of being assaulted, wrote in 1825 to the bailiff, as the chief magistrate of the borough, complaining of the gambling in inns like 'The Bell' and the 'Golden Lion' in High Street Superior, the 'Flag and Castle' in Llanfaes, and 'The Lamb' in the Watton. He

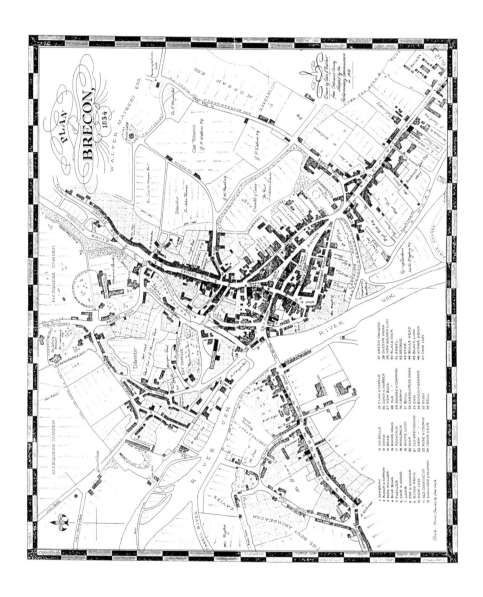

PLAN OF BRECON, 1834

Drawn by Saml Fletcher.
From Ordnance Survey. Adapted by the Bridesmeadow Commissioners in 1832.

1 CAMBRIAN
2 PLOUGH & HARROW
3 KING WILLIAM
4 BLUE BOAR
5 FOUNTAIN
6 COCK & HORSE
7 LAMB
8 FOX & HOUNDS
9 KING'S ARMS
10 NEW INN
11 OLD COACH & PAIR
12 SHOULDER of MUTTON

13 SIX BELLS
14 SWAN
15 BEAR
16 BOAR'S HEAD
17 FALSTAFF
18 WOOLPACK
19 WHITE LION
20 SHIP
21 OLD GREYHOUND
22 HEN
23 ROSE & CROWN
24 CROSS KEYS

25 PLAN & CASTLE
26 COACH & HORSES
27 NEW BUCK
28 OLD
29 SQUARE & COMPASS
30 CROWN
31 BULL
32 CARPENTERS ARMS
33 SUN
34 BUNCH of GRAPES
35 BUSH
36 BULL

37 GREEN DRAGON
38 QUEENS HEAD
39 NEW GOLDEN LION
40 BLACK COCK
41 BELL
42 GEORGE
43 STAR
44 BULLS HEAD
45 BLACK LION
46 KING'S HEAD
47 CWM INN

Scale Three Chains to One Inch

asserted that at the 'Bell', in a 'back room called the Coffee room there is a Bagatelle table with cards carried on every night to very late hours attended by young men who give much pain to their friends. There is also a table of this description at the "New Lion" attended by the lowest subjects with cards also to all hours, but the most destructive of all houses is the "Flag and Castle", Llanfaes, kept by one of the Martins, who to evade the eye of justice takes his gambling to the garret'. In his eyes these inns were dens of iniquity 'so that a decent female cannot pass the streets in safety'. The Council was slow to respond, and it was not until 1829 that a resolution was passed which prohibited the issue of any further licences for the opening of new inns.

In the mid-nineteenth century cricket was introduced into the town and in 1850 the Brecon Town and Garrison Cricket Club was founded with rules and regulations based on those which had been formulated by the Marylebone Club. There was play on Mondays, Tuesdays and Thursdays with wickets being pitched at 4.30 p.m. and stumps being drawn two hours later. The approach to the game was very relaxed, and when in August 1863 Brecon played the Welsh Wanderers, since the latter had brought only eight men, 'Brecon allowed them three to field'. The cricket scorebooks contain some acerbic comments on the quality of play of some of the cricketers. Thus while one is savouring the fact that 'Crombie did not bowl well', we are then further regaled with the caustic comment that 'he did not bat very well either'. These were also the days of the country house elevens associated with parks like Glanusk, Ffrwdgrech and Maesllwch.

In 1869 the game of football made its appearance. It contrasted starkly with the game of today as there were no rules regarding handling or off-side, and a match could be played between six scholars of Christ College and six gentlemen of Brecon. Incidents of foul play were not unusual and in April 1897, in a match between Brecon and Hereford Reserves, an S. Stenton, who throughout the match had had much to say concerning the referee, kicked a T. Williams in the leg leaving him writhing in agony on the ground. Inevitably, the game was introduced by children into the streets of the town, and two boys were summoned for kicking a ball around in those areas. One of the boys declared that he had only done so to keep warm. The case was dismissed.

Rugby football was introduced with the formation of the Brecon Football Club in 1874. A match was only decided after a goal had been scored. On Boxing Day 1874 a rugby match between Brecon and Swansea was declared a draw, two touchdowns to one in favour of Brecon, but the Brecon team had included seventeen players to Swansea's eleven.

Other physical pursuits included walking matches and cycling. Walking matches were conducted over road courses as long as twenty-five miles and excellent times could be recorded. Though the usual means of travel locally for the leisured classes was by horse and trap, the invention of the pneumatic tyre in 1887 by John Boyd Dunlop and its commercial production in 1890, led to an enormous increase in the popularity of the bicycle. At Brecon bicycles were made and sold at Fryer's, whose premises were situated at the corner of Wheat Street. A cycle club was formed, and an important annual event was the races at the cricket ground. Ladies used the bicycle to visit friends, and even to do their shopping, and Gwladys Charles, the daughter of a highly respected pharmacist living at 46, The High Street, rode 1,000 miles between March and November 1892. Riding a bicycle was not without its hazards, and in June 1897 the Express reported that 'three ladies out cycling were set upon by a horse, probably in play endeavouring to bite them, at the same time dancing around in a most frantic manner. Two of the ladies found shelter behind a hedge but the third did not come off so well as the animal caught hold of her hat'.

The pneumatic tyre and the internal combustion engine prepared the way for the advent of the motor cycle and the motor car and a well known Brecon dentist was charged by the police with 'furious' driving. It was estimated that he had ridden his motor cycle from Lloyd's Bank to Watton Pitch at fifteen to sixteen miles an hour. He was asked to pay costs of £1 5s. 6d.

The splutter of the internal combustion engine heralded the end of an era, for it led to the gradual disappearance of the horse from the streets of Brecon, and a whole way of life associated with horse-drawn traffic was to become simply a memory, a part of the rich fabric of life.

But together with the fellowship of the theatre, the inn and the great outdoors, there was another kind of fellowship in Brecon and that was the brotherhood of Free Masons. The first lodge constituted in the town dates back to Georgian times. It was formed in 1764 in the 'Sun Inn', Wheat Street. The Cambrian Lodge was formed in 1789 at the 'Swan Inn', Ship Street when Theophilus Jones, the eminent local historian, was instituted Master and he was to occupy the chair until 1804. Attendances at lodge meetings during these early years were appalling, and during his fifteen years as master, Theophilus Jones was to hold fifty meetings of the lodge, and of these thirteen had to be adjourned owing to 'insufficient Brethren being present'. The general apathy was such that in 1816 the lodge was simply opened and closed, and it is hardly surprising that the last meeting of the lodge took place in March 1819. In 1828 it was erased from the roll of lodges. Candidates came from far and wide, from Birmingham, Oxford, Bristol, Evesham, Worcester, Merthyr, Hay and Aberdare. In 1855 the Brecknock Lodge No. 936 was established, the first meeting being held at the Castle Hotel. Subsequent meetings were held at the 'Swan' until a lodge room was built adjoining the Castle Hotel and meetings were then held there until alterations to the hotel in 1895-6 led to the removal of the lodge to Ruperra House, Wheat Street. In December 1863 the Lodge number was changed to 651. Towards the end of the Victorian era the lodge had a membership of about fifty, and daughter lodges had been established at Builth and Hay.

Though life generally in Brecon, despite the considerable changes that were taking place, followed a quite orderly routine, there were occasions when the social scene was enlivened and enriched by the arrival of a personage of great distinction. One such occasion was King George IV's visit to the town in 1821. The King had been returning from Ireland when a violent storm forced the royal squadron to seek shelter in Milford Haven. The King was entertained at Priory House where he sat down to a sumptuous dinner consisting of mutton broth followed by salmon, cold partridges, ham, veal cutlets, tarts and jellies. The monarch stayed the night and slept in King Charles's room. On 26 July 1802 Lord Nelson, accompanied by Lady Hamilton, passed through the town and a local poet, W. Churchey, composed a fulsome tribute to his great achievements. Nelson, in his reply, declared that he was much flattered by Churchey's kindness 'and may say with truth that my obligation extends to the whole town of Brecon, for their flattering reception of me'.

Adelina Patti also graced local society. In the National *Eisteddfod* held at Brecon in 1889—and the pavilion had been erected on the site later to be occupied by the Girls' Grammar School— Patti was present and received a rapturous welcome. She sang a few Italian arias, and then endeared herself for ever to the Welsh people by her rendering of 'Home Sweet Home' and 'Hen Wlad fy Nhadau'. On 24 May 1897 the Queen of Song was made an honorary burgess of the borough and two years later, on 25 January 1899, at St Michael's Roman Catholic Church, she married for the third time. The groom was Rolf Cederstrom, a Swedish Count, and the event was treated as a great civic occasion by the town fathers.

Patti in the role of Gabriella

In the centre of Brecon, near St Mary's church, stands an imposing statue of the Duke of Wellington. It was made by a local man, John Evan Thomas, a sculptor of repute. The memorial is made of bronze, and the panels depict scenes from the Peninsular War and Picton's charge on the French cavalry at Waterloo. Wellington, a celebrated soldier and statesman, had died in 1852 and the statue, which was presented to the borough in 1856, was intended as a tribute to his many triumphs culminating in the defeat of Napoleon at Waterloo. But the monument, standing eight feet tall on its pedestal, with the Duke gazing haughtily over the town, seems to encapsulate such Victorian values as pride, patriotism, achievement and fulfilment. As such it can be taken as reflecting the public face of Brecon itself during that age.

NOTES

[1] Little Gate.

[2] This was the corn market. By the 1880s it was little used for commercial transactions, the farmers preferring to transact business in the principal inns and in the streets.

[3] He was born in Carmarthen in 1801 and graduated M.D. from Edinburgh in 1825. His father, Henry Lucas, was the first physician to be appointed to the Brecknock infirmary (1832) and he died in office as mayor of Brecon, 1840. Prestwood Lucas, who had only recently been appointed physician to the Swansea infirmary, after twelve years service with the Royal Artillery, now took over his father's practice in Brecon. In 1859 he became a member of the Royal College of Physicians. He was admitted a town councillor in 1866, and an alderman the following year. In addition he was a governor of Christ College and Deputy Lieutenant of the County. He died in 1871.

[4] The reformer was John Lloyd Vaughan Watkins of Penoyre. Infra, p. 114.

[5] I wish to express my indebtedness to Sister Bonaventure of the Ursuline Convent, Brecon, for this information.

Chapter 3

The Heartbeat of Administration and Representation

Until the passing of the Municipal Corporations Act 1835, the administration of Brecon had been determined by the charter which Philip and Mary had conferred on the borough in 1556. But Brecon was an ancient marcher town, and during the Middle Ages it had received a series of seigneurial charters, and in response to the privileges contained in these, a framework of municipal government had already appeared by the close of the medieval period. The bailiff had emerged as the principal officer within the borough, and he was assisted by an executive council of twenty-four capital burgesses or aldermen nominated by the general burgess body. This executive council had the authority to promulgate ordinances and bylaws for the good governance of the town though, undoubtedly, these would have had to be ratified by all the burgesses, some 120 of them by the mid fifteenth century, sitting in common hall. The council was also responsible for the collection and disbursement of the town revenue which, in 1410, amounted to £150. It was derived from three main sources: rents, the profits of justice, and the profits of trade (tolls). To enable the bailiff and council to fulfil their obligations, subordinate officers such as the serjeants or catchpolls, common attorneys (financial officials) customers (toll collectors) and constables had been appointed. The liberties over which the bailiff and council exercised jurisdiction had also been defined, and the town limits, which extended far beyond the walls, were perambulated annually, a practice which was continued down the centuries until it was made superfluous by the introduction of the Ordnance Survey Maps.

Despite the vicissitudes in its fortunes during the Middle Ages Brecon, by the commencement of the sixteenth century, had emerged as a borough possessed of very valuable privileges and having gained independence from its feudal overlords, both royal and baronial. This independence was fully confirmed in the charter granted to it in 1517 by Edward Stafford, the Duke of Buckingham, and the last of that line. The charter granted by Philip and Mary in 1556, though an important landmark in the history of the borough, was, in some respects, simply a confirmation and amplification of privileges which the burgesses had enjoyed for centuries, and a further confirmation of the degree of independence which the borough had attained. It was obtained very largely through the good offices and ample purse of Edward Games of Newton, the burgess member of Parliament, who interceded on behalf of the town with the powerful William, Earl of Pembroke, an influential figure at Court. There was a real need to remove the uncertainties and anomalies created in the minds of the burgesses by the passing of the Union legislation in 1536/43. However, Games was undoubtedly motivated also by personal considerations to press for a new charter, since the poverty of the town was such that it was unable to pay his wages as its parliamentary representative.

The charter established in the minutest detail the machinery by which the town was to be governed until the passing of the Municipal Corporations Act 1835. A bailiff and two aldermen were to be elected annually in September from the ranks of the capital burgesses and the initial holders of these offices were named. Fifteen of the 'better and honester' burgesses, of whom the bailiff and two aldermen were to comprise three, were to be designated capital burgesses, and they were to constitute the common council of the borough. They were to hold office as long as they 'conducted themselves well'. Within the Gild Hall a chamber was to be placed at their disposal for the conduct of official business. This small executive council, presided over by the bailiff, was empowered to draw up rules and regulations for the government of the town, Llywel included, and those guilty of a breach of these laws could be punished by being imprisoned and fined. Borough officers were to be appointed, and included in their ranks were the following: a recorder who had undergone legal training, and who was to hold office at the pleasure of the council; a common clerk or protonotary, likewise to hold office at the will of the council, and two chamberlains and twenty-four constables appointed in the autumn to hold office for one year. For the execution of processes and mandates, two serjeants-at-mace were required, and when the bailiff was on procession within the town and its liberties the serjeants were to bear before him gilt or silver maces engraved with the coat of arms of England. The wards—there were twelve of these—and the boundaries of the town were to remain unchanged, and the council was authorised to perambulate the boundaries from time to time. Twice weekly a court of record was to be held in the town, on Mondays and Thursdays, and it was given extensive powers to deal with all manner of cases, real, personal and mixed, arising within the borough and its liberties. There was to be a town gaol, the keeper of which was to

Old Town Hall at Brecon

(From a Drawing by the Rev. Thomas Price)

92

be the bailiff. View of frankpledge was to be held twice annually in 'le Bouth Hall' of the town. Sheriffs were prohibited from excercising any authority within the borough. The town was granted assize of bread, wine, ale and other victuals, and the bailiff was also to be the clerk of the market and regulate and supervise its activities. Three markets were to be conducted weekly, on Wednesdays, Fridays and Saturdays; and two fairs, each of two days' duration, were to be held annually, one on the Nativity of St John the Baptist (24 June) and the other on the Feast of St Leonard (6 November). On the occasion of the holding of the markets and fairs a court of piepowder was to be convened to enable problems and trouble makers to be dealt with instantly. The town was further granted the right to form a gild merchant and hanse. The burgesses could enjoy these freedoms as long as they remained continually resident within the town or at Llywel. 'Foreigners' could not produce any items for sale in Brecon, except in the time of markets and fairs, without licence from the corporation. The bailiff, recorder and aldermen were to be justices, though treason and murder were to remain outside their jurisdiction. Furthermore, the bailiff was to be coroner and escheator. The town council was empowered to levy taxes such as scot and lot on the general body of inhabitants, and the bailiff was entitled to the waifs, estrays, goods and chattels of convicted felons which were to be used for the benefit of the body corporate. Burgesses were to be free from the payment of toll throughout the kingdom, and these same freemen were also confirmed in their rights to all commons and wastes. No man could sue another for causes arising within the borough. The council was to be self-perpetuating since it was empowered to create new burgesses by gift, and they were to take the oath of obedience. In deference to the wishes of the burgesses, the annual fee-farm rent was reduced from £120 to £20 payable on the Feast of St Michael (29 September.

Though it was stipulated in the charter that burgesses, in order to enjoy their privileges, had to be resident in the town, it soon becomes transparently clear that from early in the reign of Elizabeth I, this condition had been ignored, and persons living outside the borough, and therefore non-resident, were being admitted to the freedom. Hugh Thomas, in 1698, averred that 'there are also a great number of Gentlemen that are Burgesses of this Town that dwell in the Country & in the Counties round about, as Monmouthshire, Glamorgan & other parts'. In 1723 Gabriel Powel of Pennant decided to test the legality of electing people as burgesses who were non-resident. He started proceedings which were in the nature of *quo warranto*[1] against Edward Jones of Buckland and Hugh Powel of Castell Madoc. He challenged them to demonstrate by what right they claimed to be capital burgesses of Brecon when neither of them resided within the town. Edward Jones contended that he was entitled to be a burgess by usage, and by virtue of the fact that he could hear the great bell of St Mary's toll while he sat in his parlour at Buckland some eight miles away. Surprisingly, the jury at the Hereford Assizes agreed with him, though their judgement ran contrary 'to the opinion of the court'. The case against Hugh Powel, heard initially at the Hereford Assizes, was argued further in the Court of King's Bench in 1727 and he lost the action. He appealed to the supreme court of the land, the House of Lords, but the decision arrived at earlier at the King's Bench was upheld. These legal wranglings cost Hugh Powel dearly since he apparently spent nearly the whole of his estate in defending his action. The upholding of the integrity of the charter in the courts meant that all burgesses who were non-resident, in order to avoid penalties, had to resign their office and thirty-six altogether took this action.

View of frankpledge,[2] and the appointment of the twenty-four constables to maintain some semblance of order in the twelve wards of Brecon, took place in the Leet Court of the manor of Brecon whose boundaries were not conterminous with those of the town. The court had to be held within a month after Michaelmas (29 September) each year and was presided over by the steward. The wards into which Brecon was divided for convenience of administration were as follows: Cantref Selyf (Lion Street), Heol Rydd (Free Street), Watton (a suburb to the east), Old Port Inferior (the Struet), Old Port Superior (the area comprising the castle and priory), Llanfaes (a suburb to the west), Trecastle (a distant 'vill' on the road to Llandovery), Ship Street, Morgannwg (Glamorgan Street), St Mary's, High Street Inferior and High Street Superior.

Hugh Thomas, towards the end of the seventeenth century, declared that there were 200 burgesses in Brecon, some resident and others non-resident. Since the population of the town at that time has been estimated to have been in the region of 2,069, the burgesses would appear to have constituted some 9.7 per cent of the total population. They had been reduced in number to forty-five in 1760-1 when John Hughes was bailiff, and by 1805 the borough had become so exclusive as to acquire the appearance of a closed shop. Though the population of the town had increased to about 2,898 souls, the number of capital and other burgesses had now shrunk to a mere nineteen or 0.7 per cent of the populace. It was partly to remedy situations like these, where the corporation was completely unrepresentative of the inhabitants, that the Municipal Corporations Act was passed in 1835.

Town government in Brecon, therefore, until the early years of the nineteenth century, was oligarchic in the extreme, since authority was increasingly vested in the hands of a comparatively few leading—and wealthy—families who adopted a proprietorial attitude towards the rest of the inhabitants. In Georgian times the political scene was dominated by families like the Jameses (Meredith and Thomas), the Wynters, the Cokes (father and son), the Bolds and the Morgans. Meredith James, who was three times bailiff, had been the town clerk on three separate occasions, while his son Thomas had been town clerk twice; Bartholomew Coke was a wealthy apothecary and his son became a leading Wesleyan missionary; Hugh Bold, four times bailiff, was an attorney and had occupied the office of recorder. Between 1700-1835 four of the bailiffs had been recruited from the ranks of ministers. Apart from Thomas Coke, there was Thomas James of Watton, David Williams and Archdeacon Richard Davies. However, most of the bailiffs were representative of the professional, landed and business interests of the town. This ruling junta at Brecon was also knit by family ties, and this is exemplified by the fact that Lancelot Morgan, for example, who was bailiff in 1816, and again in 1837, was the nephew of Thomas James who was three times bailiff of the borough.

The oligarchic nature of the town council undoubtedly encouraged, and even opened the doors wide, to corruption, and the town records afford occasional glimpses of practices which must be regarded as questionable. In 1666 William Aubrey had been granted a licence by the corporation to 'Keepe a taverne and to sell and utter by retayle by ye gallon or less or greater measure any manner of wyne or wynes' in his mansion house in St Mary's Street. Aubrey must have offended in some way for an informer, Mallack, started proceedings against him in March 1692 at the Hereford Assizes, and Aubrey was advised by his counsel to compound with the informer. This he agreed to do and he compounded in the sum of £50. He had also incurred legal costs amounting to £8. In 1693 Aubrey was elected bailiff, and despite his obvious transgression, the town council ordered him to be completely reimbursed by leasing the tolls of the borough to him for three years. And the conduct of the bailiffs generally was not always above reproach and beyond suspicion, for in 1670 it was ordained that they were not to 'to receive or medle with any revenue or public moneys belonging to the said borough'. The collection of the revenue was to be the sole responsibility of the chamberlains.

If there was a whiff of scandal here, in 1710 there is an entry in the Minute Book from which it would appear that bribery and corruption were the order of the day and, furthermore, were committed openly and unashamedly. It was recorded 'that William Powell, mercer, upon his paying of two gwynus (guineas) into the hands of Mr Ald. James, to be by him laid out for the reparation of the pitching and paving of ye High Street, in this towne, be admitted and sworn a burgess of the corporation. Alderman James was Meredith James who had already occupied the office of bailiff in 1708, and was to occupy it again in 1719 and 1731. The corrupt nature of town corporations, as well as their unrepresentative character, made reform of the boroughs and the way they were governed, inevitable, but these festering sores were not to be dealt with until the mid-forties of Victoria's reign.

Though town government between 1556-1835 was conducted under the terms of the charter of Philip and Mary, there was one brief interlude, in the latter half of the seventeenth century, when it was superseded. This was in 1686 when James II, in a desperate attempt to raise money, and to assert royal control over the borough, compelled the corporation to surrender its charter and to pay him a substantial sum of money for the granting of a new one in which the chief magistrate was called mayor instead of bailiff.[3] The town council incurred costs of £157 in procuring the new charter, and in order to defray this expense it was decided that the tolls of the borough over a period of eleven years should be earmarked for the purpose.

In many respects the new charter closely resembled the old, but no sooner had James 'gone on his travels' than the corporation hastily resumed its former charter. James's charter, in some instances, is more liberal than the charter of 1556 for it empowers the corporation to hold an additional fair on St George's day (23 April) annually and this has been the practice ever since. By this charter, also, the recorder was constituted one of the common council by virtue of his office and this omission was clearly an oversight in the charter of Philip and Mary. However, there was one stipulation in James's charter which would have caused a considerable flutter in the dovecots at Brecon, and occasioned many a heavy heart among the common council men. This was the condition which subjected the borough to the arbitrary demands of the Crown, as the monarch and his successors, in privy Council, and under the Privy Seal, were empowered to remove from office the mayor, recorder, common clerk, chamberlains and aldermen at his and their will and pleasure. This remodelling of the corporation was designed to secure the control of the borough by royal nominees, and since the election of the borough member was in their hands, they would be expected to return to the House of Commons a member favourably disposed towards the Crown. The successful application of this policy nationwide would have enabled James to create a Parliament of the political complexion which he wanted. It is not surprising, therefore, that the corporation should have acted with such alacrity in rejecting the charter when provided with the opportunity for doing so. During the period that Brecon was a Mayoral town, the office was occupied by four people. These were: Edward Jones of Buckland, Lodwick Lewis of Pennant, John Waters of Brecon, and William Phillips of Brecon, although the latter's term as mayor was only for a very short period.

In the procuring of this charter the Duke of Beaufort had played a leading role and it was he who, in 1684, had undertaken a grand progress through Wales. He was accompanied by a considerable entourage, including Thomas Dineley, who was to leave an interesting account of the progress. The Duke arrived at Brecon from Hay on Tuesday, 5 August, and was received, probably at the Struet Gate, by the bailiff, town clerk, town council, magistrates and officers of the town attired in their robes of office. The county militia, both horse and foot, was also there to form a guard of honour. Beaufort spent two days in the town during which time he enjoyed the hospitality of Colonel Jefferies at Priory house. On 6 August he reviewed the county militia in a meadow near the town and declared himself well satisfied with the spectacle. The militia comprised 'one troop and five companies of foot with green colours flying. The foot were clad with new hatts, blew (*sic*) cassacks, white sashes edged with blew worsted fringe, broad buff coloured shoulder belts, and red yarn stockings. The horse appeared well mounted, with buff coats, carbines, pistolls; back, breast, and pott, bridles, and collars, huisses with their cloaks strapped behind them. With officers at the head of both in good equippage'. On the following day the Duke left for Carmarthenshire, and was conducted to the borders of that shire by the High Sheriff, gentry and militia troop. He described his reception in the county and town as 'very noble'.

It was this same Duke that was called upon in 1686 to suppress an insurrection in the West Country led by Charles II's illegitimate son, the Duke of Monmouth. Monmouth, at the head of a small following, had landed at Lyme Regis, and he gained a great deal of popular support since he projected himself as the champion of Protestantism and the rightful heir to the throne. The arrival of Beaufort forced him to abandon the siege of Bristol and at Sedgemoor, on 20 June, he was crushingly defeated. He became a fugitive but on 6 July he was finally captured and beheaded on Tower Hill. Contingents from the county militia which Beaufort had reviewed at Brecon in 1684 fought under his command in the West Country. Some were doubtless killed and others wounded, and in April 1686 the justices ordered that the maimed soldiers should hand in their certificates at the next sessions to enable them to receive their pensions.

While the common councilmen could be bribed to bestow favours, the conduct of the borough officers, also, at times, left much to be desired. The twenty-four constables, elected annually and unpaid, were reluctant law enforcement officers who frequently employed deputies to serve the office. And it is sobering to discover that the serjeants-at-mace, who were responsible for executing processes and mandates as well as bearing the silver maces before the bailiff when walking on procession, could be extremely discourteous in their conduct towards the borough's principal officer. In 1698 Howell Jones, one of the serjeants-at-mace, was removed from his office 'for committing several misdemeanours in his office, and giving rude and uncivil language and expressions to Mr Bailiffe to his face, declaring he would not serve him any longer'. This kind of conduct would have been particularly offensive since the town council, small and intimate as it was, had an enhanced, even exaggerated, sense of civic pride. In 1736 it was ordained that all common councilmen should, on the first Sunday in every month, assemble and attend on the bailiff in the town hall in their gowns and from thence proceed to morning service in St Mary's church. It was important that this procedure should be followed 'in order to kepe up the solemnity of ye Corporation'. In the same order it had been laid down that the seats which had been reserved for councillors in the church, and situated between the vicar's seat and the chancel, should not be occupied by 'persons who have no rights to ye said seats, and many of them of the infferior sort'.

Such an intrusion could endanger the rights of the councillors to those seats, and constitute 'a great disparagement of ye Common Councillmen of ye said Burrough'. To exclude this undesirable element, locks were to be provided for these reserved pews, and to differentiate further between them and other seats in the church, these seats were 'to be lined ye inside with red Bays'. It would appear that the gown was regarded as a distinctive badge of office which would not only confer a degree of dignity and gravity on its wearer, but also help to distinguish him from other members of the town community. As early as 1667 it had been ordered that every common councilman, without a gown, should immediately provide himself with one before Michaelmas. Failure to comply with this injunction meant a fine of 40s or distress of his goods. There was also strict enforcement of the obligation to attend on the bailiff for worship and other civic occasions. A councilman who defaulted in this respect was to be fined 12d.

When one considers how the town council at Brecon was constituted before 1835, it is understandable that there is little evidence in its operations of any deep sense of responsibility towards the populace of the borough as a whole. Indeed membership of the corporation was regarded more as a privilege to be enjoyed than as a duty to be performed. It would appear that only the minimum of provision was made for such essentials as poor relief, education and public health. Little attention was devoted to improving the housing of the poor and alleviating their real hardships. Any relief that was forthcoming before 1834 was mainly the result of private charitable giving by well-meaning and wealthy individuals. There was also scant regard for education before the closing years of Victoria's reign. The educational needs of the town population were provided by voluntary agencies such as the Welsh Trust and the S.P.C.K. As with the poor, it needed the stimulus of national legislation before any new initiatives were undertaken. Furthermore, before the Public Health Act 1848, health was not a top priority with the corporation. There was no adequate provision for refuse collection, which was often dumped in the streets and left there to rot; the drainage was completely inadequate, and the purity of the water supply to the homes was not safeguarded, a factor which gave rise to the cholera epidemics of 1849 and 1854. However, the corporation had not been entirely neglectful in this respect, and in 1693 the condition of the conduit in the High Street had given rise to such serious concern that it was 'ordered that for the future it be kept clean and free from the usual annoyances ... That every man or male kind that shall offend contrary to this order shall be brought and put into the stocks, and there continue confined for half-an-hour; and any woman kind offending herein to bee put to sitt in the cucking stool[4] for half-an-hour'. The corporation officers were entrusted with the execution of this order and failure on their part to enforce the penalties would result in their being fined five shillings, the money to be used for the benefit of the poor. But the principal preoccupation of the corporation was, undoubtedly, with the more profitable aspects of town life such as the markets and fairs and the tolls therefrom, together with the repair and maintenance of such vital adjuncts of trade, the lifeblood of the town, as roads and bridges. Thus it was ordered in 1678 'that the summe of five pounds be forthwith levied and payd by the towne by payd rate for the repaire of the bridges on the Honddu river, and for repairs to the causeways'. In 1691 forty shillings were expended on the repair of the 'great' bridge over the river Usk and four pounds on the bridge over the river Tarell 'and the weares and stanks thereof'; a further four pounds were spent on the repair of the bridge over the Honddu near the priory, and twenty pounds were defrayed on the reparation of the highways 'out of repair within the said corporation and liberties thereof'. And the expenditure did not end there, for throughout Georgian and Victorian times, such was the pounding received by these bridges when the rivers were in flood, that they were a continuous source of considerable expense. The corporation also jealously guarded its immemorial rights to exclusive trading within the town, and in 1698 a William Lewis was ordered to pay three guineas to reimburse the expenses incurred by several tradesmen who sued him 'for intruding upon this liberty and putting up a mercer's shop therein, being noe burgess or freeman thereof'. Furthermore, the council exercised considerable vigilance in

The Stocks

ensuring that there were no illegal encroachments on corporation property. When Daniel Lloyd, a tanner, was deemed guilty of this offence in 1824, it was agreed that it should be established immediately how much land was involved before initiating proceedings.

Though it would appear that the corporation had failed lamentably in its responsibilities towards the citizens of the borough before 1835, an important mitigating factor is to be found in the limited amount of income at its disposal. Indeed, so straitened were the financial circumstances of the corporation that in 1819 it was decided to limit expenditure on the reception which followed the election of the new bailiff. Only a few of his closest friends and the gentlemen of the corporation were to be invited. Undoubtedly the main source of revenue was the tolls from the markets and fairs which, at the commencement of the nineteenth century, amounted to £64 per annum. It had become the standard practice of the council from very early days to farm these out to the highest bidder. In 1842, following the completion of the new market, the tolls, over a period of twelve months, were let for £500. Occasionally, they were even leased to the bailiff for a period of years to recompense him for any extraordinary expenditure which he had incurred, a practice, possibly, of doubtful validity. Rents were another source of income, and from 1660 onwards leases of corporation property such as lands, shops, and houses become increasingly usual. These assets were invariably let to burgesses, and this practice was exemplified in Old Port Superior in 1810 when, the lease of two houses and their gardens there to Hugh Bold having expired, it was ordered that a fresh lease of the premises for twenty-one years, at an annual rent of five guineas, should be made to his son, Thomas Bold, who was already in possession of the property (his father having died) and on which he had already expended £30 in repairs. In 1810 Sir Charles Morgan, having surrendered his interest in a parcel of land extending from Captain's Walk to the river Usk, the council decided to lease the land to the Rev. Thomas James—he had been bailiff in 1806—for ninety-nine years at an annual rent of 10s. 6d. However, Sir Charles, having released one piece of land, in the following year acquired possession by lease, over a period of ninety-nine years, at a yearly rent of three guineas, of another parcel of land at the Watergate. Other sources of income included payments on admission of burgesses, fines for breaches of municipal regulations, permits to enable 'foreigners' to trade and licences for brewing and baking. The main item of expenditure was the annual 'farm' of £20 reserved for the crown by the charter of 1556. Charles II granted this town rent to Sir Thomas Osborne who, in 1694, was created Earl of Danby. From him it descended to Francis Godolphin Osborne who, in turn, sold it to Sir Charles Morgan of Tredegar. The money for the payment of this fee farm was forthcoming from the chief rents of the manor of Brecon, which amounted in total to £23 a year. There were times when difficulties were experienced in collecting this money, and in 1829 it was resolved that the arrears should be collected by the chamberlains. Regular sums were also expended on the repair and maintenance of main roads and bridges, and such public buildings as the gild hall;[5] lesser sums were spent on paving the streets and relieving the needs of the poor. But the council found it difficult to balance its books and, in 1835, in a desperate attempt to liquidate debts which amounted to £750, it was decided to mortgage the corporation property to one Philip Vaughan.

The Municipal Corporations Act

The serious deficiencies in the manner in which old corporate boroughs like Brecon were controlled, their unrepresentative character since government was vested in the hands of a small clique of wealthy dominant families, and the bribery and corruption associated with the conduct of affairs by such juntas, were important considerations underlying the enactment of the Municipal Corporations Act 1835. These were abuses which had been highlighted by the commissioners appointed in 1833 to inquire into local administration. By the terms of the act the various constitutions of the corporate boroughs were abolished, and they were replaced by town councils appointed by the householders. These councillors, in turn, were to nominate aldermen— whose number was not to exceed a third of the total number of elected representatives—and the whole body was to be presided over by a mayor. The councillors were to be elected for three years, the aldermen for six, and the mayor for one year. The new governing body thus constituted was empowered to levy rates to cover the expenses of local government administration but the accounts were to be properly audited.

As a consequence of this legislation Brecon came to be governed by a corporation consisting of a mayor, four aldermen and twelve councillors, seventeen members in all. The first mayor elected under the terms of the act was Colonel Lloyd Vaughan Watkins of Penoyre who was appointed in 1836.[6] Samuel Church, James Prosser Snead (banker), Thomas Williams (chemist), and Thomas Meredith were nominated aldermen. Other officers appointed included Roger Thomas Watkins, solicitor, as Clerk of the Peace or Town Clerk, Thomas Armstrong, surgeon, as coroner, Thomas Lawrence as solicitor, John

Williams, grocer, as hall keeper, William Waters, weaver, as town crier, Josiah Bethell and David Davies, the elder, as sergeants-at-mace, and Jonas Williams as keeper of the town gaol. The mayor was elected annually on 9 November at noon, and each year four councillors retired but were eligible for re-election. By the Public Health Act 1872 the council was further constituted an urban sanitary authority.

The town crier was to be equipped with a suit of clothes consisting of a blue coat and waistcoat, blue trousers, and a police hat. On each side of his collar he was to wear a bell worked in white cloth. He was also to be provided with a pair of shoes, two pairs of stockings and a blue check shirt. The complete outfit was not to cost more than six pounds.

After 1835, Brecon ceased to be a 'close' corporation. The vice-like grip on the levers of power exercised by a coterie of families was finally broken, and an examination of those worthies who occupied the office of mayor from 1836 onwards is most revealing in this respect. Though the old familiar faces do not entirely disappear, especially within the first decade of the passing of the act since the Lloyds, the Powells, and the Vaughans are still there, they are now completely submerged beneath a tidal wave of new names. The Wilkinses, the Mayberys, the de Wintons, the Morgans (of Lion Street), the Gameses, the Williamses, the Thomases, the Overtons, the Riches, have come to the forefront, and there is altogether a much broader spectrum of families from whose ranks the holders of the most prestigious office in the borough were drawn. An infusion of new blood had been certainly called for, as the old body corporate had been in real danger of being afflicted by paralysis, a condition induced by continual in-breeding.

The Municipal Corporations Act marked a real watershed in the history of towns since it made possible the considerable expansion of municipal activity which became a characteristic feature of the latter half of Victoria's reign. The corporations, functioning through qualified, paid and permanent officials, were enabled to provide, on a much grander scale, such essential services as water, gas, electricity and the lighting and paving of streets which went a long way towards remedying the abuses encouraged by the former system.

From 1835 onwards, law enforcement became the responsibility of a properly constituted police force. In the following year a reinvigorated council applied to different Fire Insurance Offices for subscriptions towards the purchase of a new fire engine—the older one being beyond repair—and the erection of a new station house. The spirit of enterprise in the corporation was further demonstrated by the building of a market hall in 1838, the widening of certain streets, particularly approach roads, and the improvements to Captain's Walk, where a constable was made responsible for ensuring that it should be free of nuisances. These latter developments were undertaken, undoubtedly, to attract visitors by improving the town's aspect and amenities. The construction of a new workhouse in Llanfaes in 1839 reflected a different, if not particularly enlightened, approach towards the care of the poor. In August 1850 the council adopted the act for the better 'paving, lighting and sewering of towns'. It further elected a Board of Health with Dr Prestwood Lucas as the chief medical officer of health. The first members of the new board were: John Powell, John Lloyd, J. Parry de Winton, Walter Maybery, Lloyd Watkins M.P., T. Prothero Price, Thomas Williams, John Williams, James Sims, John Jones, J.P. Snead, Samuel Hancorn, H. Maybery, Alderman Meredith, Evan Thomas and G.R. Bevan. The town's health was further improved through the provision of cleaner water, and in 1866 new filter beds were opened above St David's workhouse. Furthermore, by 1880, Brecon had been covered by a grid of sewers. Gas had been first introduced into the town in 1822, when the corporation resolved that it was desirable for the streets and avenues to be lit. The rather paltry sum of £20 was donated from the corporation chest for the erection of the necessary pillars, lamps and fittings, and an additional £10 was set aside to cover the annual expense of procuring the gas. However, it was not until 1856 that the Brecon Gas Company was established. In the early decades of the twentieth century electricity was introduced into the borough, and in 1900 the Brecon corporation applied to the Board of Trade for permission to light by electricity, and 'to seek consent to opening of such streets as repaired by the county for the purpose of laying cables and other work'. Nevertheless it was only in 1924 that the Town Council inaugurated a scheme for supplying electricity, and by 1928 Brecon had been provided with a Municipal Power Station situated near the slaughter house in Canal Road. Towards the end of Victoria's reign education, which had been the responsibility of voluntary agencies, was taken over by the state, and new elementary and secondary schools, controlled by local officials and democratically elected governing bodies, were established in the borough. The corporation was enabled to accomplish all this—and many of these projects would have entailed the expenditure of considerable capital sums—by borrowing against the rates from central government. The period of *laissez faire* was over, and a new era of responsibility and accountability had opened.

Parliamentary Representation

PRIOR TO 1832

Brecon was first given parliamentary representation by the Acts of Union 1536/43. By this legislation each county in the principality was to be represented by one knight and each county town by one burgess. The one exception was Harlech, the county town of Merioneth, which was excused from returning any member at all on the grounds of its poverty. The knights were to be returned, as in England, according to the forty shilling freeholder franchise. But the different voting practices which prevailed in the English boroughs, precluded such uniformity with regard to the Welsh boroughs, and so the right to return the burgess members in Wales came to be vested in the freemen duly admitted through the four well-trodden avenues of birth, marriage, apprenticeship, and gift. The act of 1536 also stipulated that these members were to be paid, even though the practice of paying members was being discontinued in England, the knight receiving four shillings daily and the burgess two shillings. The burgesses' wages were to be levied not only on the shire town, but also on 'all other ancient boroughs' within the shire, though they did not have a voice in the election. This was an obvious injustice which was to be remedied in 1543. A system of contributory boroughs thus came into existence, though Brecon was not to conform to the general pattern since from the very beginning it constituted a single borough constituency without any out-boroughs.

Until the outbreak of the Civil War in 1642, the members for both the borough and county were supplied by the old county families. Brecon's members of Parliament were recruited pre-dominantly from the ranks of such leading gentry families as the Gameses of Newton, Aber-bran and Buckland; the Vaughans of Porthaml, the Prices of the Priory, and the Williamses of Gwernyfed. It was only occasionally that persons from outside the county were allowed in. The majority of Brecon's representatives had received legal training, and a few, like David Williams of Gwernyfed, were to attain positions of considerable eminence and distinction. The Roundhead triumph in the Civil Wars ended the dominance of the older gentry families, and until the restoration of monarchy in 1660 Brecon's representatives at Westminster, and this applied to the county as well, were zealous parliamentary supporters. In the eyes of the royalists these men were second rate; they were 'upstarts' drawn from the lower echelons of society, whose ascendancy had only been achieved through the power of the sword.

The Restoration saw the return of the old county families and, until the close of the century, despite the 'Glorious Revolution' 1688/9 which resulted in James II being forced into exile, there was little further change in the political scene at local level. Town and county continued to be dominated by the great houses of Gwernyfed, Buckland, the Priory and Tredegar. However, the heads of the latter three were all comparative newcomers to Breconshire politics. Edmund Jones of Llanddewi Ysgyrid had acquired Buckland about 1661 by marriage to Gladys, the second daughter and heiress of Edward Games. A little earlier, Jeffrey Jeffreys of Abercynrig had succeeded to the estate and influence of the Price family of the Priory by marrying Margaret, the daughter of Gregory Price. The Morgans of Tredegar had obtained a powerful interest in the county, when William Morgan on 4 November 1661 married Blanche, the daughter and heiress of William Morgan of Dderw. While the families of Gwernyfed, Buckland and the Priory were all 'Tory', the Morgans of Tredegar were 'Whig', though the appellations 'Whig' and 'Tory' at this time were little more than labels stuck on empty bottles. Apart from moments of crisis, political issues had little impact on electoral contests fought between local rivals. At Brecon itself, where effective control was vested in the hands of a close and self-perpetuating corporation, the situation was ripe for the rule of some patron and by 1689 borough elections had already resolved into clashes between the two families of Morgans and Jeffreys.

For electoral purposes, the voters at Brecon could be manipulated in three ways: by exercising some degree of influence over the bailiff who was the returning officer; by the mass creation of non-resident burgesses, or by strictly limiting admission to the freedom. Between 1573 and 1727, in the event of failure to win the support of the majority of the resident burgesses, the practice was to create burgesses who were non-resident. Following a celebrated court case in 1727, however, when the legality of such proceedings was successfully challenged in the law courts, non-resident burgesses were compelled to relinquish their burgess-ships in droves so that by the first decade of the nineteenth century they had been reduced in number to nineteen, a small enough group to be easily managed. As returning officer the attitude of the bailiff could be crucial, since he was in a position to admit unqualified voters, and to refuse to accept the votes of the faction to which he was opposed. In 1713 when the Priory's hold on the borough seat was broken through the election of Roger Jones of Buckland, who defeated the sitting member, Edward Jeffreys, by 114 votes to 63, two petitions were sent to the House of Commons, one from Jeffreys and the other from 'divers Burgesses, Inhabitants ... paying Scot and Lot', complaining that the bailiff, Richard Hughes, had admitted unqualified voters. In 1723, in a by-election at Brecon, John Pratt, representing the Priory interest, was defeated by Thomas

Morgan, the younger brother of William Morgan of Tredegar. A political analysis of the borough for this election reveals that Pratt had a majority of the 'inhabiting' burgesses by 69 votes to 53, but Morgan was supported by 60 'foreign residents'. Seventy freemen 'having a right as burgesses', supporters of Pratt, were presumably unpolled. The Tredegar family, having evidently acquired control of power in the borough, and lacking majority support among the resident burgesses, had admitted non-residents to the franchise while at the same time denying this right to the supporters of the rival faction. Several freemen submitted a petition to the House of Commons complaining specifically of this latter practice as a breach of accepted custom:

> That the Petitioners have severally served their Apprentice-ships, and paid Scot and Lot, within the said Borough, and most of them inhabitants there for several years past: and by the ancient usage, were entitled to the Privileges of Burgesses, and to vote for Members to Parliament; and at the last election would have voted for John Pratt Esq.: but Charles Hughes, the Acting Bailiff, refused, in open court, to poll about 57 of them, and hath returned Thomas Morgan as duly elected.

It is quite apparent, also, in this election, that open resort was made to bribery of the electorate. Thomas Morgan, in gaining victory over his rival, had incurred expenses which had amounted to the quite considerable sum of £467. This he accounted for mainly 'in small sums given to the burgesses'. Votes were being bought, and it would appear that there was no stigma attached to the practice. In this kind of situation it was the size of the purse, rather than the quality of the applicant, that determined who should be returned to the mother of parliaments.

For the greater part of the eighteenth century, the Tredegar interest prevailed in both county and borough; and change in the representation of Brecknockshire occurred not at general elections, but as the circumstances of the Tredegar family dictated. Details of election expenses underline the formality of the proceedings. The Tredegar bill for 'entertainments at Brecon'

A cartoon by Hogarth depicting the buying of votes during an election

during the county election of 1768 came to £231; that for the borough to £44. The shire by-election of 1769 cost £267, that for the borough in 1672 only £78. Though the Morgan hold on the county appeared to be impregnable, appearances could be deceptive. When Sir Charles Morgan retired in 1806 at the age of eighty, there was no Tredegar candidate to succeed him: his only son Charles was a member for Monmouthshire, and his elder grandson Charles Morgan Robinson Morgan was a mere four-teen year old. This opportunity was immediately seized on by other families with a traditional claim to share in the represent-ation of Brecknockshire. Lord Camden, son and successor of the Charles Pratt who had married the Jeffreys heiress, reasserted the Priory interest in support of the candidature of Thomas Wood of Gwernyfed for the county seat. Wood's father, in 1776, had married Mary, the only daughter and heiress of Sir Edward Williams, fifth baronet of Gwernyfed and Llangoed Castle, and Wood himself had inherited the Gwernyfed estate in 1804. Wood

111

secured the seat without a contest, and he held it unchallenged at the general election of 1812, though C.M.R. Morgan then took the borough seat at the age of twenty in place of Sir Robert Salusbury. In the election of 1818 Wood retained the county seat despite some local resentment at his supporting in Parliament in May 1817 a motion designed to relieve Roman Catholics of their legal disabilities. However, in August 1817 an agent reported to Sir Charles Morgan that 'Party matters do not I think in the least run high in this Town, the subject being very seldom mentioned or alluded to in mixed Company'.

Charles Morgan Robinson Morgan, 1st Baron Tredegar

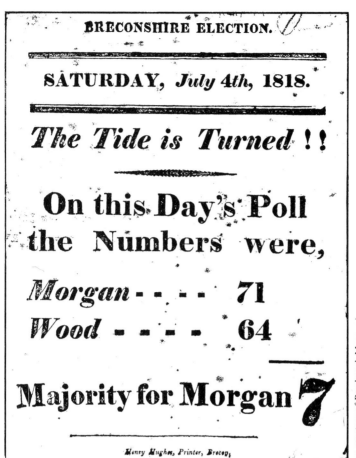

George Gould Morgan wins the Brecon seat

Wood's supporters now tried to undermine the Tredegar hold on the borough, where Sir Charles's younger son, George Gould Morgan, had been elected in June, and he continued to represent the borough from 1818 to 1830. Henceforth, the Morgans conceded the county to Wood, and retained control only of the borough where C.M.R. Morgan replaced his brother in 1830. The Morgan family had established a very firm platform within the general burgess body from which to launch their operations. In

113

1817 Sir Charles Morgan, eldest son of Sir Charles Gould (1726-1806) and two of his sons, C.M.R. Morgan and George Gould Morgan, were admitted as burgesses. Seven years later, in 1824, another son, Charles Octavius Swinnerton Morgan was admitted to the freedom. But the 'dangerous sea of reform' was soon to threaten both the Brecknockshire members. At the general election of 1831 Thomas Wood was opposed by a reformer in John Lloyd Vaughan Watkins of Penoyre, though Watkins withdrew after the first day's poll when Wood already had a lead of 282 votes to 138, and Wood continued to represent the county until his retirement in 1847. In 1832, following the enactment of the first Parliamentary Reform Act, Watkins, a Liberal, wrested the borough from Morgan, a Conservative, by the narrow margin of 110 votes to 104. Although the Tredegar family did regain the borough seat for a while (1835, 1837, 1852), these contests foreshadowed a new era in politics, when issues of policy and principle came to dominate the question of parliamentary representation. No longer would the great landowners be able to regard elections as occasions when they could flex their political muscle and assert their local dominance.

The First Parliamentary Reform Act 1832

The demand for parliamentary reform arose from two overriding considerations: there was the urgent need to extend the franchise, and a redistribution of parliamentary seats was necessary. The franchise was too narrow because elections in both counties and boroughs were effectively controlled by the great landowners, and the new barons of industry, the entrepreneurs, who were now mainly instrumental in creating the nation's wealth, were not enfranchised at all; a redistribution of seats was necessary because, as a consequence of the Industrial Revolution, large new towns like Merthyr Tydfil had made their appearance, and they were not represented in Parliament. The fall of the Duke of Wellington in 1830, following defeat on the Civil List, saw interest rekindled in parliamentary reform, which had waned in the mid 1820s with the revival of prosperity in agriculture.

Reform meetings, often accompanied by considerable violence, were held all over the country. In 1831 a mob went on the rampage in the streets of Brecon, breaking gentlemen's windows and shouting for 'Watkins and Reform'. All three reform bills were given a stormy reception in Parliament, and it was not until April 1832 that the third bill was finally carried in the House of Lords and then by the narrowest of majorities—nine only.

By the act Wales's parliamentary representation was increased from twenty-seven to thirty-two. Brecknock's position, however, remained unaltered since the county and borough still returned only one member each. In the county the franchise, which had been limited to the forty shilling freeholders, was now extended to the ten pound copyholder and the fifty pound tenant farmer. These provisions made little difference to voting patterns, since there were hardly any copyholders and few large farms to let to tenant farmers. On the other hand, the extension of the franchise in the boroughs to the ten pound householders did have an appreciable impact. At Brecon the vice-like grip of the Morgan family on the borough seat was finally loosened and a reformer was returned to Parliament in the person of J.Ll.V. Watkins, who continued to represent Brecon from 1832-4. The Morgans then reasserted their supremacy in the elections of 1835, 1837 and 1841, only for Colonel Watkins to win back the seat in 1847. However, he again lost it to a Morgan in 1852, but he regained the seat in 1854 and then retained it until 1865. From then until 1885 Brecon was represented successively by Charles Pratt, Howel Gwyn, Edward Hyde, Gwynne-Holford and finally Cyril Flower.

The Second Parliamentary Reform Act, 1867

The reformers were to be bitterly disappointed with the act of 1832. The advances made were soon demonstrated to be more apparent than real, for the electors were still those who owned property and consequently regarded as having a stake in the country. In Brecknockshire the dominance of landed families of ancient lineage is demonstrated by the fact that between 1841-74

Howel Gwyn, Esq., of Abercraf, Duffryn.
(High Sheriff 1844)

there was not a single contested county election, the seat being shared between Joseph Bailey of Glanusk Park (1847-1858) and Godfrey Charles Morgan of Tredegar Park (1858-75). The general dissatisfaction and disillusionment with the reform act gave birth to the Chartist movement and to a groundswell of popular agitation for further radical change in the electoral system, and in 1867 Lord Derby's Tory government, led in the Commons by Benjamin Disraeli, introduced a second reform bill. Lord Derby had reservations about it and he described the bill 'as a leap in the dark'. However, he allowed Disraeli to proceed with it and the bill became law. By the act Wales was given an additional member—Merthyr received an extra seat—thus increasing the total Welsh representation from 32 to 33. Since women were not enfranchised, half the population was immediately excluded, while agricultural labourers were totally disregarded. Also excluded were those thousands of industrial workers who lived outside the borough boundaries, and even within the boroughs adult male suffrage was still a dream to be realised. In Brecon, with a population of 6,308 in 1871, the number of electors was 701 in 1868, 808 in 1871 and 819 in 1877. Thus, on average over this period, the electors still represented only some 12.3 per cent of the total population. However, the increase in the number of borough electors between 1837 and

1871 was quite dramatic. When C.M.R. Morgan defeated his rival, John Lloyd of Dinas, in 1837, the total number of votes cast for both candidates was 258.[7] By 1871, the number of votes had risen to 808, an increase of the order of 213 per cent, a figure not widely disproportionate with the national average of 250 per cent for the boroughs. This expansion in the borough electorate had been achieved by conferring the vote in 1867 on all male householders rated for poor relief, and on all lodgers paying ten pounds a year rent provided that they occupied the same room for one year.

The Third Parliamentary Reform Act, 1884
The Reform Act of 1867 had created anomalies which had to be addressed. One related to the fact that while the act had enfranchised all male householders in the borough, it had failed to do so in the counties. By the 1880s there was increasing agitation for further parliamentary reform emanating predominantly from the activities of reform associations in the 1870s. Understandably, the National Agricultural Labourers' Union took up the cudgels for reform, as did the National Reform Union at its annual conference in 1883. In July of that year, at a rally of 12,000 miners in the Rhondda Valley, there were trumpet calls for parliamentary reform, and when their Lordships rejected the Franchise Bill protest meetings were held all over Wales. Agricultural workers, in particular, objected vociferously to the Lords' denial of their legitimate claims. The 1884 Reform Act disfranchised all boroughs with fewer than 15,000 inhabitants, but it also resulted in the enfranchisement of thousands of miners, tin-platers and steelmen together with workers in rural areas. All in all, Wales gained one additional seat in Parliament, thus increasing the total representation to 34. The Redistribution Act 1885 destroyed the old distinction between borough and county, and created constituencies of more equal size. Brecon was vitally affected by this legislation since the town—and Llywel—lost its right to return its own representative to Westminster. Instead it, and its offshoot at Llywel, were merged into the county of Brecknock.

The mantle of having been the last parliamentary representative of Brecon fell on the shoulders of Cyril Flower of Aston
Clinton, Tring, Herts. A Liberal, he was the eldest son of Philip
William Flower of Furze Down Park, Streatham, Surrey. He had
been educated at Harrow and Trinity College, Cambridge and
was called to the Bar in 1870. In 1886 he was Lord of the Treasury
at a salary of £1,000 a year, and between 1886-92 he was one of the
junior 'Whips'. He succeeded in wresting the borough seat from
J.P.W. Gwynne-Holford of Buckland, the sitting member, by
438 votes to 379 in 1880, and he continued to represent Brecon in
Parliament until 1885. The measure of his success can be gauged
from the fact that his opponent was a local man of considerable
standing and influence while he was a rank outsider. In an
election address in 1880 he had described himself as having come

Cyril Flower, Esq., M.P. for Brecknock

118

as a stranger among the electors of Brecon. His triumph represented a Liberal gain. In recognition of his services on behalf of the borough and its citizens—he secured for many Breconians lucrative positions in the commercial world—Cyril Flower, on Saturday, 19 October, 1885 was presented in the Town Hall with pieces of plate and a massively framed illuminated address by a grateful Town Council.

Between 1875 and the close of the nineteenth century, the county of Brecknock was represented by another Liberal, W.F. Maitland of Garth House, Builth and Stanstead Hall, Essex. The eldest son of William Fuller Maitland J.P. of Garth and Stanstead, he was educated at Harrow, and matriculated at Christ Church, Oxford, on 16 October 1862. In 1866 he entered Charseley's Hall but he left the University in 1870. He was made a J.P. of the county of Brecknock in May 1875. He first won the county seat in 1875, and he was provided with his opportunity when the sitting member, Godfrey Morgan, on the decease of his father in April 1875, was summoned to the Upper House as Lord Tredegar. Morgan's elevation to the peerage opened the door for fresh battles to be fought for political supremacy in the county. The challenge to Maitland was mounted by Howel Gwyn of Duffryn, Neath, a Conservative. Maitland, after a long-drawn out and hotly disputed contest, won by the narrow margin of 103 votes. In the elections of 1880 and 1885 he retained his seat, with greatly increased majorities in each case, by defeating Arthur John Morgan of Tredegar Park, and in 1892 he successfully withstood the challenge presented by Colonel Thomas Wood of Gwernyfed Park by 4,676 votes to 3,418.

Parliament was to be further reformed in 1918 and 1928. In 1918 Lloyd George's Coalition government enfranchised all male adults over twenty-one and women over thirty providing that they were householders or married to householders. This change came about as a result of the propaganda campaign of the philosopher J.S. Mill, the activities of the suffragettes, though often lawless and violent, and the outstanding contribution made by women to the war effort (1914-18) when they worked in munition factories and on the land. Ten years later, in 1928, Baldwin's

Conservative government enfranchised, without opposition, all female adults. This was known as the famous 'flapper vote'. The ladies of Brecon and elsewhere could finally stand shoulder to shoulder with the men and register their votes. Justice had finally been done.

The House of Commons had now become a completely democratic institution, and universal suffrage had been established. It had taken just four years short of a century to accomplish.

NOTES

[1] A writ calling upon one to show by what warrant he holds or claims a franchise or office.

[2] A system in which units or tithings composed of ten households were formed, in each of which members were held responsible for one another's conduct.

[3] This policy was pursued in respect of other boroughs as well.

[4] A stool in which scolds and other culprits were placed, usually before their own door, to be pelted by the mob.

[5] In 1832, however, it was agreed that alterations to the town hall to provide better accommodation for the assize judges were to be at the expense of the county.

[6] Vide, Appendix A.

[7] Vide, Appendix C.

Chapter 4

THE VOICE OF CONSCIENCE: THE CHURCH AND DISSENT

In 1559 Elizabeth I had drawn up her settlement of religion and the Protestant Anglican Church which was founded then became the established church in Wales down to the early years of the twentieth century. In 1914 it was disestablished and partially disendowed by the Liberals though, in the event, the act did not take effect until the end of the first World War in 1918.

Opposition to Elizabeth's church was inevitable and unavoidable and it emanated from two directions. On the left flank were the Puritans who were critical because they felt that the reform of the church had not gone far enough. Catholic survivals in worship, like bowing at the name of Jesus, were referred to as the 'rags of popery' and were anathema to them. Later, they were to attack the very pillars of the church establishment, the episcopacy, which they wanted to destroy 'root and branch'. The right flank was occupied by the Catholics, who were rigorously opposed to the new church because of its rejection of papal authority and its repudiation of the central Catholic doctrine of transubstantiation. Indeed, Protestants of all hues were unanimous in their rejection of the mass. At this time the Puritans, for the most part, were to be found within the framework of the established church despite their criticisms of what they saw as its many imperfections. The Catholics, on the other hand, remained without—the recusants—though there was a handful of 'church papists' who outwardly conformed in order to avoid the draconian penalties for non-attendance.

Gradually, the hitherto largely inert mass of the Welsh people warmed to the Anglican Church, and by the end of Elizabeth's reign it had become firmly established in their affections. The defeat and execution of the King, and the establishment of the Commonwealth in 1649, provided the sects with an unprecedented opportunity to flourish and, like the locusts from Egypt, flourish they did. Walter Cradock, the eminent Puritan divine,

121

described the gospel 'as running over the mountains between Brecknock and Monmouth like fire in the thatch', and even Cromwell was of the opinion that God 'had kindled a seed there'. Indeed, it was this seed that was to prepare the way for the harvest reaped so abundantly by the Methodists in Georgian and Victorian times. However, in Brecon town itself, the Puritans made little headway and the excesses of the Roundheads as demonstrated in their wilful destruction of effigies and tombs, the font and holy water stoup in the priory church of St John, only served to alienate still further an antagonistic populace.

In 1660 the church, which had been disestablished during the period of Puritan ascendancy, was restored with its episcopal structure intact. But it was a church which was in a vengeful mood and its persecuting nature was revealed in a corpus of laws passed between 1661-5 and referred to collectively as the Clarendon Code. The Nonconformists were now to feel the full fury of the Anglican backlash exercised through a formidable array of disciplinary agencies such as royal proclamations, the courts, and episcopal visitations. Puritan ministers were evicted from their livings, imprisoned and fined. Other Dissenters were beaten and refused Christian burial, and in the parish of Llanfihangel Brynpabuan in Breconshire, the minister had the body of a young Baptist woman exhumed and buried at the crossroads, a place usually reserved for suicides. Until the passing of the Toleration Act 1689, the tender plant of Dissent, understandably, began to wilt in the white-hot heat of persecution. But it survived, and in so doing, grew deeper and stronger roots, so that in later centuries it was able to come to full flower.

Despite the apparent strength of the established church in Wales in the Georgian era, the worm of decay was already gnawing away at its superstructure so that the whole edifice became weakened and quite unable to withstand successfully the storms that were shortly to break around it. A besetting weakness was the practice of appointing Englishmen to Welsh sees and these bishops tended to view their bishoprics simply as stepping stones to better preferment in England. Consequently, their stay in Wales was usually only too brief and there was a general neglect of their episcopal duties. Furthermore, since they were English in speech, a great divide existed between them and the lower clergy, who were for the most part Welsh in speech and sentiment. These shortcomings were exemplified in the bishopric of St David's where, between 1705-1803, eighteen bishops were appointed. They were, without exception, English, appointed for political reasons, and non-resident. Thirteen were speedily transferred to greener pastures in England, and it was not until the appointment of Thomas Burgess, who remained as bishop for twenty-two years (1803-25), that an improvement was experienced in this respect. However, in 1825, he also followed a well-trodden path since he was translated to the wealthier see of Salisbury. Apart from Burgess, these were bishops who were hardly suited as spiritual leaders, and they were completely out of touch with the common people.

Spiritually, too, the church was weak. The outlying areas of parishes tended to be neglected and, but for the Dissenters, who built their chapels there, the inhabitants of those districts would have lived the lives of heathens. The preaching office was largely ignored, and standards of pastoral care in the parishes, especially large ones, were low. Language could be a problem, since the church services were often conducted in English, a medium which a largely monoglot population did not understand. According to Griffith Jones of Llanddowror what the people wanted was plain, practical, and zealous preaching in Welsh. The situation was further exacerbated by the evil of appropriated pews, whereby the wealthier parishioners occupied the most prestigious seats in the church, a practice which alienated many. These inherent weaknesses in the church meant that those seeking to assuage a savage spiritual thirst within its portals were disappointed, and in this failure to provide such nourishment can be found one of the fundamental reasons for the success of Methodism. But the Methodists also profited from the failure of the church to adapt itself to a rapidly changing situation created by the quickening of the economic pulse, for in the industrial conurbations of south Wales, with their ever burgeoning populations, the parishes were too big and there were too few churches. This was a situation which the Methodists were to exploit to their advantage.

At Brecon a spirit of unrest pervaded the life of the church after 1660. This was exemplified in the refusal of clergymen to pay the customary visitation fees to the archdeacons; people were also refusing to pay church rates and tithes. Among the lower clergy there was a temptation to perform clandestine marriages, and there were, furthermore, examples of clerical immorality. Their betters were guilty of place-hunting, nepotism, and holding a plurality of livings. Widespread pluralism, in turn, necessitated the appointment of a large number of stipendiary curates who were ill-equipped and ill-educated. Until 1803 the archdeacons were largely non-resident and, in this respect, Thomas Payn, who was archdeacon from 1735-59, outshone everyone since he spent most of his time in Constantinople. The long succession of absentee archdeacons only came to an end in the person of Payn's successor, Edward Edwards, who was also the vicar of Llanfaes. After Edwards came a line of archdeacons who were closely associated with Brecon. An exemplar was Richard Davies, who was vicar and archdeacon of Brecon from 1803-59. The son and grandson of former vicars of the town, he was educated at Westminster School and Christ Church, Oxford. Edwin Poole described him 'as one of the most remarkable men of his time'. His interest in education was demonstrated in 1811 when he collected subscriptions from townspeople to enable the Brecon Benevolent Schools to be established. He was an effective communicator as his sermons were written in a simple and unaffected style. In two of these sermons he exhorted the parishioners to be far more regular in their attendance at communion.

It is against this background of a somewhat somnolent church which, to some extent, had lost its way, that religious developments at Brecon have to be considered in Georgian and Victorian times. Brecon, an ancient baronial citadel which had developed into a market and production centre of the first importance, together with being the county town and assize centre, had escaped industrialisation and, consequently, the power and influence of the landed gentry and the church were never seriously challenged in the Georgian era. During this period the borough remained what it had been since the sixteenth century, a bastion of Anglicanism. Dissent, as yet, had not made a deep impression, and the Catholics constituted an insignificant minority. In Victorian Brecon all this was to change dramatically when the majority of worshippers in the borough changed their allegiance and deserted the church for the chapel.

Dissent

THE BAPTISTS

The first body of Dissenters to establish itself in Breconshire was the Baptist denomination. In the 1630s the Baptists had made their appearance in the Olchon valley in west Herefordshire though their origin is still bathed in obscurity. However, their security owed much to the remoteness of their meeting place in the Black Mountains, near the frontiers of both Monmouthshire and Breconshire, a factor which made it easy for them to evade arrest by slipping over the borders to counties where the sheriff's authority did not extend. About 1649, in order to facilitate the meeting of congregations of the scattered members of the Baptist mission, it was decided to abandon Olchon and meet instead in Hay, a market town of some importance in east Breconshire. Brecon itself was possibly brought into direct contact with the Baptists for the first time in the summer of 1656, when an association of the few Baptist churches then in existence in Wales met in the town to launch a counter-offensive against the Quakers who, in 1654, had embarked upon a great missionary campaign to win converts in Wales. The broadside against the Quakers was entrusted to John Miles, who was instructed to write a pamphlet as 'An antidote against the infection of the times'. In 1720 a Baptist Association meeting was held at Troscoed, in the parish of Talachddu, and the absence of a meeting house there was rectified in 1746, when a chapel was built at Maesyberllan to which the Rev. Joshua Thomas was appointed assistant pastor in 1749. However, in 1754, he moved to Leominster, where he was to labour successfully for forty-three years.

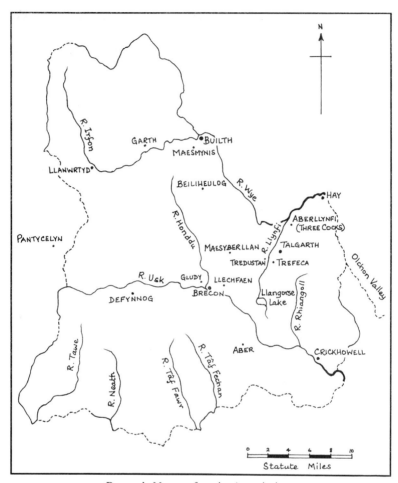

Brecon's Nonconformist Associations

A new dawn broke for the Baptists at Maesyberllan in 1784 with the appointment as minister of the Rev. David Evans of Newcastle Emlyn, popularly known as 'Dafydd Evan o Ddolgoch'. His natural ability coupled with a religious zeal resulted in hundreds being baptised during a ministry which lasted for thirty years and upwards. Shortly after he had settled at Maesyberllan, the Rev. Evans had begun to preach in the houses of some of his friends in Brecon. Conversions were made among his hearers,

126

and in 1803 it was decided to have them baptised in the river Usk, at a spot just above the bridge which spanned the river between Ship Street and Llanfaes. This was an historic event since it possibly represented the first occasion on which a public baptism had taken place at the town, though something similar could have happened during the Commonwealth period. The novelty of the event attracted a large concourse of people on a lovely Sabbath morning to witness proceedings. Many of those who watched from the bridge or from the bank on the opposite side of the river, jeered and scoffed until a water bird, which had been flying over their heads, and skimming low over the water, suddenly alighted on the head of the officiating minister, the Rev. David Evans of Dolau. The scoffers were reduced to silence, and it was in an atmosphere of some solemnity that the final act of immersion was conducted.

WATERGATE AND KENSINGTON

In 1805 premises were purchased at the Watergate, close to the junction of the Honddu and Usk rivers, and thus extremely convenient for the baptism of candidates by immersion. There a

Watergate Baptist Chapel

127

Kensington Baptist Chapel

chapel, an offshoot of the mother church at Maesyberllan, was erected and opened for worship on 1 January 1806. The total cost of ground and edifice was £700, though this debt was soon paid off through the combined efforts of the mother church and her daughter chapels. In 1809 the Rev. John Evans, the son of the founder, came to live in Brecon and he preached in Welsh, and opened a Sunday school, at Watergate. However, in 1817, he started preaching in English at the chapel on Sunday evenings. The chapel rapidly increased in numbers and prosperity, and for a period of some six years the Welsh and English members were content to sit shoulder to shoulder. Inevitably, friction arose, the concord was broken, and on 28 January 1823 an English Baptist church was formed though still worshipping at Watergate. In June 1823 this church was admitted a member of the south-eastern Baptist Association. The following year the English Baptists moved into new premises at Kensington, some one hundred yards away, the first pastor being the Rev. Benjamin Price, who had been a student at the theological college at Abergavenny. He remained a minister until 1828 when he moved to Newtown. Ministers came and went in rapid succession until the appointment in 1844 of the Rev. J.W. Evans of Dolau, who remained for thirty-three years until he was finally forced to resign his pastorate through ill-health. By 1877 the old chapel had become too small to meet the needs of an expanding congregation and a flourishing Sunday school. Furthermore, the times demanded something more modern and ornamental for divine worship. And so, in 1877, at a cost of £2,000, a new chapel, together with a vestry and schoolroom, were built. An identical situation existed at Watergate and similar considerations led to the chapel being rebuilt in 1880, also at a cost of £2,000 and again with the addition of vestry and schoolroom. The building of these chapels represented an intrusion by the Baptists into a district which had once been a stronghold of the Catholics in Brecon.

THE CATHOLICS

The numerical strength of the Catholic community at Kensington was such that there were priests ministering to their needs. The first recorded name is that of William Lloyd, who was active in Brecon between 1642-79. He was a frequent visitor at Battle End, a house thought to have been situated where Watergate Baptist chapel was built, and the home of two Catholic sisters, Mary and Margaret Thomas. During the Commonwealth period (1649-60) when the Roundhead troops occupied the town, the Catholics were hounded by the Puritan authorities. But despite the intensity of the persecution, they survived. Ironically, they may even have been strengthened by the evictions, and the lack of ministration, by Anglican clergymen. 'People', remarked a contemporary, 'were choosing to go to Rome rather than to Bedlam'.

Lloyd must have gone to ground, but that he had continued to work for the faith is indicated by the fact that in 1676, the year it was reported that there were 35 papists 'in the town and parish', he became archdeacon or head of the secular clergy in south Wales. On 1 May 1679, when the hysteria surrounding the so-called 'Popish' Plot[1] was at its height, he was indicted as a seminary priest before the Assize judges at Brecon. He was found guilty and sentenced to be hanged, drawn and quartered.[2] A week before he was due to go to the gallows, he died in the Struet gaol and was buried in the churchyard of the Priory. His death was a severe blow to the Catholics of Brecon, who were now well-advised to keep a low profile, and for over one hundred years no Catholic priest resided in the town. The flock was ministered to occasionally by visiting priests who, until the close of the seventeenth century, were made welcome in their house at Watergate by the Thomas sisters. These ladies were noted for their charitable activities and they 'educated the Catholic children in the service of God'. Mary Thomas died in 1697 and, having been denied burial in Llanddew church on the grounds that she was excommunicated from the Church of England and, consequently, had no legal claim to be laid to rest there, was finally interred in Christ College chapel 'by the general applause and approbation of all the magistrates and divines of the place'. Three years later, in 1700, Margaret Thomas also died and was buried with her sister. However, the intense and passionate nature of the persecution, and the lack of ministration by a resident priest, finally took their toll on Catholic numbers, which now dwindled rapidly. Indeed, a great weariness had descended on the Catholic community. Many of the local gentry, who had remained loyal for over a century, and who had maintained chaplains in their homes to minister to the spiritual needs of relatives, friends and neighbours, as well as to their own households, now changed their affiliations. There were, of course, gentry who remained steadfast in the faith and the Jones family of Llanarth, outside Abergavenny, continued to support a priest who, every two or three months, visited the Catholics in Brecon and the Senni valley.

The recusancy returns, by which the Anglican clergy provided their bishops with information about the numbers of known Catholics in their parishes, demonstrate starkly how Catholic numbers had been decimated. According to the returns made in 1767, there were two Catholics in Hay, both milliners; seven in Brecon, an apothecary, a shoemaker and some servants; four in Crickhowell; a similar number in Merthyr Cynog, all farmers; three in Partricio, again farmers; one each in Llangattock and Llanelli, widows of forgemen; three in Llanigon, all farmers; six

St Michael's Catholic Church

in Llansanffraid and three in Llangynidr. In the parish of Defynnog, where fifty had been recorded in the late seventeenth century, there were now only twenty-nine. This area was referred to locally as the 'Roman Dingle', and the influence of the Havards and Powells was paramount. From the 1767 returns, therefore, it would appear that there were only sixty-three

Catholics in the entire county, and though this figure is possibly on the low side, it still compares most unfavourably with the estimated 250 for the shire in 1680. In 1783, doubtless with an eye to impressing the hierarchy at Rome, and to boost morale, the Catholic bishop with responsibility for Wales declared that the flock in the Senni valley numbered almost 200 and that they were in need of a pastor.

In the latter half of the Georgian period the nerve centre of Catholic activities in Brecon was probably still at the Watergate, in the house once occupied by the Thomas sisters. The Rev. John Jones of Llanarth visited the house in October 1784 and found there 'a Tabernacle that deserves not the name, an old tattered vestment, 2 old pewter candlesticks, with a room about 12 foot square'. The Catholics, inded, were in dire financial straits. In 1788 a resident priest was appointed to Brecon, a development made possible by a generous donation towards a priest's stipend by a Mrs Elizabeth Heneage, a wealthy widow from the Isle of Wight. The Rev. John Williams now came to the town and it was he who, in 1792, informed his bishop that 'there were two boys upon the hills of Brecon who had vocations to the priesthood'. The following year he reported that scarcely any of his flock had been confirmed, and he further complained that his Watergate chapel 'is a sad place'. It is significant that, apart from Brecon, only two other towns in Wales had a resident priest at this time. These were Holywell and Abergavenny.

For the Catholics spring was in the air at the commencement of the nineteenth century. Some of the legal restrictions on their activities were being lifted, the number of priests was increasing, and the influx of clergy and religious from the Continent, fleeing from the French Revolution, brought fresh hope and vigour. The resurgence in Catholic confidence was felt in Brecon, and the property at Watergate was sold in 1805 for £200 to the Particular Baptists, who promptly built a chapel there. The Catholics now bought a property between Wheat Street and St Michael's Street which included an inn known as the 'Three Cocks'. Presumably this inn then served as a chapel and a residence for the priest, although it is recorded that Mass was also celebrated in a hayloft behind the cottage now identified as 4, St Michael Street.

In the Catholic parish records the names initially are those of the Havards and the Powells, with the Kellys, Fords, Furys and other Irish names, together with those of army personnel, becoming common in the 1830s. By 1850 there would appear to have been 120 Catholics in Brecon, and a further hundred at Senni, Craig-y-Nos and Abermorlais. Edwin Poole observed how the Catholic priest at Brecon used to strap his vestments and communion plate on his back, and make frequent journeys on foot from the town to Abergavenny, and other neighbouring towns, for the purpose of ministering to a few scattered adherents of the church.

When, in 1829, Catholic Emancipation was foremost on the political agenda, a public meeting had been held in the Town Hall in Brecon, and most of the gentry present had petitioned Parliament opposing the move. A notable dissentient was Penry Williams, the squire of Penoyre, who had declared himself strongly in favour. But despite stern opposition, the bill conferring normal civil liberties on Catholics became law, and they were now able to practise their religion openly. The time had therefore become propitious for the building of a proper church and a noted Catholic architect, Charles Hansom,[3] was engaged for the purpose. The new church, built in the Gothic style at a cost of £1,000, was opened in 1851. During the time that the church was being built, it would appear that the Catholics returned to Kensington and worshipped in what had formerly been a farm house. In March 1851 they had been in occupation of this 'temporary' accommodation for nine months. The new church could seat 150 people, although in 1866 the recorded attendance for Mass was only sixty. This was in sharp contrast to the situation at St Mary's where the attendance on Sundays was 380.

The Congregationalists or Independents

In the early days of Nonconformity, when it was subject to persecution under the penal code, a Dissenting church was somewhat different from what it is today, for it comprised members drawn from a very wide area—occasionally from a whole county and beyond—who met privately in various places for common worship and mutual exhortation. Inevitably, this kind of 'gathered church', scattered so broadly, had more than one meeting place, and the whole church would sometimes be known by the name of its chief place of meeting. As the Nonconformists increased in number, and a greater liberty of worship came gradually to be granted, first under the terms of Indemnity Acts, and later of the Toleration Act (1689), it was natural that those widely scattered meeting places of the one mother church should become separate churches, each with the right of self-government, but the process was a gradual one, and the various stages in this devolution of authority are not clearly delineated.

The Plough

The Plough church in Lion Street, Brecon, had its roots in the widely scattered Breconshire church, known as the Llanigon church,[4] because its chief meeting place was in the parish of Llanigon, near Hay. It also met secretly in the early days of persecution in many other places throughout the county, and even without in villages like Merthyr Tydfil and Cefnarthen. One of those numerous meeting places was Aberllynfi, about ten miles to the north-east of Brecon, near what is now known as Three Cocks junction. Here congregated those who were afterwards to become the founders of the Tredustan, Plough and Beiliheulog churches, and from the records of the Presbyterian Board, London, a certain Rees Prytherch is mentioned as minister of the church at Aberllynfi from 1690-93. The fact that this congregation was able to maintain a minister of its own, instead of relying on the services of an itinerant preacher, indicates that they had put to good use the generous bequest of Richard Williams who, in his will dated 26 March 1689, left a farm of one hundred acres called Tŷ Rhydymaen, in the parish of Merthyr Cynog, for the maintenance of the ministry of the Nonconformist meeting place at Aberllynfi. This farm, until fairly recent times, was still in the possession of the Plough Chapel. It has now been disposed of.

134

There is no extant evidence to indicate when the daughter church at Aberllynfi became separated from the mother church at Llanigon, though it is possible that the Toleration Act was mainly instrumental in encouraging the scattered communities to reform into individual churches, exercising self-government and having their own pastors. Neither is it recorded when the congregation at Aberllynfi moved into Brecon, since the worshippers, for the most part, lived in or near the town. Though it is certain that there was still a church at Aberllynfi in 1693, it is probable that, as early as 1689, some members had already moved to Gludy, a farmhouse between Brecon and Aberyscir, and the home of Richard Williams. At that date Gludy is described as 'a place appointed by the Protestant Dissenters for the exercise of their Religion within this county'. After a short stay at Gludy, the congregation moved to a house in Ship Street, Brecon. Until then the church had been without a chapel, but on 19 August 1697 a certain Edward Williams and his wife, Anne, sold to Edward Havard of Tylecrwn, for five shillings, a plot of ground in that part of the town known at Cantercelly (Cantref Selyf) for the purpose of building a place of worship. The public house known as 'The Plough' had stood on this spot, and this helps to explain the name given to the new chapel. It was completed on 5 October 1699 and, on 1 November, it was licensed as a place of worship under the terms of the Toleration Act by William Williams of Maes-llwch, justice of the peace. The first recorded minister is James Watkins, who is mentioned in 1714 in certain trust deeds of the church. He was still officiating there the following year, when it appears that he also had charge of a little church in Cwmiau on the border of Herefordshire. The congregation at this time numbered eighty, and among them were eight landowners. John Williams, minister of Cefnarthen, is the next to be mentioned, and between 1752-7 David Jones, who had previously been minister at Gellilibion, in Gower, appears as pastor. About 1760, William Williams, the pastor of Aber, near Talybont-on-Usk, took over as minister at the Plough as well, and for some fifty years subsequently the ministers of Aber were to officiate at the Plough. This arrangement was not conducive to the development of the town church since, for half a century, it was treated as an appendage to a country church seven or eight miles away. When William Williams was 74, Evan Davies of Pencader became his assistant, and following the death of the aged pastor in 1800, he took over as sole pastor of the two churches for a period of eleven years. The decease of Evan Davies at a comparatively early age was greatly lamented, for he had been a learned and pious man.

The Plough now severed its connection with Aber, and gave a call to Thomas Powell of Denbigh, who ministered there for twelve years (1814-26). In collaboration with the Rev. J. Jones of Talgarth, he laboured strenuously to promote the Sunday School at the Plough, and he succeeded in evoking an enthusiastic response from young people. In 1826 he left Brecon for Brynbigo and was succeeded at the Plough by Timothy Evans, a native of Cilcennin, who had been trained at the college in Carmarthen. Following Evans's departure for the Established Church, the pastorate was offered to Griffith Griffiths of Newport, Mon., who ministered in the town for eight years. The old dilapidated chapel had now become much too small. It had successfully

Plough Chapel, Lion Street

136

Independent Chapel and Sunday School in Glamorgan Street

served its purpose for over 140 years with only a slight extension in 1817. A much larger chapel was now built near to the old, and was formally opened on 29 and 30 December 1841.

Between 1849-73 the Plough was served by two ministers who had been trained at the Brecon theological college. These were Caleb Gwion (1849-60), and Richard Solomon Williams (1867-73). R.S. Williams was a pulpit giant, such was his eloquence, and after his departure from Brecon he became minister at Bethesda, Caernarvonshire. He occupied the chair of the Welsh Congregational Union in 1897 and died three years later in 1900.

It was during the ministry of his successor, the Rev. John Bowen Jones (1874-1901), who had been pastor at the Tabernacle, Bridgend, that the Plough was thoroughly renovated, enlarged and transformed into one of the most beautiful chapels in south Wales. Furthermore, a magnificent pipe-organ was installed. The opening services were performed on 30 June 1897. The new minister, J.B. Jones, was a man possessed of a strong personality and considerable scholastic gifts. His preaching was characterised by a philosophic calm, bordering on the stoical,

though he never failed to be refreshingly original and inform-
ative. He also attained the highest distinction which his
denomination could confer on him, namely, the chairmanship of
the Welsh Congregational Union (1895).

There was another Independent chapel in Brecon situated in
Glamorgan Street. This church owed its origin to an English Congregational minister, the Rev. David Blow, who had moved from
London to Brecon in 1833. The town appeared to him a desirable place of residence and a suitable vineyard for his labours.
His house was in St Mary Street, which later was to be taken over
by the Independent College. Blow started preaching in English in
this large house, which was licensed for the purpose. It soon
became evident that he was striking a chord, and his preaching
attracted so many hearers that it was decided to build a chapel in
his spacious garden to the rear of his residence facing Glamorgan
Street. The chapel was opened for worship in 1836. David Blow
moved to Monmouth in 1843 and was succeeded in the pastorate
at Brecon by Professor Henry Griffiths—his son became principal of University College, Cardiff—who had become theological
tutor at Brecon in succession to Charles Rice Davies. Griffiths
remained pastor until 1849 when he retired from his post owing to
an increasing workload at the college and the demands of his
many other preaching engagements.

Henry Griffiths, a namesake and an old pupil, followed in his
master's footsteps in 1849. This Henry Griffiths was the son of
the Rev. G. Griffiths, who was minister at the nearby Plough
chapel from 1840-48. In the chapel in Glamorgan Street he
laboured for almost a quarter of a century, and for twenty-three
years he was secretary of the College Committee. During his
ministry he was responsible for the founding of the first Band of
Hope in Brecon. He resigned from his pastorate in 1873 and
moved to Swansea on his appointment as Deputation Agent of
the Bible Society. Many persons prominent in the life of the local
community were members of his congregation. These included
Miss Mary Buck who, for sixty years, was principal of the
Boughrood House Ladies' College and Mr Edwin Poole, editor,
publisher and local historian. Edwin Poole became a superin-

tendent of the extremely successful Sunday School conducted at the chapel, and he was also a tireless worker for the Band of Hope.

During the pastorate of G.W. Cowper-Smith (1878-80), the chapel was renovated at a cost of £400, and additional changes were made to the fabric during the ministry of John Evans B.A. who officiated between 1894-1905. At the close of the Victorian era the chapel was continuing to hold its own both numerically and financially despite the fact that, owing to the anglicisation of the town, almost all religious services were now conducted in English. Many other shepherds had tended the fold in Glamorgan Street, and in their ranks were Edmund Goodison (1875-78), of Spring Hill College, B.L. Thomas of the Memorial College, (1882-86). Melchizedek Evans of Cardigan, and A.R. Ezard of Cardiff.

The Methodists

BACKGROUND

The Georgian period bore witness to a religious revival in both England and Wales. The great evangelists in England were the brothers John and Charles Wesley and George Whitefield; in Wales there appeared impassioned preachers of the stature of Howel Harris of Trefeca in Breconshire, Daniel Rowland of Llangeitho, William Williams of Pantycelyn, Howell Davies and Peter Williams, all household names. The Methodists, as they came to be called, were appalled at the low standards of public and private morality; they were revolted by the vice, drunkenness, gambling, profanity and the desecration of the Sabbath which were so prevalent in society. The souls of a benighted people had to be saved, and Satan well and truly put in his place with his empire in ruins about him. The Established Church was in no condition to meet the challenges of the times; it was impoverished, inert and supine. And the soil had also been prepared for the seed by the Dissenters, and by the Circulating Schools of Griffith Jones of Llanddowror. The Methodists received active support from Dissenting ministers, and it is

139

Howel Harris

Daniel Rowland

extremely significant that early Methodism flourished where Dissent was strongest. As for the Circulating Schools, their appearance certainly signified the emergence of a new dawn, since the advance in literacy went hand in hand with the development of Methodism.

The faith was disseminated in the town and county through the tireless labours of Methodist missionaries. Foremost amongst these was Howel Harris, who was born at Trefeca Fach in 1714 and educated at the Nonconformist academy at Llwyn Llwyd. A sermon delivered by Pryce Davies, the vicar of Talgarth in 1735, led to his spiritual conversion, and he embarked upon an evangelical mission. Harris preached in every town and village in the county, and those hearers who were deeply moved by his preaching established societies (*seiadau*) to create and perpetuate a warm spirit of Christian fellowship. He was in the congregation at Defynnog church in 1737 when, for the first time, he heard Daniel Rowland preach. A firm friendship grew up between them and they resolved to work together. A sermon which Harris preached in the churchyard at Talgarth in 1738 changed the whole course of life of a young man who had ambitions to become a doctor. This was William Williams of Pantycelyn. He now took

Holy Orders and became, for a time, a curate at Llanwrtyd where the vicar was Theophilus Evans, an unbending Anglican, and a literary figure of considerable stature.[5] William Williams, however, is best known as the hymn writer of the movement and over a thousand of these lyrical masterpieces flowed from his pen.

But Methodism in Breconshire also owed much to the labours of John Wesley. He often preached at Maesmynys church near Builth and he inspired the unfailing loyalty and devotion of three of Brecon's ark-bearers: Dr Thomas Coke, Hugh Bold and the Rev. John Hughes. Dr Coke was the son of a wealthy apothecary of the town and he was educated at Christ College before entering Jesus College, Oxford when he was sixteen years of age. He preached on numerous occasions in the county before departing as a missionary to America and the West Indies. Hugh Bold, whose father was 'trumpeter to the Corporation of Brecon' became an attorney, with a practice in the town and, despite his humble beginnings, he rose in the social scale to become bailiff of Brecon on four separate occasions: 1773, 1783, 1791 and 1804.

Countess of Huntingdon   John Wesley

141

He was a close friend of John Wesley and became a strong pillar of Welseyan Methodism in Brecon. His son was the Rev. Hugh Bold of Boughrood Castle. The Rev. John Hughes was the son of a Brecon hatter. He used to preach in the Methodist chapel in Lion Street and in north Wales, but the latter years of his life were spent in England. Besides pamphlets, sermons and commentaries which were of considerable value to the revival, he was also the author of *Horae Britannicae,*[6] a substantial tome in two volumes published in 1818 and 1819.

Charles Wesley, the eminent hymnist, also participated in the evangelising mission in Breconshire. One of the patrons of both John and Charles Wesley during their missionary journeys through the county was Marmaduke Gwynne, a magistrate in the parish of Llanllywenfel. He was a member of one of the county's leading landed families, and had been led into the arms of Methodism by Howel Harris. In 1749 Charles Wesley married his daughter, Sarah, in the parish church.

These early Methodist missionaries were subjected to cruel persecution at the hands of clergymen, magistrates and the mob. Howel Harris was denounced by the local clergy as a deceiver of the people; Marmaduke Gwynne of Garth had gone to listen to him preach at Llanwrtyd churchyard with a copy of the Riot Act

The 'Bull's Head Inn' (centre of painting) with the Methodist Chapel opposite

in his pocket fully intending to commit him as an incendiary; and when George Whitefield attempted to preach in the Bulwark, Brecon, the rabble completely silenced him. At Defynnog Methodist preachers were pelted and mobbed. The combined efforts of priests, magistrates and mobs having failed, in 1774 the Grand Jury at the Brecon Assizes decided to take matters into their own hands and made a presentment to the presiding judge. They submitted that the Methodists were guilty of illegal assembly; that they drew together great numbers of disorderly people; and that they so 'confounded' and 'disordered' the minds of their listeners that this might lead to the overthrowing of good government in both church and state. Whatever the outcome of this appeal, the Methodists were not to be gagged and chained, and their ministry continued unabated.

Welsh Methodism in Brecon

It was in 1780 that a Welsh Calvinistic chapel was built by Lady Huntingdon in the Struet, on leased land opposite the 'Bull's Head'. Here, in 1795, Evan Edwards, a weaver, began keeping a Sunday School. About 1800 the lease expired, and William James of Traedyrhaearn, with the aid of a few friends, purchased the old chapel for £125. In 1820 the chapel was rebuilt, but it soon proved too small to accommodate a rapidly expanding congregation. The 'Old Lion' premises were purchased in 1859 for £1,100, and a further £1,200 were expended on building a chapel there. It was thus that Bethel was born.

In the winter of 1807 the Welsh Wesleyan missionaries came to Brecon. The work of forming a society in the town was successfully prosecuted under the guidance of William Batten, who was then stationed in Merthyr Tydfil as a Welsh missionary. In 1822 the Revs. David Evans and Lewis Jones were appointed to Brecon. Shortly after their coming they succeeded in securing a very desirable site in the Struet for a chapel and a minister's house. The Tabernacle chapel, a 'neat and commodious' structure, was opened on 24 August 1824. In 1871 the property was disposed of for £600 to a Mr James, a grocer, who converted it

143

The Tabernacle Chapel. Until recently a Hardware Store

The Wesleyan Chapel, Llanfaes c. 1900

into business premises and it was to remain a grocer's shop until comparatively recent times. At the present moment it is a photographic shop. A new chapel was erected in Walnut Square, Llanfaes in 1873 where the services were regularly held in Welsh until 1885 when, owing to a fall in numbers, it was amalgamated with the English chapel in Lion Street, which later came to be known as 'Dr Coke's'. During the interval between the sale of the chapel in the Struet, and the opening of a new chapel in Llanfaes, the worshippers had assembled in a disused Baptist chapel in Newmarch Street. This Baptist chapel had come into existence following a schism in the ranks of the congregation at Watergate. The rebellious faction had withdrawn and erected this chapel. Time, however, proved a greater healer; the dissensions were resolved, and there was a gradual return to Watergate.

English Methodism in Brecon

The decline in the use of Welsh owing to the increasing anglicisation of the borough led to the establishment of the English cause in Brecon. In 1756 John Wesley—the founder of English Methodism—preached in the Town Hall and his influence led to the formation of an English Wesleyan Society, which was accustomed to meet in the houses of William Gilbert and Thomas James. The need for a proper sanctuary soon arose, and to fulfil this purpose, William Gilbert generously gave a corner of his orchard where John Wesley used to preach in the open air during the warm summer months. The chapel was erected at the corner of Free Street and Little Free Street in 1770—the year in which the English Circuit was formed—and, in addition to this gift, Gilbert subscribed £100. In 1815 this chapel was thoroughly revamped and, at the time, it was jointly used by the English and Welsh Wesleyan Societies of the town, though their services were held at separate times. Their Sunday Schools were also conducted at different venues, the English at the top of Heol Rydd and the Welsh at the 'Fountain Inn', where they also worshipped for a time owing to a disagreement with their English brethren. The English Society, whose members were of good social and economic standing, did not partake of the Lord's Supper in their own place of worship; rather did they attend communion in St Mary's Church. In 1834 a new Wesleyan chapel, with accommodation for 400 people, was built in Lion Street, near the birthplace of Dr Coke, on a piece of land purchased from Penry Williams for £200. The new edifice cost £2,000 to build, and most of the pews were soon let. The chapel was re-seated, cemented and completely renovated in 1800 at a cost of £280.

The increase in the number of English speakers in the borough also created a demand for an English Calvinistic chapel and, in 1866, such a place of worship was provided in the Watton—the Watton Presbyterian Church. The foundation stone of this

Dr Coke's Chapel and Memorial Schools. The site is now occupied by Leos

146

Gothic-style structure was laid on 17 January 1866 by Mrs Mordecai Jones, and it was opened for public worship on Monday, 28 January 1867. The total cost of the building amounted to over £2,300. Meetings of the English cause had been held in Brecon prior to this date, the first being held in the Town Hall on 14 August 1864 when the Rev. Lumley of Cardiff officiated. The Rev. D.W. Davies was chosen to be pastor of the new church, and he laboured successfully there until he left for Newport in December 1876. He will always be remembered with affection and gratitude as the founder of the Brecon Literary Institution.

By mid-Victorian times the religious scene at Brecon had been completely transformed. The Anglican Church, which for centuries, had retained the loyalty and respect of the vast majority of the worshippers in the town, lost its hold on the affections of most. Hitherto, it had remained virtually unassailable, since people felt that it pointed the way to salvation as it offered the true way of life and belief, and the gentry, the backbone of society, were giant pillars of support. But the church was sadly in need of reform, and a growing number of people of the middle sort were becoming disillusioned. The defences of the church were undermined to such an extent that in the nineteenth century it was finally overwhelmed by a great Nonconformist tide. The changed situation in Brecon, and elsewhere in Wales, is demonstrated in the religious census of 1851. The primary purpose of this census was to ascertain the extent to which the means of religious worship had kept pace with the increase in population since the beginning of the century. Horace Mann, one of the senior officials at the Census Office, was entrusted with the task of supervising the work. Inevitably, criticisms were voiced concerning the reliability of the returns, as Mann had to rely on the goodwill of those individuals responsible for collecting the information. Places of worship could be omitted, worshippers could be counted twice, and attendances could be based on estimates. But despite these deficiencies, this mammoth task was completed with a fair degree of accuracy. The following table, compiled from the returns made for the Brecon churches, clearly illustrates the dominant position of Nonconformity in the town by mid-century:

The Church of England

Church	No. of Worshippers		
	Morning	Afternoon	Evening
St John	370	520	-
St Mary	757	-	600
St David	152	-	132
	1,279	520	732

Grand Total = 2,531

Nonconformists

Wesleyan Methodists

Struet (Tabernacle)	15	60	80
Lion St (Dr Coke)	200	-	300
	215	60	380

Grand Total = 655

Calvinistic Methodists

Struet	200	149	231

Grand Total = 580

Baptists

Kensington	160	-	140
Watergate	300	-	500
	460		640

Grand Total = 1,100

Independents

Plough	550	-	800
Glamorgan Street	130	-	150
	680		950

Grand Total = 1,630

Catholics

Kensington	191	51	-

Grand Total = 242

Altogether there were 6,738 attendances at places of worship in Brecon on that last Sunday in March. Of these, 2,531 or 37 per cent were Anglican communicants, while 3,965 or 59 per cent worshipped at one or another of the Nonconformist chapels. The remainder, the Catholics, with 242 attendances, constituted some 4 per cent of the worshippers.[5]

The returns not only enable comparisons to be drawn between the relative positions of the Established Church and Protestant Nonconformity at Brecon; they also throw considerable light on the relative strengths of the various Nonconformist denominations themselves in the town. By the mid-nineteenth century the Independents were by far the largest single Nonconformist persuasion. Next came the Baptists and, finally, at the bottom of the league table, came the Methodists with the Wesleyans considerably stronger than the Calvinists.

The officials making the returns were also expected to indicate the number of 'free' and 'other' sittings. The object was to discover what proportion of the provision of seats was available for the poorer classes. Though some of the officials might not have understood exactly what was required, the published figures still provide useful indicators as to the extent to which the provision of church sittings was freely available. The statistics for Brecon show that 41 per cent of the provision was free, a figure that compares favourably with the 45 per cent for south Wales. In England and Wales, on the other hand, an estimated 37 per cent of places were free.

The period 1801-51 witnessed a phenomenal expansion in the population of Brecon, for it rose from 2,898 to 5,827 (the military excluded), an increase of the order of some 101 per cent. There was adequate space in the three medieval churches of Brecon to accommodate 1,815 worshippers. While there would have been ample room for Anglican worshippers in 1801, this would certainly not have been the case fifty years later when the population had leapt by almost 3,000. This overnight dramatic increase caught the church napping, and the chronic insufficiency in the number of places for worship was rectified not through the provision of new churches, or the extension of older edifices, but rather by the construction of chapels. Between 1800-50 five new Nonconformist chapels made their appearance, while two others were entirely rebuilt. Not only had the worshippers in Brecon rejected the Anglican Church in significant numbers; they had also provided themselves with alternative places of worship.

In Wales, from about 1840 onwards, there was a regeneration in church life. The parliamentary reforms of the 1830s, the Established Church Bill (1836), the Pluralities and Non-Residence Bill (1836), the Dean and Chapter Bill (1840), and the establishment of the Ecclesiastical Commissioners greatly facilitated the work of church reform. The root causes of its failure in previous centuries, pluralism and non-residence, were suppressed at all levels, and church resources were released allowing for the augmenting of stipends, and the restoration and extension of ancient fabrics. From 1803 onwards, archdeacons at Brecon ceased to be non-resident, and Richard Davies was not only an effective preacher of sermons from the pulpit, but he also actively promoted the provision of educational facilities in the borough. At the Priory of St John the Evangelist the ravages of centuries of neglect were tackled, a beginning being made in 1836 when Lord Camden had the chancel covered with slate. Furthermore, a glass screen was erected between the choir and the nave, and the church was re-pewed with 250 sittings free. Between 1836-60, at a cost estimated at £1,000, St John's was subjected to 'tinkering' operations which saw some of its most beautiful features hidden under coatings of plaster and whitewash. In 1860, Sir Gilbert Scott submitted a detailed report on the state of the building and, as a result, proper restoration work was undertaken, though it was limited to the eastern end of the church where a grained ceiling was built over the chancel under the perpendicular roof. This work again was financed by the Marquis of Camden. Following another report by Scott in 1872 the church, between 1873-5, was thoroughly renovated at a cost of £5,500. Altogether, from 1860-75, it has been estimated that £12,000 had been spent on restoration work.

But the renewal was not confined to the major church in the borough. The builders were also busy in St Mary's though some minor improvements had already been effected in 1805. The cost of the reparations in 1857 amounted to £3,280. Two years later, in 1859, St David's church, which had collapsed in 1852, was restored at a cost of £1,500. All the Anglican churches in Brecon, built in the Gothic style, had now been given a face-lift and this, undoubtedly, was one of the most spectacular aspects of church reform in the town. But the church had acted rather belatedly, as

The Priory Church of St John

151

St Mary's Church from the Bulwark. Note the Wellington Memorial

the Nonconformist chapels, some also built in the Gothic style, were already in position.

But despite this rash of chapel building and church reconstruction, it is nevertheless true that a substantial number of the population of Brecon had no formal connection with any organised religion, and this applied particularly to the workers and the poor. For the middle class element in the town, on the other hand, membership of church or chapel was certainly an essential feature of their life styles; equally, and this was so important to them, it conferred a measure of respectability.

NOTES

[1] In 1678 a scoundrel by the name of Titus Oates declared the existence of a plot by the Catholics to murder King Charles II and place his brother James (the future James II) on the throne of England with the assistance of the French army. Following accomplishment of this design, Roman Catholicism would be restored in the country.

[2] This was a particularly horrendous way to meet one's Maker. The victim would first be hanged, though not until he was dead, then cut down and disembowelled while still alive. The body was then dismembered.

[3] He was the brother of Jospeh Hansom of Hansom Cab fame.

[4] The first pastor was Henry Maurice who was descended from north Wales gentry stock. The elders of the church were, without exception, men of substance.

[5] His best known work was *Drych y Prif Oesoedd* (A Mirror of the First Ages) which is regarded as one of the classics of Welsh prose.

[6] Hours of Britain.

[7] Another method of estimating the relative strengths of the Anglicans, Nonconformists and Catholics in the town is to base the calculation on the best-attended service whether it was morning, afternoon or evening. Assessed by this method there would have been 3,841 attendances at places of worship. Of these 1,429 or 37 per cent were Anglican and 2,221, or 58 per cent, Nonconformist. The Catholics, with 191 attendances, would have comprised 5 per cent of the worshippers. The correlation between the two sets of statistics is impressively close.

Chapter 5

LET THERE BE LIGHT: THE EDUCATIONAL SCENE

There was a tradition of educational provision at Brecon, both formal and informal, stretching back for centuries. Even during the Middle Ages, all was not gloom and doom since, for a small privileged band of promising young scholars, there were opportunities for cultural advancement. Though the concept of education for the masses did not exist, even remotely, in anyone's mind, schools, of one kind or another, were to be found. At the Priory of St John the Evangelist, overlooking the Honddu, there was a school for novices; and the education of the boys might not end there, since monks could be transferred to larger monastic schools before proceeding to university. St Mary's church housed a Song School at which, in addition to music, the rudiments of reading and writing would also, presumably, have been taught. Such education as was given in the Middle Ages was often imparted by well-disposed parish or chantry priests who would instruct the brighter and more hopeful children. And in the bigger and wealthier households there would sometimes have been a household chaplain who performed this function. However, together with these more formal agencies for learning, there was also a more informal, and very practical, education through a system of apprenticeship, and the six trade gilds of Brecon enforced a lengthy apprenticeship which must have constituted an educational experience of considerable importance. Finally, there was the bardic tradition, which imparted a wide liberal education embracing gentry and poets alike, and visiting bards entertained not only the chieftain in his hall; they also taught his children.

During the Tudor age, at Brecon, an advance in educational provision of a momentous nature took place since, on the site of the dissolved Dominican friary in Llanfaes, an endowed grammar school was established. Christ College was the first of its kind in Wales, and within its walls scholars were introduced to

154

the Classics through the teaching of Latin grammar and literature together with a little Greek. Some provision was also made for Religious Education and, as the school's founder in 1541, Bishop William Barlow, had encouraged it, a little time might have been devoted to singing. Several factors underlay the establishment of this school. One was the need to produce good upright citizens who would be obedient to the laws of both state and church, and who would bend the knee readily to the will of King, bishop and magistrate. Another was Barlow's desire to advance Protestantism in the town of Brecon and the eastern half of his vast diocese. He was an ardent Protestant and the first with such views to become bishop of St David's. Finally, there was the need to provide better educational facilities for the clerics in his diocese.

During the Commonwealth period (1649-1660) the Puritans, as part of their great missionary campaign to spread the light of the Gospel in the dark places of Wales, established schools. Under the terms of the Propagation Act of February 1650 the commissioners were to appoint suitable men to act as school-masters at a salary not to exceed £40 a year and to be drawn from the sequestered revenues of the church. Christ College was not interfered with and it was for this reason, together with the influence which powerful local parliamentarians like Sir William Lewis could exert in high places, that the Commonwealth school was established not in populous places such as Hay and Crick-howell, but in the tiny remote village of Llangorse.

Though Christ College continued to exist, its efficiency during the Commonwealth period was seriously impaired. The College buildings were plundered, with the result that the school had to continue in a building in the Struet, a suburb to the north of the town. The master of the school was one Philip Williams (appoint-ed in 1650) and in 1652 he was provided with an usher, Hugh Powell. The restoration of monarchy in the person of Charles II in 1660 witnessed a change for the better in the fortunes of the College. The foundation was now restored to the newly conse-crated bishop of St David's, Dr William Lucy, and he displayed his considerable interest in it by having it 'wholly rebuilt again'.

Christ College

This rebuilding was completed by 1666, and the bishop's personal involvement with the College was now further demonstrated by his presentation to it of a silver flagon weighing 47 ounces. This period, appropriately enough, has consequently been described as the 'Lucy Era'. But though the College owed much to his vigour the church, on the other hand, at a critical moment in its history, was to suffer grievously from his lack of wisdom and fiery temper, for he was to display little or no sympathy with Wales and her culture.

The Restoration also bore witness to the eviction of the Puritan master and usher and their replacement by Anglicans. The new appointments were very much in keeping with the general Anglican practice of choosing local clergymen for their school-masters. The master, Meredith Penry, who was thirty-three when he took over the reins, had been rector of Llanhamlach since 30 November 1661 and vicar of the Priory church of St John the Evangelist since February 1662. To assist him in his work he was provided with the services of an usher, Hugh Jones. Both took a substantial drop in salary, for while the Puritan authorities had been generous in their remuneration of schoolmasters, the master and usher at Brecon receiving £40 a year between them, at the Restoration the salaries reverted to their former levels arising from the original benefaction. Thus Penry received £13 13*s.* 4*d.* while Hugh Jones was paid £6 6*s.* 8*d.*, both sums amounting to the original endowment of £20 a year.

For the remainder of the seventeenth century the College was conducted with reasonable efficiency and in 1688 the bishop of St David's described the master and usher as being 'sober and of good conversation (i.e. character) and well qualified'. Considerable attention was devoted to ridding the school of any taint of Puritanism, and the scholars were catechised regularly, and taken to the parish church every Sunday and feast day where they were expected to behave modestly and quietly. At all times the master was to impress upon their minds the truths contained in the Scriptures and inculcate the rules of right conduct. The concept of what constituted a good education was still rather narrow and bigoted, and would not apear to have represented any advance on that which prevailed during the period of Puritan domination.

At the turn of the century, in 1699, matters began to go badly wrong for the College owing to the maladministration of Thomas Watson, who had become bishop of St David's in 1687. His misconduct led to his suspension, trial and deprivation. Amongst the charges laid against him was one to the effect that he had removed the College's original charter of foundation together with other muniments. Fortunately, his successor at St David's was George Bull, an honourable and capable bishop. He resided in Brecon, was widely respected, and with him a start was made on restoring the tarnished public image of the College. However, in 1716, the school was still in an unsatisfactory condition both with regard to its buildings and the education provided there. John Jandrell the master, writing to Bishop Ottley, declared that 'the dilapidations at the school amount to about £80'. He then further declared that 'I have now about forty scholars and believe the number will considerably increase between this and Whitsuntide; I shall use my utmost endeavour to retrieve the character of the school'. Some success must have attended his efforts, for in a report on the school in 1725 it is stated that 'the Schoolmaster performs his duty with great care. His salary or pension is £16 per annum paid out of the tithes of the Rectory of Mothvey by the Bishop of St. David's for the time being. The schoolmaster has besides the said £16 a further stipend of about £5-10 payable by the prebendary of St Harmon's, Llangunllo, Llandrindod and Trallong'.

Ruslow Barrer was appointed master in 1736 and he was followed by Rees Powell. But then came the man who made by far the greatest impact on the College. This was David Griffith, who became master in 1757. Under his influence came boys who were later to achieve considerable distinction in various walks of national life. Amongst these luminaries were Theophilus Jones, the historian of Brecknockshire; the Reverend Edward Davies, author of *Horae Britannicae*; Dr Thomas Coke, the famous Wesleyan Methodist and missionary; Thomas Price (Carnhuanawc), one of the leading Celtic scholars of his day; and Dr John Jones, the litigious theologian and scholar. Such an impressive list speaks well of the school and the quality of its educational provision.

Together with enlightened masters, the College during this century was to benefit from the fact that it found a generous benefactor in the person of Sir Jeffrey Jeffreys of St Mary Axe, London, who represented the borough of Brecon at Westminster from 1689-1709. But it was a sad commentary on the state of the finances of the school, arising very largely from financial mismanagement, that the revenue from its endowments had to be augmented in this fashion from private means.

Generally speaking, then, the eighteenth century was a period when, despite the peaks, Christ College was in a state of stagnation, even decline, and financial mismanagement, even corruption, had a great deal to do with it. Even the universities were somnolent, and they had become very largely institutions where young men of good family could go to prepare themselves for entry into polite society. And within that society promotion and advancement were not related to ability but were controlled by patronage. Consequently, there was no stream of well-qualified young hopefuls leaving the higher institutions of learning to take up teaching appointments, and grammar schools, like Christ College, suffered as a result.

The bishops of St David's, whose duties embraced the government of the grammar school at Brecon, have also to shoulder part of the blame for the decline in the fortunes of the College. Most were English, appointed for political reasons, and they spent but little time within the diocese. During their absences they delegated their responsibilities for the school to the prebendaries in residence, who lacked the financial means to take any effective action.

In 1808 Bishop Thomas Burgess appointed as headmaster of Christ College the Reverend Thomas Williams, a man of excellent education. He was, furthermore, a person of integrity and possessed of considerable private means. The new headmaster took immediate steps to erect a more suitable schoolroom to replace the old premises which had become unfit for use, and he contributed the substantial sum of £200 from his own pocket towards the building fund.

Christ College was a fee-charging institution, junior pupils paying four guineas and senior pupils six guineas a year. The scholars received a classical education, though Bishop Burgess had established a theological course at Brecon, something which he had also instituted in the three other grammar schools licensed by him in the diocese, namely, Carmarthen, Lampeter and Ystrad Meurig. This course of action was dictated by the need to secure better trained candidates for ordination. Christ College, as a result, attracted more pupils and the number of scholars varied between forty and sixty. However, the venerable bishop now embarked upon an initiative which was to threaten the very existence of the school at Brecon; he began to collect subscriptions for the funding of a college in Wales to prepare men for holy orders. Such success accompanied his efforts that in 1822 he was able to lay the foundation stone of St David's College, Lampeter. The new college threw open its doors to candidates in 1825 and such was its appeal that the number of pupils for ordination at Brecon rapidly diminished. In 1825 Bishop Burgess was translated to Salisbury, and his departure represented a sad loss both to the diocese and to the school at Brecon.

159

The early decades of the nineteenth century witnessed the grammar schools being subjected to considerable criticism over their curricula. Radical reformers such as Edgeworth, Bentham and Cobbett wrote vigorously concerning the limitations of a purely classical education which led to many schools being regarded as the preserves of the middle and upper classes. The decline in numbers owing to the opening of the college at Lampeter, and the narrowness of the curriculum, were both contributory factors in the decline of Christ College at this time. It is hardly surprising, therefore, that the Charity Commissioners should have found the school in an unsatisfactory condition in 1836. Though the College was described as a 'free' grammar school, the observation was made that 'it does not appear to have been at any time conducted purely as a free grammar school, the scholars being required to pay between £2-2s. and £4-4s. per annum, with the exception of two or three who were placed on the foundation'. In other words the school had become the kind of establishment so criticised by the radicals. The number of pupils had been reduced to seven, their ages varying between six and fourteen. In the curriculum were included the three Rs and the classics, but the school was now at an extremely low ebb.

The remuneration of the master was £43-12s.-4d. annually though this sum was augmented from other sources since he was also the recipient of the rents of two cottages, the schoolroom, and a small stable adjoining it, amounting in all to £11-3s. The master was provided with an usher though, not surprisingly, the commissioners disputed his 'right to the assistance of this person's services' because of the small number of pupils.

In 1840, the newly appointed bishop of St David's, Connop Thirlwall, was of the opinion that 'the best thing that could happen to the chapel of Christ College was to let it fall quietly to the ground', an opinion which he was soon obliged to alter as a result of the force of public opinion locally. The chapel had by now lost most of its roof, and neighbouring farmers used it as a stable on market days. As for the school, for much of its work, it had been forced to migrate to rooms in the town itself, in Lion Street and Bell Lane.

In 1840 the collegiate church at Brecon was dissolved and a contemporary observer, the Reverend Jermyn Pratt from Suffolk, described the school which had been attached to it in the following terms: 'The school, however, was kept up until 1845, but from the inefficiency of the schoolmaster it dwindled away to a very few boys and now there is neither school nor service nor lecture. The small building set apart for the schoolroom is perfectly unfit for the purpose and indeed would be a disgrace to the smallest population in any parish'. The College was now at the very nadir of its fortunes.

Pratt's report provoked an acrimonious correspondence between Sir Benjamin Hall of Llanover Court, situated four miles south of Abergavenny, and Bishop Connop Thirlwall concerning the state of the school at Brecon, the bishop vainly attempting to defend it against Pratt's criticisms. The debate led to a scheme being prepared in the Court of Chancery in 1851, and the Christ College Act of Parliament, embodying its proposals, became law in 1853. It was by the terms of this act that a modern public school, with a board of governors, emerged in 1855. The act provided for the election of a headmaster, who was to be in holy orders, a second master who was to be a member of the

Christ College in a ruinous state

Church of England, and a lecturer in Divinity, an office which could be held by either of the foregoing. The right of placing boys in the school was vested in the governors, and the election of 'free' scholars was never to exceed the ratio of one in three of the number on roll at the time. The amalgamation of Christ College and Lampeter was considered but the idea was dropped. The curriculum was laid down. In addition to Religious Instruction, the course of study was to include Greek and Latin, English Grammar, Writing, Geography, History, Arithmetic, Mathematics and such other languages and branches of literature, art and science as the governors should prescribe and direct. Boys were not to be admitted until they had attained the age of eight and had received certain preliminary instruction determined by the headmaster with the approval of the governors.

Although in 1860 Pratt had declared that nothing had been done at Christ College during the thirteen years since he had brought the unhappy state of affairs at the school to the public notice, in 1861 a beginning was made with the provision of new buildings and a master's residence at an estimated cost of £10,000. This building programme, which included dormitories and other necessary accommodation for forty boarders, was completed in 1864.

By this time annual examinations conducted in mid-summer by chosen inspectors were becoming an important feature of the school, and they contributed greatly to the raising of academic standards. In 1867 a full report of the examination conducted by Christopher Wordsworth of Winchester College appeared in the *Brecon County Times*. From this report it appears that the boys were given oral and written examinations in the Classics, Mathematics, History, Geography and French. In the Mathematics examination the Euclid papers were good throughout and the work in Arithmetic and Algebra was satisfactory. With regard to the Classics, Wordsworth was particularly pleased with the style of construing in the upper classes, especially in the sixth form. The English History and Geography papers were found to be very correct and painstaking. The examiner concluded his report by declaring that the standard of construing at Christ College compared favourably with that at Winchester, Harrow and Wellington. Christ College, he opined, was becoming a very good school, and a foundation stone had been laid for one of the great schools of Wales.

Invaluable light is cast on the condition of Christ College by the Taunton Report. The assistant commissioners of the Taunton Committee visited the endowed grammar schools in 1865-6 and their report was published in 1868. That on Christ College was the work of James Bryce, a well known Mathematician, Geologist and ambassador. There were 53 boys in the school, more than half of whom were day scholars. They were the sons of professional men and the wealthier shopkeepers of the town. For the smaller tradespeople and artisans the annual fee of £8 was too high. The parents included builders, painters, bank clerks, farmers, surveyors, surgeons, solicitors, clergymen, coachmakers, bandmasters, drapers, curriers, and iron founders. Free education was provided for certain foundations 'to be elected at a general meeting of the governors from amongst the most meritorious candidates for admission, whether then in the school or not'. The practice was for the examiner to report to the headmaster upon those boys who had most distinguished themselves, and for the headmaster to recommend these boys, or some of them, to the governors for selection. Preference was generally given to poor scholars. In 1870 the number of foundations was fixed at three.

Within the school the bias throughout was towards the teaching of the Classics—there is no mention of Welsh as a subject or as a medium of instruction—and, according to the commissioners, the school resembled on a small scale the great classical boarding schools of the south of England. At this time few of the scholars entered Oxford or Cambridge, though the number was increasing, and many of those who had gained admission into these universities from Brecon had distinguished themselves.

Taken as a whole, the work done at the school, while not exceptional, was found to be sound and good, a tribute to the earnest and careful teaching of the masters. The commissioners were of the opinion that the school should cater for three categories of boys—day scholars, boarders from wealthy homes, and boarders whose parents could not be described as affluent. The town of Brecon did not provide more than forty of the boys, and there was need for a hostel or cheap boarding house to attract boys from the densely populated industrial valleys of Glamorgan and Monmouthshire. The commissioners also advised a modification of the curriculum to give greater prominence to Arithmetic and the Natural Sciences, though they were very anxious to preserve the classical character of the school.

From the report it becomes evident that the revenues from College lands were still by far the most important single item of income, while the greatly improved salaries of the masters accounted for the largest single item of expenditure.

The next official investigation was conducted by the Charity Commissioners, whose enquiries were made between 1874-80. Richard Durnforth, later the bishop of Chichester, as representative of the commissioners, met the mayor and council of Brecon in the town hall on Friday, 12 April 1873. He later visited the school and submitted a report on his findings. His main recommendations were that Christ College should be primarily a training college for the Welsh clergy and should meet the requirements of the people of south Wales. Though he considered that room could be made for one hundred boarders, he could see no advantage in filling the school with English boys. He would divide the school into junior and senior departments, and thought that there should be room in both for day boys. In this way he would attempt to make the school into a 'local' one while still making it attractive for boarders.

This new scheme was approved and authorised to be enforced on 28 July 1880. The governing body with its corporate rights was continued and the number of governors fixed at seventeen, six ex-officio, seven representative and four co-optative. Brecon Town Council was to be represented by one member only. New school buildings, with accommodation for 150 boys, were to be erected on the site of the old school. The salaries of the headmaster and lecturer were to be £200 and £100 per annum respectively and the headmaster, in addition to his salary, was to receive a capitation allowance. The entrance fees were not to exceed £1 in the junior department and £2 in the senior. Tuition fees were to range from £10 to £15 in both departments. Boarding fees were not to exceed £30 in a hostel, or £45 in a master's house.

Twenty pounds a year were earmarked for special prizes for boys who showed proficiency in the study of the Greek Testament, early Christian history, and the doctrines and formularies of the Church of England. Scholarships were to be maintained in the school as exemptions, total or partial, from the payment of tuition fees. The recipients were to be called 'Foundation' scholars, and they were never to exceed one-tenth of the boys on roll. The governors could keep in reserve a number of these foundation scholarships to be competed for by boys who were being educated, or had been educated, at public elementary schools in south Wales or in Monmouthshire for not less than three years. Twenty-four other scholarships to be called Saint David's Scholarships, each of the annual value of £20, were established though this stipulation was later amended to read 'not less than five nor more than twenty-four other scholarships'.

Some of these scholarships were to be awarded on the results of an examination which included the Welsh language so that half of the scholarships would be awarded to boys born and resident in Wales, and the other half to boys seeking a classical education with the object of entering Holy Orders. Boys whose parents were financially secure were excluded from the scheme.

In addition to these special prizes and scholarships there was also the Parry de Winton exhibition of £40 a year tenable at the Universities of Oxford and Cambridge. The scheme of 1880 had established the school on a firm basis and the advantages of its endowments were made available to boys from all parts of the United Kingdom.

Further interesting insights into the state of Christ College are provided by the Aberdare Report (1881). This was the result of an inquiry into the state of intermediate and higher education in Wales. Evidence was taken at Brecon in December, when the school was described as being in the first grade, whose income from its endowments amounted to about £1,200. However, this income was 'temporarily' burdened owing to a large expenditure on improving and extending the buildings which, when completed, would be amongst the best and most convenient in Wales. They would provide accommodation for 200 boys, inclusive of 60 boarders. Other boarders 'are now received in the houses of assistant masters'. The number of pupils in attendance had swollen to 131, of whom 83 were boarders and 48 day scholars and, of these, 100 were domiciled in Wales. Greek was taught to 108, and Natural Science to about 60. Most of the pupils attended church, 12 only being Nonconformists. The fees charged for boarding had escalated to £42 per annum; tuition fees for the lower school were £8-8s. and for the upper £10. The headmaster, Daniel Lewis Lloyd, had found, on his appointment, 15 scholars in attendance, a figure which he had succeeded in augmenting to 131. Lloyd, who was later made bishop of Bangor (1890), had been headmaster of Friars' school in that town, and it was reported that many boys from that school had followed him to Brecon. The Nonconformist pupils were not constrained to attend worship inconsistent with their religious principles and the religious instruction provided was not of a strictly denominational character.

In 1889 Mr Edgar Thomas returned very complete answers to queries sent to Brecon Town Council by the Charity Commissioners with regard to Christ College. The number of boys on roll was now 150, of whom 108 were boarders, and nine came from outside Wales. The majority of the pupils had middle-class backgrounds being the sons of clergy, doctors, lawyers, army officers, non-conformist ministers, tradesmen, mining agents and gentlemen of independent means. The average number proceeding to the universities of Oxford and Cambridge over the previous ten years was seven; other boys on leaving the school entered such professions as law, medicine, engineering, banking and the army. It was noticeable that the boarders invariably went to the universities. Education costs, *per capita*, excluding boarders, were approximately £13. The headmaster's salary was £200 per annum, though he also received capitation payments of £4 for upper school pupils and £2 for lower school pupils. The eight assistant masters, all resident, received £175 per annum. Tuition fees were £10 for upper school and £8 for the lower. Boarders paid £42 for tuition and board. The entrance examination to the school was not difficult and very few boys were rejected. However, despite the ease with which entry could be gained, the external examination results achieved by the pupils placed Christ College twelfth in the entire kingdom. The examinations taken were those of the Oxford and Cambridge Examination Board and, in 1889, 16 Higher and 15 Lower Certificates were gained. From 1890 onwards the annual Speech Day became an institution, and the headmaster's report provided a veritable quarry of information on the academic achievements of the school.

D.L. Lloyd whose energy and zeal had raised the College to a pre-eminent position amongst Welsh schools, was succeeded as headmaster by the Reverend M.A. Bayfield and it was during his time that the oak floors and the oak choir stalls were introduced, both at the expense of Richard D. Cleasby of Penoyre. Bayfield proved a controversial appointment since the rumour was spread, at a time of growing national consciousness, that he was anti-Welsh in his sympathies. Though Bayfield strenuously denied the charge, an article in the *Brecon County Times* in 1892 made it clear that it would 'prove to be of little avail'.

In 1896 the Education Committee of Brecon County Council, in its efforts to meet the requirements of the Welsh Intermediate Act of 1889, sought the co-operation of Christ College in providing places for boys who held Intermediate School Scholarships. There was at the time considerable opposition to the idea of building a county school on the grounds that it was not needed at Brecon and would undermine the position of Christ College. The governors of the College, eager to preserve its public school character, rejected the idea and negotiations fell through.

The objectives of the school at the turn of the century were admirably summarised by the headmaster, the Reverend R.H. Chambers, in his annual report in 1900. He declared that he wished the pupils to be provided 'with an intellectual training of the highest kind, a sound body, and a high character'. He judiciously added that it was not for him to judge to what extent the

The Rev. D.L. Lloyd,
Headmaster 1879-1890

The Rev. M.A. Bayfield,
Headmaster 1890-1895

school had succeeded in its objectives though the examination results would appear to provide a partial answer.

Primary Education—Pre 1870

THE CHARITY SCHOOLS

The succession of Charles II to the throne in 1660 enabled the Tory squires and churchmen, who had suffered so grievously during the period of Puritan ascendancy following the execution of the King in 1649, to exact their 'pound of flesh'. The intolerant and persecuting nature of the restored Anglican church was reflected in the Clarendon Code, that draconian legislation enacted by the Cavalier Parliament between 1661-65. And yet there was an essential dichotomy in Restoration society, for despite the severity of the persecution of the Dissenters under these laws, a characteristic feature of the age ushered in by the 'Merry Monarch' was a concern for piety and good works. The wealthy were exhorted to utilise some of their wealth, in their own lifetimes, for charitable purposes and assume responsibility for the welfare of the underdog, the old, the infirm and the poor. Such solicitude for the physical and spiritual needs of one's fellow beings was regarded as a sure passport to eternal salvation.

This emphasis on piety and good works represented a reaction against the low standards of private and public morality, themselves an indirect product of the strict Puritan regime. There were those who were appalled by the vice, profanity, gambling, and drunkenness so prevalent in society, and they were determined on a 'Reformation of Manners'. Societies were formed for this purpose, the first being established in London, but they soon spread to Wales, and through prosecutions in the law courts it was hoped to compel people to mend their ways.

Similar developments were taking place in Germany under the influence of Philipp Jacob Spener and Hermann Francke, and it was as a result of the influence of these Pietists that the London reformers came to the conclusion that penal action alone was insufficient. What was also required to achieve higher moral standards was to diminish the ignorance of the masses through a system of religious education. This desire to improve 'manners' (conduct) through education led to the establishment in 1674 of the Welsh Trust, which represented the first attempt by a voluntary agency to establish schools in Wales. Moderate men of differing religious persuasions, who prided themselves on their 'latitude', became patrons. They included future bishops as well as leading Dissenters; the lion, indeed, was to lie down with the lamb.

Thomas Gouge, the principal architect of the Welsh Trust, was a Puritan divine who had been ejected from the living of St Sepulchre, in Southwark, London, in 1662. His first flirtation with Wales occurred in 1671-2 when he undertook some itinerant preaching on the 'skirts of Wales'. It was this experience that convinced him of the need to establish schools and to provide devotional literature in Welsh. The realisation of these twin aims necessitated the raising of funds, and, on his return to the Capital, he established the Trust. The movement, therefore, from its very inception, was London-based.

The emphasis within these Charity Schools established for the education of poor Welsh children was on the teaching of reading, writing and arithmetic, a severely practical curriculum. The medium of instruction was English, since it was held, and espec-

169

ially by the Puritans, that because English was the key which un-
locked so many doors, the interests of the children would best be
served by their acquiring a mastery of that language, whereby
they would be 'more serviceable to their country and live more
comfortably in the world'. Furthermore, the London patrons of
the movement did not regard Welsh as a fitting vehicle for the
communication of eternal truths. The books mainly employed in
the instruction of the pupils were the Bible, the Church Catechism, the Apostles' creed, *The Practice of Piety*[1] and the *Whole
Duty of Man.*[2] The schools, therefore, aimed not only at pro-
ducing pupils who would be good in this world and happy in the
next, but also at moulding children who would be useful citizens,
since they would have been taught obedience to the powers that
be, irrespective of whether that authority was wielded by magistrate or minister. There was also inculcated into the minds of the
young a hatred of Popery, because they were taught that the
Church of Rome was the mother of ignorance and superstition
and her ways were those of the Devil. By 1675, eighty-seven
schools had been established in the chief towns of Wales, and of
these two were established in Brecknockshire, one in Brecon
town itself and the other in Hay. The Brecon school had twenty
pupils and was under the jurisdiction of Meredith Penry, vicar of
St John's and Dan(iel) Herberth, churchwarden. It is probable
that this was the Meredith Penry who was master at Christ
College. However, it is possible that he was not the master in the
charity school, though it was he and Herberth 'who certified the
truth thereof under their hands'. This school could not have
lasted for long, since it is not included among the schools listed in
the Trust's report for 1678.

One of the reasons for the failure of the Brecon school was
undoubtedly the fact that it was conducted in English and most of
the children, at this time, would have been monoglot Welsh.
Another may well be found in the strength of the Anglican
tradition at Brecon, so that the local gentry, and the church
authorities—particularly Bishop Lucy of St David's, who
actually resided in the town—would have frowned on any organisation which included Dissenters in its ranks. The venerable

bishop would have been further alienated by the publication by the Trust in 1678 of a new edition of the Welsh Bible, as this was an area which bishops generally regarded as exclusively their own.

The work of the Welsh Trust was continued by another philanthropic organisation, the S.P.C.K. (The Society for the Promotion of Christian Knowledge), founded in London in 1699. Brecon was to derive considerable benefit from the activities of the S.P.C.K., and the fact that a Trust school had earlier been established in the town was helpful to the Society as it was able to breathe new life into dying embers. However, the Society differed markedly from the Trust in one very important respect. While the Trust had been non-denominational, the S.P.C.K. was composed solely of members of the Church of England. Its aim was to combat the vice and profanity so prevalent in society by means of the establishment of schools and the distribution of religious literature, and in this latter respect Brecon was to be served by the central library of the diocese of St David's situated at Carmarthen.

The Society operated through a system of residing and corresponding members. The former lived in and around London, while the latter lived in the localities and were to be found, for the most part, in the chief market towns. The Society's agent in Breconshire and Radnorshire was Humphrey Jorden and on 18 March 1716 he had written from Brecon thanking the Society for the packet of books received there. A packet of books had also been sent to Brecon gaol 'for the use of the poor prisoners'. But the most important function of the S.P.C.K. was the establishment of schools, and ninety-six were set up in Wales. Eight were to be found in Breconshire and, of these, three were situated in Brecon town itself.

A characteristic which these schools shared with the Trust schools was that the curriculum was virtually the same. The three Rs were taught, and the main text books used were the Bible, the Catechism, the Prayer Book and some books of devotion. The emphasis was on teaching children to read the Bible and on catechising them so that they would reject the dogmas of both

171

Nonconformity and the Church of Rome. However, pupils did receive instruction in some useful trades, though this aspect of their education was not given the prominence that it received in the English schools. Thus, the boys were taught a craft, while the girls were given instruction in sewing, spinning and knitting. In a few schools Music was also introduced. The medium of instruction in most was English, and this factor was to reduce considerably their effectiveness.

Usually the Society's schools were conducted in parish churches, though unoccupied houses, suitably altered, were frequently used. The course of study lasted four years, and the school day extended from 7 a.m. to 5 p.m., the morning session finishing at 11 a.m. and the afternoon session beginning at 1 p.m., although it was customary during the cold, dark winter months to start at 8 a.m. and finish at 4 p.m. The teachers were invariably vicars or curates who had undertaken the work in order to supplement their meagre earnings. As it was, the payment they received as schoolmasters was pitiful enough, as it amounted to only £4 or £5 a year. A master was expected to be not only a member of the Church of England, but also 'of a sober life and conversation, not under the age of twenty-five, one that frequents the Holy Communion, hath a good government of himself and his passions, of a meek temper and humble behaviour, of a good genius for teaching, who understands well the grounds and principles of the Christian religion ... who can write a good hand and who understands the grounds of Arithmetick'. To maintain standards a regular system of inspection of the Society schools was instituted, the work in the counties of Brecon and Radnor being performed by Humphrey Jorden. He was also a great benefactor of the movement, since in these two counties he paid for the schooling and books annually of fifty-seven children in four small schools.

At Brecon the work of collecting subscriptions began in 1716 and in a letter dated 29 March Jorden stated that 'a subscription is setting on foot at Brecknock Town for the Girls by the Gentlewomen of the Place, that the school is opened and fourteen Girls are cloath'd and taught in Prospect of a great number'. The cost of clothing for a girl at this time was approximately 17*s*. 1*d*.; for a boy it was 18*s*. 6*d*. These ladies were organised by Mrs Henry Williams, the wife of an attorney of the town, and she was one of thirty women patrons who played a vital role in the Society's work from 1699-1740. In April 1718, Jorden could declare that 'the school erected for fourteen girls is in a flourishing condition, the children being able to read well, and say their cathechisms in the church readily, and answer most of Lewis's Exposition, although they could before speak but little or no English. The School is visited once a week by the contributors and is increased to eighteen girls'. From this correspondence it can clearly be inferred that the language of instruction in the Society's schools in Brecon was English, a factor which must have contributed to the gradual anglicisation of the town. From the same letter it is discovered that another school 'for twenty boys, cloath'd and supported by the gentry of the town had been erected' and this was to be an example of a school being built for a particular educational purpose.

In 1720 a third school had appeared, made possible through a charitable bequest by a gentleman whose identity is, unfortunately not known. This was a school for twenty poor boys, and twenty appears to have been the favoured number when providing charity schools for boys. It is interesting, in this respect, to note that at the foundation of Christ College, £24 was set aside annually for the maintenance of, again, twenty poor scholars.

There was considerable discord in Brecon in 1723 and the vicar, Richard Davies, a corresponding member of the Society, declared 'that a division lately in the town had liked to have destroyed the Charity Schools of that place, but by the application of some worthy Gentlemen with himself, those prejudices were overcome and the Subscriptions ran higher this year (1723) than ever before'. It could be that the first flush of enthusiasm of the inhabitants of Brecon for the charity schools had begun to wane in the face of rising demands. Whatever the reason, Brecon was fortunate that a man of Davies's qualities was present to iron out the difficulties.

These schools must have been fortunate in their staffing, for there is evidence in the S.P.C.K. correspondence to suggest that all three must have survived from between sixteen to twenty years. Their Anglican tone would also have been most helpful since that factor would have endeared them to the local gentry who were staunch in their support of the Established Church. These schools represented by far the most successful attempt to date at establishing elementary education for the poor children of the borough. What happened at Brecon compared favourably with other towns in Wales, as only Glasbury in the same county catered for a greater number of pupils, while Monmouth and Pembroke made provision on a similar scale.

By 1727 the halcyon days were over. The leaves had begun to fall after 1715, and from the death of Queen Anne to 1727 only a further twenty-eight schools were established in Wales. After 1727 there were none. Several factors accounted for this sad decline: the withdrawal of support by gentry who had Jacobite sympathies, as schoolmasters were subject to intense pressure to demonstrate their loyalty to the Hanoverian George I; the employment, in the majority of the schools, of English as the vehicle of communication; the difficulty of convincing parents, many of whom lived at subsistence level, of the value of education since the labour of their children was required on the land and in the workshop, and these same children were even expected to beg for their food. But the Society also lost ground to Private Adventure Schools and, in 1694, a David Thomas and a Watkin Walter were presented for trial in Brecon for keeping schools without licence.

Wales was now to derive inestimable benefits from the untiring and dedicated efforts of an educationist who had served as a schoolmaster in the S.P.C.K. schools, an experience which enabled him to avoid many of the pitfalls which had beset that Society. This was Griffith Jones of Llanddowror and although his aim was basically the same as that of the Welsh Trust and the S.P.C.K., to save souls by teaching the people to read the Bible, and by catechising them, the movement inaugurated by him, though his ideas were not entirely novel, differed in three

174

important respects. First, he used Welsh as the medium of instruction; secondly, his schools were designed not only for children, but also for adults of all ages; and thirdly, the schools were organised on a circulating basis, remaining not more than three months in any place.

Griffith Jones's approach was to seek the support of the incumbent of a parish and the use of his vestry. If this was not forthcoming, then the school would be held in a barn, farmhouse, cottage or almshouse, all of which were easily accessible. An itinerant teacher, carefully selected and trained by Griffith Jones himself at Llanddowror, would then arrive and set up school for three months—considered a long enough period to teach reading only—in the autumn or winter when work on the land was at its slackest. Although the schools would appear to have been unduly restrictive in scope, as they concentrated on one task only, that of teaching children and adults to read, in Wales as a whole they proved enormously successful and helped greatly to create a literate laity. Their success can largely be attributed to the ability and enthusiasm of the masters, 'God fearing members of the Church of England' who were paid a miserable pittance of about £5 a year for their labours, and the co-operation of clergymen.

At one time or another about 147 of these schools had been established in Breconshire though from the *Welch Piety*, Griffith Jones's annual report, only one school would appear to have been set up in the town of Brecon. At this school sixty-one pupils are recorded as having been in attendance, but as there is no further mention of it in any report or correspondence, one must conclude that it can only have lasted for that brief period of three months.

Since the small hamlets of Merthyr Cynog and Talachddu each had schools with sixty-six pupils on the roll it is, perhaps, rather surprising that the movement should have failed to kindle the imagination of the inhabitants of Brecon. The reason is certainly not to be found in the fact that the town was already adequately provided with schools; nor was it that the anglicisation process had proceeded so far as to make schools, conducted entirely in

Welsh, impracticable. Rather was it that the religious climate in the town was uncongenial. Brecon was an Anglican stronghold, and it is more than possible that the local vicar was cold, even hostile, in his attitude because these schools, particularly in their early days, were tainted with Methodism. Nevertheless, one must not underestimate the impact made on the town by this one school, since many of the inhabitants, adults as well as children, would have been taught to read.

Together with the schools established in Brecon during the Georgian age, which were the products of national charity movements, there were also elementary schools which owed their existence to the benevolence of charitable citizens. In 1686 the Reverend Rees Powell of Boughrood gave the manors of Upper Elvel, Aberedw and Carreg, together with other property in the county of Radnor, in trust for charitable work. Sixty-five pounds were assigned annually towards setting up poor children as apprentices. The remaining money was to be employed for educational purposes. Thus £25 was to be used for the maintenance of two poor scholars at Jesus College, Oxford, preference to be given to the donor's kin; a further £11 a year were to be employed towards the remuneration of 'an honest careful man to teach and instruct poor children, natives of the said borough of Brecon, in the English language, the better to enable them to serve God and manage their respective trades and occupations'. The emphasis was to be on teaching the children to read. This school was established in the Struet, in a house known as Boughrood, and here the schoolmaster also lived rent free. A plaque in the south-west wall of the Priory Church commemorates Rees Powell's piety and charity and he deserves his niche, for his school flourished continuously until 1855 when it was amalgamated with the National school, Pendre.

In 1722, Nicholas Jeffreys of Brecon Priory, left £100, the interest on which was to be paid to a 'Charity School of the Blue-Coat Boys in the town' and in 1723, Mr Henry Williams, junior, gave £20 towards the same object. The following year Mrs Catherine Games of Newton donated forty shillings annually for the Charity School for girls. The most probable site of the school

Boughrood House in the Struet

known as the Blue Coat School with its two departments, one for the boys and the other for the girls, was Pencraig, Brecon. It is known that the boys and girls were clothed, as well as educated, the uniforms probably consisting of blue coats for the boys and blue coats, gowns and stockings for the girls. The school flourished very largely because its benefactors, led by Mrs Games and her sisters, Mrs Walker and Mrs Lucy, were among the most influential and well-to-do people in the town at the time. In 1759 additional provision was made for the school when Mrs Mary

Williams left £100 in her will for the maintenance and clothing of poor girls attending the 'Blue Girls School' thus consolidating still further its financial position.

Another organisation which made provision for the education of poor children was the Brecknockshire Agricultural Society, founded in 1755 chiefly on the initiative of Charles Powell, the squire of Castell Madoc. It did this by establishing Spinning Schools to teach children the art of weaving and to keep them out of mischief. One such school was established in Brecon in 1756 when a Mrs Tedman was appointed headmistress at a salary of £5 a year. In 1757 a further £10 were paid to the headmistress for introducing children to the spinning of flax. However, Mrs Tedman proved a most unsatisfactory appointment, and her services were terminated in September 1757 when two new mistresses were appointed, a Miss Christian Tallon and a Miss Elizabeth Grant. Instead of a fixed salary, each was paid 2s. 6d. a quarter for every child taught to spin. They were also paid a further 1s. for each child admitted into the school so that it was to their advantage to recruit freely. A Mr Daniel Wynter was appointed to supervise the work of the Spinning Schools, and although it has not been possible to establish the number of children in attendance, they included both boys and girls, and their ages ranged from under twelve to eighteen. As for their activities, yarn was spun and linen manufactured.

The school continued until 1758-9 when the rent paid to a Mr Meredith for the use of the premises where the school was held amounted to £8. The establishment must have been of some obvious benefit since similar schools were opened at Llangorse and Talgarth in September 1759. However, after this date, there are no further references to any Spinning Schools.

It has been estimated that by the end of the Georgian era only half the child population of Brecon, a town of some 2,898 inhabitants, had been provided with any kind of schooling, while a study of wills and inventories reveals that only about the same percentage could write their own names so that there was little room for complacency or satisfaction. Two educational traditions had been established in the town: one was the Charity

School tradition which aimed at the saving of souls; the other was the Grammar School tradition, which had far greater antiquity and was certainly more secular and political in its aims. But both traditions helped to familiarise the children with the English language and English modes of thought and contributed to destroy the hitherto Welsh ethos of the town.

During Victoria's reign the further development of the Charity School movement in Brecon was very largely the province of the Brecon Benevolent Schools. The movement was inaugurated by a sermon which Archdeacon Richard Davies preached in Brecon on 25 October 1809, when he alluded to the 'mechanic and the husbandman who earn a hard subsistence by their daily labour (whatever parental tenderness may suggest) can seldom afford their children many opportunities of literary instruction ... It is the object of this institution, which I wish to recommend to your notice, to teach such children to read their mother tongue; to write, and to perform some of the most generally useful operations in arithmetic'. His pious hopes were that pupils should be enabled to 'acquire a rational knowledge of the doctrines and precepts of religion, or of the duties of morality'; enable them to communicate with absent friends, and to manage 'those little transactions which pass among them'. In the wake of this sermon, and to mark the occasion of George III's jubilee (1810), a meeting was held in the Shire Hall when it was agreed to build a school for the children of the poorer inhabitants of the town. Before the conclusion of the meeting £250 were subscribed towards the construction of schoolrooms, and £150 for the support of a boys' and girls' school. The Mary Williams' charity, which had provided for the maintenance and clothing of the Blue Coat School for Girls, was used to supplement the Girls' Benevolent School, while the Boys' Blue Coat School was merged with the Boys' Benevolent School. Though the principal aim was to improve the moral standards of the children, there was also an underlying note of pragmatism since writing and arithmetic were taught and, for the girls, some needlework.

The Brecon Benevolent Schools began their work on 14 February 1811 and in December 1814 an account of their work was delivered to a general meeting of subscribers, the eminent local antiquary Theophilus Jones being one of them. John Parry Wilkins, the treasurer, declared that over the past four years a total of £1,424 had been received in subscriptions, while £558 had been spent on building schoolrooms. At this meeting it was agreed to increase the headmistress's salary to £42 per annum 'for her attention to the duties of her situation'. In 1815 this was increased to £52-10s. but, significantly perhaps, there was no mention of a similar increase for the headmaster. The subscribers obviously felt that good work should be rewarded since a sum not exceeding £10 a year was also to be spent on the purchase of books to be presented to children 'as rewards for good behaviour and proficiency in learning'. A public examination of the top class of both schools was to take place every year in December in the Town Hall, an admission fee of one shilling being charged. Such was the success of the schools that it was resolved to establish offshoots in other parts of the county, and the first branch school to be opened was at Llanfihangel Talyllyn, when the Archdeacon 'very liberally purchased at his own expense a building there to be converted into a schoolroom at the price of £105'.

It would appear that during this period 172 boys were admitted to the boys' school, and of the fifty that had left, thirty-five had

The Commissioners—Lingen, Symons and Vaughan Johnson. A caricature

180

successfully completed the course planned for them. Ten boys had left under a cloud because of the irregularity of their attendance. If the financial situation of the parents was such as to warrant it, the boys were given four or five guineas to enable them to find apprenticeships. The number of girls enrolled during the same four year period was 163, and thirty had been obliged to leave for continual absences. Fifty had reached the top class, and their parents were also provided with financial assistance to prepare them for employment.

The Benevolent Schools were profoundly influenced by the methods and procedures employed in the British and National Schools. The British and Foreign School Society had been founded in 1808 by Joseph Lancaster, while the National Society had been established shortly after, in 1811, by Dr Andrew Bell. In these the monitorial system was introduced whereby the older pupils taught the younger children. Archdeacon Davies, having examined both systems very closely, decided to adopt Dr Bell's principles for teaching pupils to read, but the Lancasterian method was adopted for arithmetic and writing. The Benevolent Schools in Brecon had seven classes altogether. No lesson was to be longer than one hour in duration and, together with the three Rs, considerable attention was paid to a study of the Bible and the Church Catechism. The school day was not unduly long, since it began at 9 a.m. and ended at 2 p.m. On Sundays, lessons were confined to learning the Catechism, and attending morning service at St Mary's Church. However, on Wednesdays and Fridays school could end at 1 p.m. 'if Catechists deserve it, otherwise not till Two'.

In these schools much emphasis was placed on personal cleanliness, and the monitors were made responsible for ensuring that the pupils in their classes had clean hands and faces. Archdeacon Davies attempted to shame children into adopting clean personal habits as boys with dirty hands and faces were made to wash in the girls' school and girls, in a similar condition, in the boys' school.

It is very surprising, therefore, considering the apparent success of these Benevolent Schools, that in the report of the commissioners appointed to inquire into the state of education in

Wales in 1846, much should have been found that was unsatisfactory. The chief commissioner for Breconshire was J.C. Symons, and he was assisted by three others. They praised the pupils in the girls' school, now known as St John's School, for being so well-informed on the Bible, but their knowledge of Geography and grammar, on the other hand, was very limited. However, despite these criticisms, they still regarded the school as the best they had visited. As for the boys, they considered their school to be badly conducted, the pupils being backward in most subjects. They were frequently beaten so that they gave the impression of being very cowed.

In 1855 both the Boys' and the Girls' Benevolent Schools were placed under the control of the National Society. Within them, and this applied to the other local charity schools as well founded on the initiative of the Established Church and those who worshipped there, learning was by rote, and the methods of teaching were very mechanical. The curriculum was extremely limited, and it is doubtful whether there was much comprehension. However, it is imperative that they should be judged in the context of the age and not from the perspective of more modern times.

The only other school which was the result of local charitable endeavour was the Workhouse School in Llanfaes established in 1840. The room in which the school was conducted was favourably commented upon by Symons, since it was light and cheerful and supplied with ample furniture, maps and books—unusual advantages for those days. The twenty-six year old master had not received any training and was an ex-labourer. His annual salary was £15 but he had been provided with a house and garden rent free. The number of children on roll was seventeen and, unlike the situation in the other charity schools in the town where attendance was sporadic, these were, not surprisingly, always present. Despite the fact that the children had been in attendance for two years, they were found to be singularly uninformed. A few of the boys read tolerably well, though with little understanding, but they were taught little else. However, the girls did receive instruction in sewing in another department.

These charity schools paved the way for the Monitorial Schools. The British Society (1808) was a primarily Nonconformist Institution, while the National Society was closely linked with the Established Church. Indeed this society was established in 1811 to counter the threat posed by the Nonconformists to the dominance of the Church in the field of religion.

Though the Boughrood School and the Boys' and Girls' Benevolent School owed much to the patronage of the Church, they were not official Church institutions. There was, however, in Llanfaes a school which was a church school in every sense of the word. It was conducted in a building situated in the yard of St David's Church. Though originally intended as a Sunday School, it was the first school in Brecon to apply to the National Society for aid. The application was made on 21 July 1834 when £65-12s. out of an estimated cost of £149 had already been collected. When Symons visited the school in 1846 he found a well-attended day school in progress. He reported that 'it is chiefly a school for girls. The master is a painstaking quiet person and evidently desirous to do the best, but very much in need of more instruction. He was certainly at fault both in grammar and pronunciation . . . they (the pupils) were unable to answer the most simple questions on the New Testament. Their knowledge of the meaning of words was imperfect, though all of them understood English . . . In general knowledge they were extremely deficient and none knew the number of days or weeks in a year. In arithmetic they were exceedingly backward, none could do a sum in compound subtraction and none could read 2501 . . . a few wrote tolerably well. The master is an amiable and teachable person'. There were sixty-six children enrolled of whom forty-three were between five and ten years of age and the remainder over ten. The master was paid £27 per annum in addition to the £15 he received from school pence. The method of teaching was the monitorial system—children teaching children—and the whole process of learning was very routine. It represented a system of mass production in education.

In 1833 Earl Grey's Whig government made a state grant of £10,000 available to each of the two voluntary societies, the

The National School at the Postern

National and the British, inspectors being appointed in 1839 to ensure that the money was properly spent. In 1846 the government sponsored an enquiry into the state of education in Wales, and the report of the commissioners, which came to be dubbed by its critics as *Brad y Llyfrau Gleision* (Treason of the Blue Books), was published in the following year. Despite its grave deficiencies —the commissioners knew little about education and less still about the Welsh—the report concentrated attention on the frailty of elementary education in Wales, and led the National Society to conduct its own enquiry into the state of church education. At Brecon these commissioners concluded that central National Schools were required, and that more provision should be made for infant education.

In August 1847 a meeting was held in the Shire Hall, chaired by John Parry de Winton, for the purpose of establishing a school for 150 girls and 150 infants in the town of Brecon. The school was to be erected on a site given by Mr John Powell at the Postern and subscriptions were collected. The document of conveyance

184

was signed on 20 January 1849. The three messuages or dwelling houses, together with a garden, at the Postern in the parish of St John's, were given to provide a school for infants and girls of 'the labouring manufacturing and poorer classes and for no other purpose which said school shall always be in union with and conducted upon the principles and in furtherance of the ends and designs of the Incorporated National Society'. By now the Church was responsible for the education of nearly 400 children in the town. The time had come for a complete overhaul of the system.

The Postern Schools for girls and infants were opened in 1850. The government grant towards these schools amounted to £214-10s. while the National Society's contribution was £106. Other contributions came from local subscribers. The vacated girls' school at Pendre was now occupied by the boys and came to be known as St John's Boys' School. At a meeting held in the Town Hall on 22 October 1857, an education board was established for the purpose of promoting the education of the children of the poor within the Archdeaconry of Brecon. In 1858, in order to

The National School at Pendre

improve and maintain standards within the church schools, an organising visitor was appointed for the whole diocese of St David's and £200 were allocated to cover his expenses. In 1860 the curriculum for the National schools in Brecon was established. Religious Knowledge was given pride of place, and reading and Music were made complementary studies. The history and geography of Wales were ignored. Very little practical work was to be attempted, and there was no scope for creative work on the part of the pupils. What was required of them was not imagination or originality but a mastery of selected facts and passages. This code was revised in 1861, when a uniform standard in the three Rs was prescribed for all state-aided schools and an annual inspection and examination were to be held.

The foundation stone for a new school for boys at Pendre was laid in August 1867 and the school was completed in the following year together with a house for the master. The new building was spacious and well-adapted for the purpose of instruction. The buildings, with accommodation for 180 boys, cost £1,083-10s. and the donor of the land on which they were built was the Marquis of Camden.

By 1870 the standards in the National Schools at Brecon were generally very satisfactory though, from time to time, there were criticisms of the boys' school. But the schools were housed in good buildings, the girls at Postern and the boys at Pendre, both in close proximity to the old priory church of St John's, and the quality of the fabrics certainly provided grounds for hope for future development.

The British Society, unlike its counterpart, the National Society, was very laggard in establishing schools in Wales. One reason for this was lack of funds since the Nonconformists were very reluctant to accept government aid to supplement voluntary subscriptions. In its first Annual Report in 1815 the British Society included Brecon in 'A list of Places at which schools have been formed in whole or in part on the British System'. Undoubtedly this was a reference to the Benevolent Schools established in Brecon by Archdeacon Davies which were partly organised on Lancasterian lines. Locally, however, these were never referred to as British Schools and they had no direct connection with the Society.

A British School at Brecon is mentioned in the reports between 1823-9, the only detail provided being that it was a school for boys. This raises the question as to whether this was a new British School which lasted for six years, or whether the report referred to the Boys' Benevolent School at Pencraig. The most likely explanation is that a boys' school was founded in Brecon in 1823 according to the British School System, that it continued for six years, and thereafter ceased to exist from lack of funding.

At an important conference of the Voluntary Society (*Y Gym-deithas Wirfoddol*), composed of Nonconformists opposed to state aid, it was resolved to establish a Normal College at Brecon for the purpose of training teachers, and to organise a system of voluntary schools throughout south Wales supported by sub-scriptions. Brecon was chosen as the home of the new college because it 'was a central spot, easy of access, on account of its facilities of conveyance from all parts of the country'. The college was opened on 1 January 1846 with eighteen students on roll, though none from Brecon, and Evan Davies, a graduate of Glasgow University, as Principal. Though the Society hoped one day to occupy better premises, it was glad of the opportunity to rent a building, on a three-year lease, at an annual payment of £50. The students had greatly differing occupational backgrounds but they were all working class. The youngest, Thomas Jones, aged 18, had been an assistant in a grocer's shop while the eldest, Warriatte Edwards, who was 30, had been a schoolmaster for five years at Swansea. Amongst the other students were a tailor, a carpenter, a miner, a shoemaker, a blacksmith and a number of farm servants. They came from all over south Wales, and their early schooling had ranged from a few weeks to some six years. Their working day was extremely intensive and provided few opportunities for leisure, only some 2¾ hours in a working day which began at 5.30 a.m. and finished at 10.45 p.m. This was no place for the weak or the indolent. Evan Davies proved a forceful Principal and his views on education were, for the times, quite enlightened, since he stressed the

Site of the British Normal College and School in Lion Street

importance of developing the mind rather than simply stuffing it with knowledge. In conjunction with this training school, a British Model Elementary School was established which opened its doors at the same time, and arrangements were entered into whereby the students at the college were able to participate in the instruction. Today, the buildings can be identified with those lying on each side of the archway in Lion Street, behind the Gild Hall. This was the site of the now defunct Golden Lion Inn and in the time between the closure of the inn, and the opening of the college and school, the premises had been employed as a depot by the military.

Symons, when he inspected the school in 1847, was favourably impressed. It appears from his report that the master was a Mr Evan Evans who had been trained for nine months at the Normal College. The school was held in a very large and commodious room, situated on the ground floor and formerly used as an assembly room. This schoolroom opened on to an extensive play-ground supplied with a circular swing, and on one side of the playing area were the outbuildings. The number of scholars on roll, all boys, was 96 and, at the time of Symons's visit, nearly all were present. The emphasis was on the three Rs, reading being taught entirely from the Scriptures. However, some attention was paid to Music, both vocal and instrumental. It was in this manner that the school attempted to dispel ignorance among the poor, and by so doing, produce law-abiding citizens.

Considering that Symons regarded the school as one that was full of promise, it is rather surprising that it should have survived for only a few years. But its fate was clearly linked to that of the adjoining college which, because of lack of funds, was transferred in 1849 to a far more populous area, Swansea. It is more than likely that the Model British School closed at the same time or immediately afterwards.

The failure of the British School to promote bilingual teaching did not provoke any adverse comment locally at the time, and it is quite evident that while in the sixteenth and seventeenth centuries there had been a predominantly Welsh-speaking population in the town, this situation was changing rapidly during the Victorian period, and the town was now becoming anglicised. Many factors accounted for this change but chief among them, undoubtedly, was the fact that in all the elementary schools established in Brecon, apart from the Circulating School of Griffith Jones, Englich was the medium of instruction.

Despite the growing Nonconformist element in the town, part-icularly after 1848, the British Society was making little progress. This was partly due to the fact that Brecon was already well served by the National Society; another was the removal of the Normal College to Swansea, which led to a shortage of trained teachers in the area. But Brecon itself now compounded matters for the Society by building two schools which were undenominational in character and where scholars were at liberty to attend whichever place of worship they or their parents might choose. These were the Dr Coke Memorial Schools. They were to receive grant aid from the government and were open, consequently, to govern-ment inspection. These were schools primarily designed for boys and girls of the middle and poorer classes.

Dr Coke was a Wesleyan missionary and the founder of the Methodist Episcopal Church of America. The concept of honouring his memory by erecting the Dr Coke Memorial Schools owed its inspiration to the Reverend Edwin Thornley. He appreciated that the illustrious doctor, born the son of an apothecary in the town and educated at Christ College, was a greatly admired figure. Considerable sums of money were raised locally, and a portion of the garden of the George Hotel was acquired for £16-15s. On 6 January 1868 the schools were opened under the headmastership of Mr Jabez Jenkinson, who had been trained at the Wesleyan Normal Training College at Westminster. On the first day 82 scholars were admitted and they were divided into two sections: the infants under Miss Emily Wyatt and the remainder under Mr Jenkinson. The schools were an immediate success until they were destroyed by fire in 1890. By 1870 the Nonconformists, through the agency of these Memorial Schools, were assuming a greater share of the burden of providing an elementary education for the children of the town of Brecon. Indeed, the borough had now been provided with facilities for elementary education which compared favourably with those existing in any town in Wales of comparable size.

But despite all their efforts the voluntary agencies were not succeeding in keeping pace with the demands of a rapidly growing population for greater educational opportunities. The short stay of the pupils at the schools, and the irregular and non-compulsory nature of the attendance, were serious drawbacks. Westminster grants, and with them an ever-expanding degree of governmental control, were increasing every year. The enactment of Forster's Education Act 1870 had become inevitable.

Dame and Private Adventure Schools
The inadequacy of the more formal agencies for the provision of elementary education led inevitably to the appearance of private schools run by individuals for their own profit, meagre though that was. They ranged from mere child-minding establishments to schools which provided a reasonably sound standard of education in adequate buildings.

190

Such schools had existed in Brecon certainly since the latter years of the seventeenth century. In 1694 David Thomas and Watkin Walter were presented before the Consistory Court by Marmaduke Powell, a churchwarden, for keeping school without licence in the parish of St David's.[3] In 1705 one Abel Phillips was guilty of a similar offence, and on 17 October 1728 David Morgan and Evan Price were to incur the wrath of the Court.

Symons and his three assistant commissioners found five private schools when they visited the town in 1846 .They classified the four schools run by women as 'Dame Schools', and the solitary one conducted by a man as a 'Private Adventure School'.

The four Dame Schools were all day schools with no provision for boarding. The teachers were untrained and derived a meagre living from school pence brought by the pupils. The education provided was of an exceedingly low standard—not even the Catechism or hymns being taught—and the lessons were conducted entirely in English. In the parish of St John's there were schools run by a Mrs Price and a Mrs Maund; a Mrs Jones had a school in the parish of St Mary's, and in the parish of St David's there was

A Private Adventure School

191

to be found Mrs Rees's school. Before taking up teaching Mrs Maund had been a grocer, Mrs Jones had been a domestic help, and Mrs Rees had been a seamstress. Two of these ladies were also rather elderly, Mrs Maund being 67 and Mrs Jones 62. These Dame Schools were basically establishments where parents could send their children so that they could be taken care of for at least part of the day. Little or no genuine teaching was attempted, and the children's stay was brief.

The fifth school, the Private Adventure School, was run by a Mr Morgan, an ex-timber merchant who was 66 years of age. It was situated in a 'back lane in the suburbs of Brecknock' and within it a genuine attempt was made at providing some kind of education, however limited and unimaginative. He taught 'reading, writing and cyphering after the old fashion'. The pupils read tolerably well, and spelled with remarkable correctness even words such as 'Physician'. Mr Morgan's labours brought him £25 a year, considerably more than the mere pittance which was received by the four ladies since Mrs Price only earned £8 per annum, Mrs Maund and Mrs Jones £4 each, and Mrs Rees £10. Considering the advanced age of most of the teachers, it is hardly surprising that within a few years all these schools had disappeared from the scene.

However, private schools continued to spread like mushrooms and by 1860 a fresh crop had appeared. Richard Bonner and Emma Crogan had each opened a school in the Watton; Mary Buck had started a Boarding and Day School in the Struet; Elizabeth Duncan conducted a school in the High Street; William Evans another in Lion Street; Catherine Pearce had a Boarding School in Bellevue; and Susan Roberts and Evan Watson had opened schools in Llanfaes and the Watton respectively. Few details relating to these schools can be found. Though they were referred to as 'respectable academies', there is little reason to believe that their standards were any better than those of their predecessors for, with the exception of the Mary Buck school, which survived for over forty years, not one continued until 1871.

In the report of the newly constituted School Board, established in the wake of Forster's Act, mention is made of three private schools in the town, all of them Dame Schools. These were: Mrs Roberts's School, Mrs Williams's School and Miss Morgan's School. Two of these were conducted in private dwelling houses, and it is more than possible that the third was also. The accommodation was completely unsuitable since, for the most part, the rooms were badly ventilated and ill-lit.

The Sunday Schools

It is very largely to the organising genius of Thomas Charles of Bala that Wales owes its Sunday Schools. Charles was a rigid Sabbatarian, and he adopted the system of Sunday Schools with great reluctance. However, he felt reassured by the actions of men like Morgan John Rhys and Edward Williams of Oswestry, both firm upholders of the principle of conducting schools on Sunday. And, if he needed further convincing, across the border in England, there was the example of Robert Raikes of Gloucester, an extremely active promoter of the idea of Sunday Schools.

About 1789 Thomas Charles embarked on the task of establishing Sunday Schools not so much to prevent delinquency, as was the case with the English schools, but with the avowed purpose of 'making pupils proficient in reading their native language so as to become acquainted with the word of God'. Apart from the basic aim, the Welsh Sunday Schools differed from their English counterparts in two important respects: first, the teachers were volunteers and unpaid; and secondly, there was a mixture of classes and ages. They were never the preserves of the poor or the young, and adult classes were a distinctive feature from the very beginning.

The Sunday Schools spread quickly and became extremely popular because they were not handicapped by the imposition of fees, and they did not interfere with the normal working week. The commissioners, who visited Brecon in 1846, found twelve thriving Sunday Schools there. Despite their personal prejudices, they were agreed that the general effect of the Sunday Schools was beneficial. Symons was of the view 'that three-fourths of the correct answers made in day school examinations had been the result of Sunday School teaching'. Even though the Nonconformist Sunday Schools were conducted almost entirely in Welsh, the commissioners were of the opinion that they were more effective for the purposes of Religious Instruction than those of the Church.

Nonconformist or Dissenting Sunday Schools

Nonconformity in Brecon embraced the following denominations: the Calvinistic and Wesleyan Methodists, the Baptists, and the Congregationalists or Independents. Sunday schools were attached to all these chapels, scattered as they were about the town and its suburbs, and within them adults as well as children were taught. The numbers attending these schools were very considerable indeed. In the Welsh Calvinistic chapel in the Struet there were, in 1846, 153 on the books. Of these 56 were under fifteen, and 97 were over this age. Furthermore, 120 of these scholars were fairly regular in their attendance. Similarly, in the English Calvinistic Church in the Watton, the Sunday School was in a very flourishing condition and in 1885 the average attendance was over 80, taught by some fourteen to fifteen teachers.

But while the commissioners of 1846 were generally pleased with the manner in which they were conducted in Brecon, a note of criticism was occasionally heard. Symons, while delighted with the progress made by the boys in the Welseyan Methodist Sunday School held in a comfortable and spacious room at the back of the chapel situated in the Struet, found the girls, on the other hand, 'bashful and uninformed'.

At Kensington there was an English-medium Baptist Sunday School, and in 1846 there were 27 boys, 22 girls, nine men and eight women on the books and, of these, 60 were in regular attendance and were taught by six men and five female teachers. Between 1879-1902 the average attendance was 115, a significantly high figure.

But the Independents were not to be outdone, and the commis-

194

sioners in 1846 declared that the Sunday School attached to their chapel in Glamorgan Street was 'about the best conducted in the county of Brecknock' with teachers who were more efficient than most, as many were students at the Independent College situated nearby. The school was composed, for the most part, of children and young people about the age of twenty, and the period of instruction lasted 3½ hours and was supervised by the minister. Both English and Welsh were employed as media of instruction.

These Sunday Schools did far more than create a literate public at Brecon by teaching children and adults to read, mostly in Welsh, and thus counteract to some extent the powerful anglicising influences already at work. In this respect they may well have helped to preserve the language from complete extinction in the area. Their activities were far more diversified than this. Annual outings were organised to places of interest locally, and extremely popular were the trips by train to Llangorse and by barge to Pencelli. Branches of the Band of Hope were established to promote temperance principles and, to encourage attendance at these meetings and inculcate the practice of thrift, Penny Banks were opened. In the evenings programmes of singing and recitation were presented with the occasional address for the children. It is small wonder that by the end of Victoria's reign the Sunday Schools should have become the religious, intellectual and social power-house of Welsh Nonconformity.

While Symons, who was an Anglican, was generally pleased with the state of the Nonconformist Sunday Schools in Brecon, he was not similarly impressed by the Church Schools. Instruction in these, for the most part, consisted of the 'rote system and the mechanical exercise of reading'. Compared with the Dissenting Sunday Schools, which were efficiently and enthusiastically conducted, the Church Schools 'wanted life. The whole system was spiritless and monotonous, and repulsive instead of attractive to children'. There were three Church Sunday Schools in Brecon: those of St Mary's, St David's and St John's, and while Symons's strictures might have applied to the latter two, they certainly had no relevance where St Mary's was concerned, since this school was described as an excellent one. Here, the Scriptures were explained as well as read, and the Church Catechism 'instead of being presented to the child's mind as a string of words for the barren exercise of memory . . . became a living letter of doctrine'. The Church Sunday Schools of Brecon can best be described as extensions of the day schools; they were conducted entirely in English and catered exclusively for children.

The Sunday School at St Mary's was established in 1831 and was for girls only. There were 165 of them on the books in 1846, and they were taught by thirteen female teachers, two of whom were paid. Seven girls, over fifteen years of age, were described as 'scholars'. Seventy-eight of the girls were able to read the Scriptures, and this was one of the few Church Sunday Schools where a real education was imparted.

St David's Church Sunday School was established in 1828 and, in 1846, there were 44 boys and 76 girls enrolled taught by twelve male and nine female teachers, one of whom was paid. Ninety of these children could read the Scriptures and, unlike St Mary's, where the school day was only of an hour's duration, it was 3½ hours long at St David's.

The Sunday School at St John's first made its appearance in 1840, and again was for females only. On the roll there were 110 girls under fifteen years of age, and twelve over that age. They were taught by thirteen female teachers, two of whom were paid. Thirty-four of the children could read the Scriptures.

These schools were conducted in the churches until the opening of the National Schools in 1850 when they came to be held in the Boys', Girls' and Infants' Schools. They then became, in effect, day schools held on Sundays with perhaps a little more emphasis placed on the Scriptures and the Catechism.

A feature of these Church Sunday Schools was the annual excursion to Senni or some other local beauty spot. The highlight of the day was a tea-party, and the expenditure on this was greater than that on books for teaching purposes though, it has to be said, a parochial library was established in 1867 to encourage reading. It was housed in the High Street and the librarian then was a Mr Charles Hughes. By 1873 there were 600 volumes on its shelves.

By 1869 there were altogether 290 children on the books of the Church Sunday Schools with an average attendance of 214. The Book of Common Prayer was regularly taught together with the Catechism. After 1850 the practice of paying the teachers was discontinued. Though these Church Sunday Schools came to be firmly established, they were never accorded the degree of support provided for the Church Day Schools, and particularly did this apply to the upper echelons of local society. The Dissenting Sunday Schools were fortunate in that they had never suffered from such considerations of class distinction.

Elementary, Secondary and Higher Education—Post 1870

ELEMENTARY EDUCATION

During Victoria's reign the clamour for greater educational provision continued to escalate. In the workshop, machines were replacing labour by hand, and even transportation by land and sea was becoming mechanised with the advent of the railway and the steamship. Such developments made a knowledge of machinery and mathematics essential. Politically, the Parliamentary Reform Act of 1867 had extended the franchise to embrace large sections of the working classes, and if they were to use this vote intelligently, then they had to be properly educated. The deficiencies of the Voluntary system were such that the challenges presented by these novel changes could not be adequately met. Attendance at the schools was very irregular, and they were also deficient in resources and trained staff. Another serious impediment was the apathy of parents who, because of their straitened financial circumstances, needed to supplement their income by such wages as their children might earn. In 1870 Forster's Education Act was passed to remedy these weaknesses by plugging the gaps in the Voluntary system.

The Act laid the foundations of a national system of elementary education. Government grants to Church Schools were to be continued and increased, but where Church Schools did not exist, or were inadequate, state schools were to be introduced controlled by a board of local ratepayers known as the School Board. Hence the schools came to be known as Board Schools. The Boards were empowered to make attendance by children compulsory to the age of thirteen, and parents were to pay ninepence a week, though very poor parents could apply for a free ticket. By the Cowper-Temple Conscience clause attendance at the daily Scripture lesson was to be purely voluntary.

On 16 February 1871 the first meeting of the Brecon Board took place under the chairmanship of Mr Mordecai Jones. A census of all children of school age in the borough taken in May revealed a total of 1,210, 265 aged between three and five years and 745 aged between five and thirteen. Another survey of school accommodation to determine whether a Board School was necessary showed that 1,035 places were available, a shortfall of 75. The disposition of school places was as follows:

National Boys	176
National Girls	109
National Infants	111
Dr Coke's Memorial—Mixed	231
Dr Coke's Memorial—Infants	108
Union Workhouse—Mixed	60
Roman Catholic	40
Mrs Roberts's—Dame	21
Mrs Williams's—Dame	13
Mrs Morgan's—Dame	11
Military—Mixed	131
Military—Infants	24
	1,035

Considerable discussion took place as to whether the Barracks' Schools should be considered as open to the children of the town. These schools, with accommodation for 155 pupils, were reserved for the soldiers' children, who numbered thirty-nine. The decision was ultimately made not to make use of this accommodation.

A school not hitherto mentioned was the Catholic School. It had been established in 1847, and had only sixteen children on roll with an untrained mistress in charge. There was little evidence of anything but Religious Instruction being given there. In 1871 this school was for girls only, and was held in a large club-room in an inn which, on fair days, was used for drinking purposes. The lighting was poor, the ventilation inadequate, and it was ill-adapted for holding a school.

The decision having finally been taken to build a school, a site was acquired in Orchard Street, Llanfaes. The building was officially opened on 18 January 1875 and the entire cost of site, buildings, gas fittings, fixtures, furniture and drainage amounted to £1,943-3s.-1d. From the forty applications received for the post of headmaster, a Mr W. Jones was appointed and, since the number of children registered on the first day was 86, more staff had immediately to be appointed. Town by-laws, making attendance compulsory for all children between the ages of five and thirteen, were now introduced, and to enforce these regulations an attendance officer was appointed.

On 14 November 1890 an event happened which necessitated the building of another Board School. This was the destruction

Mount Street Board School

by fire of the Dr Coke Memorial Schools. Temporary premises were secured at Ruperra House, and the Parish Room was also made available by the Reverend Williams, the vicar of St Mary's. The increasingly stringent requirements of the Education Department, coupled with inadequate funds, proved effective barriers to the re-erection of the schools on the same site by the Wesleyans. They now decided to transfer control of the Mixed and Infant Schools to the Brecon School Board, which immediately embarked upon the work of erecting a new school at Mount Street. This school was built to provide accommodation for 450 children, and included classrooms for boys, girls and infants, together with cloakrooms. It was constructed on two floors in native stone and roofed with the best Bangor slates. The playground was spacious and divided between boys and girls. The foundation stone was laid on 18 March 1892, and all the children of the local public elementary schools attended. Much to the satisfaction of the citizens of Brecon, the headmaster, David Fisher, and staff of the Dr Coke Memorial Schools were now placed in charge.

Within all the elementary schools in Brecon before 1902, repetition and rote learning were the order of the day, and much of the curriculum was dull and lacking in variety. Even after the abandonment of payment by results in 1890, no radical changes were discernible in the work of the schools. Still, satisfactory standards were achieved in the three Rs, Religious Instruction, Music (Tonic Sol-fa), Geography, History, Needlework, Drawing and Grammar (Analysis and Parsing). Little attention was devoted to Physical Education and, as a local Derby, an annual football match was arranged between them.

Notably absent from the curriculum of these elementary schools in Brecon was Welsh. The language, literature, history and geography of Wales were completely ignored. The town *Eisteddfod* was regarded as nothing but a nuisance by the schools, and headteachers complained that it disrupted the work of the schools for a whole week. The Welsh National Anthem was never sung, not even in English, and the festival of the patron saint of Wales was not celebrated. However, this was an indifference to national culture which was not confined to Brecon.

Despite the presence of an attendance officer, securing regular attendance still presented problems. Among the reasons for absence recorded in the school log books are such factors as potato picking, picnics, Sunday School treats, adverse weather conditions, selling papers and helping in the market. Punishment for this offence could take the form of a stroke of the cane and, for persistent offenders, committal to the Quakers' Yard Truant School, Merthyr, for a period of three months.

As far as the teaching environment was concerned, Brecon was fortunate in having, after 1870, two new Board Schools, but conditions in the classrooms in the National Schools and the Dr Coke Memorial Schools, before the latter were burnt down, were unsatisfactory. Heat was supplied by stoves so that those near the fires were scorched, whilst those furthest away shivered with cold. Ventilation was achieved by vertical flues assisted by a gas fire, and gas lighting was employed in all the schools, though the teachers were encouraged not to keep them lit for extended periods of time. Sanitary conditions were below acceptable standards with the result that, periodically, there were outbreaks of diseases such as measles, scarlet fever and influenza. A terrible outbreak of measles occurred in Llanfaes in August 1885 and 'seven deaths having taken place, the schools were closed by order of the Medical Authority'. In 1891 an outbreak of scarlet fever in the Barracks' School resulted in the children being confined to quarters for several weeks.

Attempts were made to maintain a degree of warmth and a certain standard of cleanliness within the schools. In April 1892 it was decided by the School Board that the school cleaner at Llanfaes should light the fires by 7 a.m. to ensure that the school was thoroughly warm before the children arrived; the school was also to be washed at least once a fortnight.

The elementary schools at Brecon, as elsewhere, were most unhappy places for children. Learning processes were arid and unimaginative, and discipline very severe. Children could be expelled for stealing and, apart from strokes of the cane, they

201

could be cuffed about the head. Conditions for teachers were also most unsatisfactory. Their remuneration was generally very low and, between 1862-90, had been determined under a system known as 'payment by results'. In 1897 Mr Fisher, the headmaster of Mount Street, was paid £16-13*s*.-4*d*. a month; his six members of staff, on the other hand, were paid sums ranging from £2-3*s*.-4*d*. to £8.-6*s*.-8*d*.

Secondary and Higher Education

PRIVATE SECONDARY PROVISION

Despite the existence of Christ College, there was still room for private schools providing some form of secondary education, particularly for the children of upper middle class parents, and a few of these also acted as preparatory schools for entry into Christ College and other public schools.

The most important of such schools at Brecon was established in 1877 by Thomas Butcher, who had previously been an assistant master at Christ College for ten years. His school was set up, to some extent, in opposition to the College, and catered mainly for the sons of Nonconformists. He called it the 'Middle Class School', and his pupils, whose ages ranged from six to twenty, were the sons of 'professional men, farmers, tradesmen, and the better class mechanics'. His fees varied from four or five guineas per annum for day scholars to £31-10*s*. for boarders. Mr Butcher enjoyed an enviable reputation. An ex-pupil, Councillor David Lewis, M.B.E., who became Chairman of Breconshire Education Authority, vividly remembered him as an excellent teacher, greatly loved and respected by his pupils. His discipline was firm but sympathetic, and he took a personal interest in each of his scholars. This Middle Class School lasted until the opening of the Boys' Intermediate School in 1896 when most of its pupils transferred to the new establishment, which was temporarily situated at Dr Coke's, and Mr Butcher was enrolled as second master.

There were three similar schools open to the girls. These were the Boughrood House Academy, the Miss King School, and the

202

Miss Butcher School in the High Street. The Boughrood House Academy was held in the same premises as the Boughrood Charity School had been before it was amalgamated with the Boys' National School in 1855. The Academy was run by Miss Mary Buck, who was principal until 1901. Though the Girls' Intermediate School was opened in 1896, this development had no adverse effect on its fortunes, and it was still in a flourishing state in 1902.

A smaller, but seemingly equally successful school, was that of Miss King which opened in 1892. In this institution instruction was provided in English, French, Music, Elementary Science, Elocution, Drawing, Needlework and Calisthenics. Miss King also ran a preparatory class for boys.

Miss Butcher's school in the High Street was extremely short-lived possibly because it only offered instruction in Music and Painting. She was, in all probability, a relative of the headmaster of the Middle Class School.

In 1884 a private Preparatory School for boys was established by W.P.J. le Brocc M.A., a former student of Christ College. He had gained honours in Science at Cambridge, and had been assistant master at Maidstone Grammar School from 1882-5. His school was situated opposite Christ College, and the pupils were allowed the use of the College's spacious grounds on payment of a nominal fee. After 1900 no further mention is made of the school in the press, and so it can reasonably be assumed that it had closed its doors that year.

State Secondary Education

THE INTERMEDIATE SCHOOLS

The demographic explosion during Victoria's reign meant that the number of grammar schools in Wales was hopelessly inadequate. Furthermore, there was a growing appreciation that before the three new University Colleges of Aberystwyth (1872), Cardiff (1883) and Bangor (1884) could function effectively, more secondary schools had to be established to prepare students for admission. A committee set up to inquire into the state of intermediate and higher education in Wales, under the chairmanship of Lord Aberdare, published its report in 1881. It found that only 1,540 boys and 265 girls were receiving secondary education in grammar schools. Lord Aberdare recommended both the extension of existing schools, and the establishment of new ones by direct grant from the government. The recommendations of the committee were incorporated in the Welsh Intermediate Act 1889. The new County Councils (1888) were empowered to raise a $\frac{1}{2}d.$ rate for secondary education, and a Treasury grant was to be made to each county equivalent to the amount raised.

The provision for secondary education at Brecon, apart from Christ College and a few small private schools like Thomas Butcher's, was completely insufficient. On 16 February 1895, therefore, in response to the Act, it was resolved at a meeting of the school managers of the Brecon County School District held in Mount Street School, with J.A. Jebb, the mayor of the borough in the chair, to build two separate secondary schools. One was to be a boys' school and the other a girls'. This decision was taken despite objection from those in the town, and among them were

The Girls' Intermediate School at the Elms in the Struet

The Girls' Intermediate School at Cerrig Cochion Hill

many Nonconformists, who felt that the answer was for Christ College to admit local children. Three months later it was resolved unanimously that the most suitable site for the erection of both intermediate schools was a field belonging to the Marquis of Camden situated on the right hand side of Cemetery Road now known as Cradoc Road. A request was made to the marquis who agreed to make conveyance of the land as soon as the committee was ready to build.

It now became evident that the distance from the railway station to the proposed site was too far for 'any but the strongest girls', and a battle of the sites raged before a decision was finally made in January 1896 to build the girls' school in Cerrig Cochion Road. The local community responded magnificently to the appeal for funds, and a site in the field where the National *Eisteddfod* had been held in 1889 was purchased. In the interim period while the schools were being built, temporary accommodation was found for the girls at The Elms[4] in the Struet, and for the boys in two rooms at Dr Coke's Methodist Church in Lion Street. Miss Margaret Davies, Inter B.Sc., assistant mistress at Whitland Intermediate School, was appointed headmistress at a salary of £120 a year together with a capitation allowance of £1 per pupil. A Miss E.H. Short B.A. (London) was appointed second mistress. Mr Nathan John B.A. (London), second master at the Pembroke Dock Intermediate School, was appointed headmaster of the boys' school at an annual salary of £150, together with a capitation allowance. His assistant was Thomas Butcher, formerly headmaster of the Middle Class School.

The girls' school opened at The Elms on 1 May 1896 and for the benefit of those girls who lived too far away to travel daily, a carefully prepared list of suitable lodging houses was compiled. The school was open to girls between the ages of ten and eighteen who had passed an examination equivalent to the fifth standard of a public elementary school. On the first morning there were only thirteen girls present. The boys' school was not opened until 22 September 1896 and at the end of the first week there were forty-seven on roll, a few of whom were boarders.

The Boys' Intermediate School at Cradoc Road

Before the Central Welsh Board (C.W.B.) was instituted in 1896, both schools entered their scholars for the examinations of the College of Preceptors. The most difficult problem confronting both establishments in these early days was the provision of an education adapted to the needs of children of diverse abilities and widely differing social and educational backgrounds. The spectrum extended from those children who wished to leave after a year or two—by 1900 more than half the boys and girls who had left the schools had stayed for one year or less—to those who wanted to enter the universities. They also came from disparate primary schools whose standards were by no means uniform.

The fees payable by both sets of pupils were the same. These were: tuition, £5; boarding, not more than £30; Music, £2-5s; stationery and the use of text books, 7s. 6d. each. The C.W.B. inspectors were generally pleased with academic progress and standards in both schools, despite the difficulties with accommodation, and this satisfactory state of affairs was reflected in most gratifying examination results, with the girls displaying a slight superiority to the boys.

After considerable delays the new schools were officially opened on their respective campuses on 10 July 1901 by Charles Morley M.P. The girls' school at Cerrig Cochion was opened first, and then the whole concourse, comprising the County Governing Body, managers, parents and pupils marched across Brecon to Cradoc for the opening of the boys' school.

The most impressive extra-curricular activity was the Cadet Corps of the boys' school established in February 1901. Despite the strong military tradition in the town, there was much opposition to this initiative and letters were published in the local press condemning the whole idea on the ground that scholars would be made into soldiers. However, the headmaster, Mr John, stood firm and much of the heat was taken out of the dispute when, in a letter to the *Brecon County Times*, he declared that the idea of a Cadet Corps was not 'to make Soldiers instead of Scholars but to make men of Scholars'. After this the corps went from strength to strength.

The Boys' Intermediate School at Dr Coke's. The headmaster, Mr Nathan John, is seated in the centre of the photograph

In 1902 the Balfour Education Act abolished the School Boards of 1870, and handed over control of education to the Borough and County Councils. It was in this manner that the 'Council Schools' came into existence.

Higher Education

A Higher Education had fleetingly been provided at the Normal College (1846-9),[5] but an institution with a far longer pedigree was the Congregational College, which was first established in 1839. In St Mary's Street a substantial house was found and purchased for £1,000 though another £300 had to be spent to adapt it for its new role. The building, which has had a chequered history, is now home to the Conservative Club. The College was opened on 20 February, and was called the Brecon Independent College. Charles Davies was appointed as first principal, and he proved a controversial choice since he had a penchant for regarding matters from a purely English standpoint. During the principalship of his successor, James Henry Griffiths, two significant developments took place: first, the College was thrown open to a limited number of non-ministerial students and secondly, in 1851, it was recognised as one of the colleges of the University of London.

In 1862, as a memorial to those Nonconformist ministers who had been evicted from their livings as a result of the Act of Uniformity 1662, it was resolved to build a new college in Brecon. A quite delightful site was obtained in Camden Road, and the Memorial College, built at a cost of £12,000, opened its doors in 1869.

In the academic life of the College, Welsh was accorded its rightful place and, indeed, it rapidly became one of the strongest subjects on the curriculum and helped to stem the tide of anglicisation which was threatening to engulf the town. The students were prepared for the examinations set by the *Senatus Academicus*, and the first batch of pupils to gain the coveted A.T.S. left the College in 1880. In 1883 it was decided to send the students to the newly-established University College of Cardiff (1883) to

The Congregational College in St Mary's Street

pursue a two year course in Arts. Following completion of this course, they returned to Brecon to finish the Divinity course.

Together with the two colleges, there were other agencies in Victorian Brecon for the cultural and physical advancement of adults. These included the Brecon Literary Institution, founded in 1875 by the Reverend D.W. Davies to foster good taste in reading, and provide the citizens of Brecon with the opportunity of becoming acquainted with good literature; the local and, occasionally, National *Eisteddfod* which did much to further literary education by stimulating reading and research; university extension organised first, by the University of Oxford, and then by the University of Wales following its foundation in 1893; the Gymnasium, with its winter sessions, to promote physical training and general well-being; and finally the theoretical and practical instruction provided under the auspices of the Brecknock Agricultural Education Committee.

When Victoria breathed her last in 1901, the town of Brecon was provided with seven adequate elementary schools, two efficient Intermediate schools, a reputable public school and an impressive theological college. There also existed a network of evening classes which made additional provision for adult education. Indeed, the range, diversity and quality of the institutions available were such as to make Brecon one of the more fortunate towns in Wales.

NOTES

[1] This extremely popular book was written by Lewis Bayly, the bishop of Bangor. It was published at the beginning of the seventeenth century.
[2] The author was Richard Allestree, a royalist divine, who took up arms for the King during the English Civil War.
[3] Supra, p. 174.
[4] Today this building is the headquarters of the Brecon Rugby Club.
[5] Supra, pp. 187-8.

210

APPENDIX A

Bailiffs and Mayors of Brecon in Georgian and Victorian Times

Bailiffs

Year	Name
1714	John Price
1715	Henry Thomas
1716	Henry Williams
1717	Daniel Wynter
1718	Jenkin Price
1719	Meredith James
1720	Daniel Wynter
1721	Thomas Jones
1722	Hugh Powel
1723	Jenkin Price and Charles Hughes
1724	William Morgan
1725	Richard Hughes
1726	Rice Edwards
1727	Edward Williams
1728	John Morgan and John Bullock
1729	John Phillips
1730	Charles Sandys
1731	Meredith James
1732	Walter Jeffreys
1733	Gabriel Powell
1734	Edward Williams
1735	Rowland Hughes
1736	Thomas James
1737	Bartholomew Coke
1738	John Bullock
1739	John Phillips
1740	John Hughes
1741	Samuel Walters
1742	Thomas Mitchel
1743	John Phillips
1744	Edward Morgan
1745	Owen Evans (Pennant)
1746	Thomas James
1747	James Parry
1748	Hugh Edwards
1749	William Morgan
1750	John Phillips, junior
1751	Charles Hughes
1752	Thomas Morgan, junior
1753	Charles Powel
1754	John Bullock Lloyd

211

Year	Name
1755	Thomas Phillips
1756	George Williams
1757	George Devereux
1758	Bartholomew Coke
1759	John Phillips
1760	John Hughes
1761	Owen Evans
1762	Thomas James
1763	Charles Davids
1764	Henry Davies
1765	John Morgan
1766	Samuel Hughes
1767	James Parry
1768	Charles Morgan
1769	George Devereux
1770	Thomas Coke
1771	John Bullock Lloyd
1772	Charles Davids
1773	Hugh Bold
1774	George Morgan
1775	Henry Davies
1776	Charles Pritchard
1777	Thomas Williams
1778	Walter Jeffreys
1779	John Morgan
1780	Samuel Hughes
1781	Charles Morgan
1782	Charles Davids
1783	Hugh Bold
1784	George Morgan
1785	Edward Morgan
1786	Henry Davies
1787	Charles Pritchard
1788	Thomas Williams
1789	William Jones
1790	Charles Gould
1791	Hugh Bold
1792	Samuel Hughes
1793	Sir Charles Morgan (vide 1790)
1794	Thomas Meredith
1795	Hugh Bold, junior
1796	Walter Jeffreys
1797	Charles Pritchard
1798	William Wynter
1799	William Williams
1800	Samuel Homfray
1801	Richard Davies, junior

Year	Name
1802	Charles Morgan
1803	Henry Davies
1804	Hugh Bold
1805	Hugh Bold, junior
1806	Thomas James
1807	?
1808	William Williams
1809	David Williams
1810	Thomas Meredith
1811	John Lloyd
1812	Hugh Bold
1813	William Williams
1814	Charles Morgan Robinson Morgan (elected but resigned) Hugh Bold
1815	Thomas Bold
1816	Lancelot Morgan
1817	Samuel Church
1818	Thomas Bold
1819	William Williams
1820	David Price
1821	Charles Griffith
1822	Thomas Williams
1823	John Brown
1824	William Williams
1825	John Powell
1826	Philip Vaughan
1827	David Price
1828	John Church Morrice
1829	Richard Davies
1830	Philip Vaughan
1831	Charles M.R. Morgan
1832	Thomas Bold
1833	Lancelot Morgan
1834	Charles Griffith
1835	John Wilkins (last bailiff)

Mayors

1836	John Lloyd Vaughan Watkins (Penoyre) First Mayor
1837	John Parry Wilkins
1838	John Lloyd
1839	James Prosser Snead
1840	John Powell (refused to serve and fined 1*s*) Henry Lucas died in office) John Powell

Year	Name
1841	Walter Maybery
1842	Philip Vaughan
1843	John Jones (Glanhonddu)
1844	George Rees Bevan (Priory)
1845	David Watkins Lloyd (Aberllech)
1846	Howell Jones Williams
1847	Henry Maybery
1848	Thomas Prothero Price
1849	Thomas Williams
1850	John Powell (Watton)
1851	Evan Thomas (afterwards Pateshall)
1852	Thomas Williams
1853	John Powell
1854	Mordecai Jones (Morganwg House)
1855	George Rees Bevan
1856	William Pearce (Ffrwdgrech)
1857	David Thomas
1858	John Williams
1859	William Laurance Banks (Watton House)
1860	James Williams
1861	W.L. Banks
1862	Joseph Joseph
1863	William Pearce
1864	George J. Williamson (died in office)
	John Williams
1865	George Cansick
1866	John Prothero
1867	John Davies
1868	Philip Bright (Greenfields)
1869	William de Winton (Maesderwen)
1870	William de Winton
1871	Herbert Charles Rich (Watton)
1872	George Overton (Watton)
1873	William Games (Struet)
1874	David Thomas (Watton)
1875	William Games
1876	David Thomas
1877	William Games
1878	Thomas Williams (Llanfaes)
1879	Thomas Conway Lloyd (Dinas)
1880	Thomas Conway Lloyd
1881	William de Winton
1882	Lewis Jones
1883	Lewis Jones
1884	John Morgan (Lion St)
1885	John Morgan (Bridge St)
1886	Edwin A. Wright (Bridge St)

Year	Name
1887	Jas. Williams (Jubilee mayor)
1888	John Morgan
1889	John Morgan
1890	John Morgan
1891	John Morgan
1892	John Morgan
1893	Lewis Williams
1894	J.A. Jebb
1895	J.A. Jebb
1896	John Williams
1897	William de Winton
1898	Aneurin George
1899	John Morgan
1900	John Morgan
1901	W. Powell Price
1902	David Powell (Coronation Mayor)

APPENDIX B

Brecon's Parliamentary Representatives in Georgian and Victorian Times

Dates	Name
1713-22	Roger Jones of Buckland
1722	William Morgan of Tredegar
1723	Thomas Morgan of Dderw
1727	Thomas Morgan of Dderw
1734-54	John Talbot of Lincoln's Inn
1754	Thomas Morgan the Younger of Ruperra, Glamorgan
1761	Thomas Morgan
1763	Charles Morgan of Dderw
1768	Charles Morgan
1769	John Morgan of Tredegar
1772-78	Charles Van of Llanwern, Mon.
1778	Charles Gould of London
1780	Sir Charles Gould
1784	Sir Charles Gould
1787	Charles Gould, son of Sir Charles
1790	Charles Gould
1796	Charles Gould. Re-elected as Charles Morgan
1796	Sir Robert Salusbury of Llanwern
1802	Sir Robert Salusbury
1806	Sir Robert Salusbury
1807	Sir Robert Salusbury
1812-18	Charles Morgan Robinson Morgan of Tredegar
1818-30	George Gould Morgan of Tredegar
1830-32	C.M.R. Morgan
1832-4	John Lloyd Vaughan Watkins of Penoyre
1835	C.M.R. Morgan of Ruperra
1837	C.M.R. Morgan
1841	C.M.R. Morgan
1847-52	John Lloyd Vaughan Watkins
1852-4	Charles Rodney Morgan of Tredegar
1854	J.L.V. Watkins
1859	J.L.V. Watkins
1865	J.L.V. Watkins
1866	John Charles Pratt of Bayham Abbey, Sussex
1866-8	Howel Gwyn of Duffryn, Neath
1869	Edward Hyde (Villiers)
1870-80	James Price William Gwynne-Holford of Buckland
1880-85	Cyril Flower of Aston Clinton, Tring, Herts. The last member for Brecon
1885	Borough of Brecknock and Llywel ceased to return a separate member and became merged in the county

APPENDIX C

Election of 1837

AN ALPHABETICAL

LIST OF THE POLL,

FOR THE

BOROUGH OF BRECON;

AT THE GENERAL ELECTION IN 1837.

FREEMEN.

Names.	Residence.	Profession.	Morgan	Lloyd.
Bold, Hugh	Brecknock	Esquire	—	
Church, Samuel	Ffrwdgrech	Solicitor	—	
Churchey, Walter	Brecknock	Town Clerk		—
Davies, Richard	Brecknock	Clerk	—	
Morgan, Lancelot	Brecknock.,	Esquire	—	
Powell, John	Brecknock	Solicitor	—	
Vaughan, Philip	Brecknock	Solicitor	—	
Williams, William	Brecknock	Esquire	—	

217

Brecon Borough Election.

Table of the Poll.

MORGAN 156

LLOYD 102

TOTAL POLLED........ 258

MAJORITY FOR C. M. R. MORGAN, ESQUIRE........ 54

ELECTORS

Who voted in respect of Property occupied within the Borough of Brecon—the extraparochial districts of Christ's College and Brecon Castle—and the Town of Llywell, in the County of Brecon.

Names.	Residence.	Profession.
Armstrong, Thomas	Bulwark	Surgeon
Awbrey, George	High Street	Saddler
Bass, Joseph	High Street	Grocer
Batt, Thomas	Bulwark	Surgeon
Batt, F. C.	Bulwark	Surgeon
Bevan, Geo. R.	Lion Street	Solicitor
Bevan, Thomas	Watton	Serjeant
Bevan, William	Struet	Inn-keeper
Brown, William	Orchard Street	Inn-keeper
Brown, William	Church Street	Skinner
Brien, Patrick	Ship Street	Gardener
Bishop, Thomas	Ship Street	Solicitor
Bold, Hugh	Struet	Clerk
Brace, John	High Street	Inn-keeper
Brock, Benjamin	High Street	Book-keeper
Cole, William	Mainwaring's Court	Hatter
Cook, James	Priory	Carpenter
Davies, David	Trecastle	Inn-keeper
Davies, Richard	High Street	Shoemaker
Davies, Thomas	Wheat Street	Currier
Davies, David	Horn Lane	Maltster
Davies, David	High Street	Inn-keeper
Davies, David	Lion Street	Serjeant at Mace
Davies, David	High Street	Painter
Davies, Richard	Orchard Street	Carpenter
Dorrell, Thomas	Ship Street	Inn-keeper
Duncan, John	High Street	Druggist
Dunn, Joseph	Watton	Coal Merchant
Edwards, Edward	Orchard Street	Inn-keeper
Edwards, Jonathan	Castle	Inn-keeper
Edwards, Samuel	Struet	Weaver
Evans, John	High Street	Banker's Clerk
Edwards, Thomas	Watton	Yeoman
Esmand, Joseph John	Watton	Office Clerk
Evans, John	High Street	Shop-keeper
Evans, William	Ship Street	Gentleman
Evans, Rees	Ship Street	Tailor
Evans, Thomas	Lion Street	Accountant
Evans, Thomas	Trecastle	Inn-keeper
Evans, William	Trecastle	Inn-keeper
Gayton, Thomas	Dinas Road	Basket Maker
Griffiths, Thomas	Orchard Street	Shop-keeper
Griffiths, Charles	Glynkelin	Clerk
Griffiths, Thomas	Watton	Builder
Griffiths, John	High Street	Grocer
Gunter, Thomas	Watton	Innkeeper

219

Names,	Residence,	Profession.
Griffiths, John	Pendre	Gardener
Griffiths, William	Struet	Painter
Gwillym, Thomas	Slwch	Farmer
Hall, James	Ship Street	Inn-keeper
Harries, Evan	High Street	Shop-keeper
Harris, David	Castle Street	Inn-keeper
Hancorn, Samuel	Orchard Street	Builder
Havard, Lewis	Wheat Street	Catholic Priest
Hughes, Charles	Wheat Street	Inn-keeper
Hughes, Charles Marcus	High Street	Shop-keeper
Hughes, William	Bridge Street	Maltster
Hunt, Edward	Ship Street	Shop-keeper
James, James	Watton	Wharfinger
Jeffreys, William	Watton	Cooper
Jenkins, David	High Street	Draper
Jenkins, Edward	High Street	Wine Merchant
Jenkins, John	Watton	Wharfinger
Jenkins, Thomas	Watton	Wharfinger
Jenkins, Thomas	Wheat Street	Maltster
Jehu, Hugh	Struet	Skinner
Jones, David	Struet	Millwright
Jones, John	Struet	Clerk
Jones, William	Baileyglaes	Land Surveyor
Jones, Thomas	Watergate	Woolstapler
Jones, John	Christ's College	Currier
Jones, Thomas	Trecastle	Shop-keeper
Jones, Thomas	Bridge Street	Inn-keeper
Jones, Thomas	Bridge Street	Wheelwright
Jones, Thomas	Orchard Street	Gentleman
Jones, John	Bridge Street	Shop-keeper
Jones, Daniel	Church Street	Shop-keeper
Jones, John	Orchard Street	Painter
Jones, Miles	Saint Mary Street	Seed Merchant
Jones, John	Ship Street	Shop-keeper
Jones, Walter	Ship Street	Shop-keeper
Jones, John	High Street	Druggist
Jones, John	High Street	Butcher
Jones, John	High Street	Hair Dresser
Jones, Thomas	High Street	Gentleman
Jones, Thomas Baskerville	High Street	Brewer
Jones, William	High Street	Inn-keeper
Jones, John	Glanhonddu	Solicitor
Jones, Hugh	Castle Street	Auctioneer
Jones, John	Saint Mary's Ward	Cabinet Maker
Jones, David	High Street	Carpenter
Jones, Morgan	Lion Street	Builder
Jones, Richard	Watton	Boat Builder
Jones, Rees	Watton	Inn-keeper
Jones, John	Watton	Wheelwright
Jones, William	Watton	Inn-keeper
Jones, John	Watton	Maltster
Knowles, Robert	Struet	Inn-keeper
Lewis, Evan	Orchard Street	Blacksmith
Lewis, Thomas	Venny fach	Farmer
Lewis, William	Struet	Weaver

Names,	Residence,	Profession.
Lloyd, David Watkins	Lion Street	Esquire
Lloyd, John	Dinas	Esquire
Lloyd, John	High Street	Watchmaker
Lloyd, Watkin	Trecastle	Esquire
Lucas, Henry	Bulwark	Doctor of Medicine
Matthews, William	High Street	Shopkeeper
Matthews, John Powell	Watton	Esquire
Maybery, Walter	Glamorgan Street	Esquire
Maund, Howell	Struet	Gentleman
Mainwaring, John	Struet	Inn-keeper
Martin, Thomas	Gwttws	Huntsman
Matthews, William	Orchard Street	Inn-keeper
Morgan, Llewellin	Newgate Street;	Inn-keeper
Meredith, Thomas	Wheat Street	Esquire
Milner, Joseph	High Street	Shop-keeper
Morgan, Edward	Watton	Shop-keeper
Morgan, William	High Street	Brazier
Morgan, Michael	Watton	Inn-keeper
Moore, Thomas	Horn Lane	Sheomaker
Moore, Francis	Watton	Inn-keeper
North, James Price	Church Street	Carrier
Parker, Thomas	Morgannog Ward	Esquire
Parker, William Henry	High Street	Stationer
Parry, Watkin	Watton	Inn-keeper
Parry, John	Ship Street	Shoemaker
Parry, William	Wheat Street	Inn-keeper
Patrick, Charles Paul	Watergate	Gentleman
Parry, John	Mount Street	Gentleman
Parry, Thomas	Postern	Labourer
Price, Thomas	Gaer	Auctioneer
Phillips, Joseph	Old Port Inferior	Brickmaker
Price, (the elder) Lemuel	Cwmtoyddur	Farmer
Powell, William	Watton	Coal Merchant
Probert, Thomas	Struet	Pump Maker
Price, Benjamin	Mount Street	Serjeant
Powell, (the younger) Abel	Struet	Inn-keeper
Prothero, William	Old Port Superior	Carpenter
Parry, Rees,	Cwm Inn	Inn-keeper
Powell, Aythau	Mill Street	Shop-keeper
Price, John	Factory	Weaver
Price, (the elder) John	Honddu Mill	Miller
Price, (the younger) John	Honddu Mill	Miller
Price, (the younger) Lemuel	Old Port Superior	Haullier
Powell, Joseph	Ship Street	Brazier
Price, Job	Old Port Superior	Labourer
Powell, William	Pantycorred	Farmer
Pritchard, David	Derwengroes	Inn-keeper
Peirce, Joseph	Mount Street	Banker's Clerk
Phillips, Philip	High Street	Breeches Maker
Powell, John	High Street	Butcher
Powell, Abel	Watton	Inn-keeper
Powell, Samuel	Ship Street	Brazier
Powell, John	High Street	China Seller
Powell, Thomas	Lion Street	Shoemaker
Price, John	Cantercelly Ward	Draper

Names.	Residence.	Profession.
Price, Thomas	Watton	Shop-keeper....
Price, Thomas	Watton	Maltster........
Prosser, John	Ship Street	Inn-keeper.....
Prosser, Thomas	Kefnbrynich	Farmer........
Prosser, Walter	Kefnbrynich	Farmer........
Prosser, Roger	High Street	Druggist.......
Powell, Howell	Orchard Street	Cabinet Maker..
Pow-ll, Richard	Orchard Street	Hawker........
Powell, Howell	Gwttws	Labourer......
Prosser, David,	Bridge Street	Inn-keeper.....
Price, Rees	Penypentre	Inn-keeper.....
Powell, John	Newgate Street	Weaver.........
Powell, Thomas	Back Street	Mason.........
Prothero, David	Christ's College	Turner........
Parry, David	Trecastle	Clerk.........
Powell, Thomas	Trecastle	Gentleman......
Price, John	Trecastle	Inn-keeper.....
Richards, William	Trecastle	Shop-keeper....
Rees, Thomas	Cantercelly Ward.	Shop-keeper....
Richards, Robert	Watton	Ironmonger.....
Rowlands, William	High Street	Clerk..........
Rees, Howell	Orchard Street	Inn-keeper......
Sims, James	Watton	Coachmaker....
Smith, Richard	Bulwark	Flour Merchant..
Stephens, William	Watton	Flour Merchant ..
Symmonds, Thomas	High Street	Boot-maker ....
Snead, James Prosser	Graiglais	Banker........
Thomas, David	Bridge Street	Grocer........
Thomas, (the younger) William..	Bridge Street	Grocer........
Thomas, (the elder) William	Bridge Street	Grocer........
Thomas, John	Struet	Tailor........
Thomas, John	Struet	Gentleman.....
Thomas, Thomas	Struet	Tailor........
Thomas, John	Castle Street	Sculptor.......
Thomas, David	High Street	Solicitor......
Trew, George	Cantercelly Ward.	Haberdasher....
Trew, Elijah	Watton	Butcher........
Trew, Thomas	Watton	Butcher........
Thomas, Evan	Orchard Street	Inn-keeper.....
Vaughan, Thomas	Priory Hill	Clerk.........
Vaughan, Thomas	Watton	Inn-keeper....
Vaughan, William	Bulwark	Gardener......
Vaughan, John	Mount Street	Yeoman........
Wallace, Robert	Ship Street	Gardener......
Wathen, Richard	Watergate	Shop-keeper....
Watson, Evan	Watergate	Schoolmaster....
Watkins, William	Horn Lane	Blacksmith....
Watkins, Rees	High Street	Hair Dresser.....
Watkins, John	Penkelly	Coal Merchant..
Watkins, Rees	Watton	Grocer........
Watkins, Howell	Bridge Street	Ironmonger....
Watkins, John	Bridge Street	Wheelwright....
Williams, (the younger) William..	Orchard Street	Mason........
Williams, Griffith	Orchard Street	Watchmaker....
Williams, Thomas	Bridge Street	Inn-keeper....

Names,	Residence,	Profession.
Williams, (the elder) William....	Back Street...............	Mason ....
Williams, Thomas.............	High Street...............	Clerk..........
Williams, Thomas	Trecastle	Inn-keeper .....
Winston, Evan	Struet	Grocer ....
Winston, William.............	Struet	Brewer ....
Winston, David	Struet	Carpenter ......
Winston, Penry	Struet	Chandler ....
Winstone, Evan.............	Pendre..................	Builder ....
Webb, William..............	Struet	Shop-keeper....
Wood, Oliver	Pennant	Farmer ....
Watkeys, Thomas	Held	Farmer ....
Watkins, Lewis	Struet	Surgeon ....
Watkins, Thomas	Struet	Painter ....
Watkins, William.............	Bridge Street	Road Surveyor..
Watkins, John...............	Blackboy	Beerhouse-keeper
Williams, David	Old Port Superior Ward....	Maltster ....
Williams, William	Court	Labourer ......
Williams, Thomas	Old Port Superior Ward....	Farmer ....
Watkins, Roger Thomas	Struet	Solicitor ....
Williams, John	Struet	Banker's Clerk..
Williams, Thomas	Bryndu..................	Farmer ....
Webb, Thomas...............	Mount Street..............	Inn-keeper .....
Wharton, William.............	Watton..................	Esquire ....
Williams, Thomas	High Street...............	Druggist ....
Williams, Howell	Ship Street	Shop-keeper....
Williams, Walter.............	Ship Street..............	Ironmonger ....
Williams, Watkin	Watton	Labourer ......
Williams, John.............	Ship Street	Inn-keeper .....
Williams, James.............	Ship Street	Shop-keeper....
Williams, William	Castle Street..............	Tailor ....
Williams, David	Mount Street	Gardener ......
Williams, John	Cantercelly Ward	Shop-keeper ....
Williams, William	Lion Street	Watchmaker ....
Williams, Howell.............	Penkelly	Coal Merchant..
Williams, William	Skethrog	Farmer ....
Williams, Rees...............	Mannest	Farmer ....
Williams, William	Watton..................	Gardener ......
Wiliams, Theophilus	Wheat Street	Organist ....
Wilkins, John Parry	Maesderwen	Esquire ....

BIBLIOGRAPHY

Since this volume is aimed at the general reader, no attempt has been made to provide a bibliography which has any pretensions to be exhaustive. Rather, only those books and articles which are generally available, and are of particular importance, relevance and interest have been included.

However, it would be extremely remiss of one not to make particular mention of the herculean labours of Theophilus Jones, a local solicitor, whose *History of Brecknockshire* undoubtedly constitutes the best of the Welsh county histories. This work is a veritable mine of invaluable information, and any researcher is immediately made conscious of the debt of gratitude that is owed to him. To write the history of his beloved county, he relinquished the practice of the law and, living upon his private means, devoted some eight years of a comparatively short life—he died when he was only fifty-one—to its compilation.

Lord Glanusk, who always displayed a lively and abiding interest in county matters, while studiously avoiding any material interference with the original concept of the renowned antiquary, continued the history to his own time, and one is also greatly obligated to him.

A *General*

Hadfield, Charles, *The Canals of South Wales and the Border*, Cardiff, 1960.

Jones, Owain and Walker, David (eds.), *Links with the Past: Swansea and Brecon Historical Essays*, Llandybïe, 1974.

Jones, R. Tudur. 'Religion in Post-Restoration Breconshire, 1660-88', *Brycheiniog*, viii (1962).

Jones, Theophilus, *History of the County of Brecknock*, ed. J.R. Bailey, Brecknock, 1909.

Jones, T.P., 'The History of Education in the town of Brecon to 1902', Unpublished M.A. (Ed.) thesis of the University of London, 1965.

Jones, T. Wynne, *Wesleyan Methodism in the Brecon Circuit*, Brecon, 1888.

Lewis, Michael, *From Darkness to Light : The Catholics of Breconshire 1536-1851*, Abertillery, 1992.

O'Keefe, M.C., 'Three Catholic Martyrs of Breconshire', *Brycheiniog*, xvii (1976-77).

Parry, E.G., *Christ College, Brecon: An Illustrated History*, Pontypool, 1991.

Id., 'Cholera Epidemics in Brecon', *Brycheiniog*, 22 (1986-7).

Parry, V.J., *Brecon and Merthyr Railway*, Brecon, 1970.

Poole, Edwin, *The Illustrated History and Biography of Brecknockshire from the Earliest Times to the Present Day*, Brecon, 1886.

Jones, I.G. *Explorations and Expanations*, Llandysul, 1981.

Jones, I.G. and Williams, D. (eds.), *The Religious Census of 1851: a Calendar of Returns Relating to Wales*, Llandysul, 1981.

Lloyd, John, *The Early History of the old south Wales Iron Works, 1760-1840*, London, 1906.

Price, Cecil, *The English Theatre in Wales*, Cardiff, 1948.

Williams, W.R., *The Parliamentary History of the Principality of Wales, 1541-1895*, Brecon, 1895.